T0301770

GLOBAL BUSINESS STRATEGY

Asian Perspective

Second Edition

GLOBAL BUSINESS STRATEGY

Asian Perspective

Second Edition

Hwy-Chang Moon

Beijing Normal University, China
Seoul National University, Korea
Institute for Policy and Strategy on National Competitiveness, Korea

NEW JERSEY · LONDON · SINGAPORE · BEIJING · SHANGHAI · HONG KONG · TAIPEI · CHENNAI · TOKYO

Published by

World Scientific Publishing Co. Pte. Ltd.

5 Toh Tuck Link, Singapore 596224

USA office: 27 Warren Street, Suite 401-402, Hackensack, NJ 07601

UK office: 57 Shelton Street, Covent Garden, London WC2H 9HE

Library of Congress Cataloging-in-Publication Data
Names: Moon, Hwy-chang, author.
Title: Global business strategy : Asian perspective / Hwy-Chang Moon,
    Beijing Normal University, China, Seoul National University, Korea,
    Institute for Policy and Strategy on National Competitiveness, Korea.
Description: Second edition. | New Jersey : World Scientific, [2022] |
    Includes bibliographical references and index.
Identifiers: LCCN 2021021108 | ISBN 9789811236174 (hardcover) |
    ISBN 9789811236587 (ebook) | ISBN 9789811236594 (ebook other)
Subjects: LCSH: International business enterprises--Asia. |
    International business enterprises--Management. | Business planning--Asia.
Classification: LCC HD62.4 .M846 2022 | DDC 658.4/012--dc23
LC record available at https://lccn.loc.gov/2021021108

British Library Cataloguing-in-Publication Data
A catalogue record for this book is available from the British Library.

For any available supplementary material, please visit
https://www.worldscientific.com/worldscibooks/10.1142/12254#t=suppl

Desk Editors: Balasubramanian Shanmugam/Lum Pui Yee

Typeset by Stallion Press
Email: enquiries@stallionpress.com

Printed in Singapore

Preface

It has been over ten years since the first edition of this book was published. Despite the many changes that have occurred over the last decade in the international business environment, often coined as the "post-golden age of globalization," I have found that most of the theories and concepts introduced in the first edition still possess explanatory power in this era. Building upon these approaches, this second edition includes more recent business theories, techniques, and cases within the field of global business strategy. For example, this book includes creating shared value, the global value chain, platform strategy, and business ecosystem. These theories and techniques are shown to be important for competitiveness and sustainability among firms in today's rapidly changing environment. This is very much evident today given the critical challenges arising from the trade tensions between the United States and China, emerging technologies such as artificial intelligence and digital transformation, and the unprecedented disruptions brought on by the coronavirus pandemic.

This book provides novel insights on how a firm can formulate a successful global business strategy from both the Western and Asian perspectives. There are substantial differences between firms from these two regions that multinational corporations should not ignore. Without a proper understanding of Asian business practices and the environment, even the most successful Western multinationals, such as Walmart, will find themselves struggling in the Asian market. However, this does not mean that the differences outweigh the similarities. Many of the key formulas for success may work equally well on both sides of the world. The main point is that either overemphasizing or underestimating the differences could lead to undesirable outcomes. To avoid such misguided approaches, this book aims to bridge the Western and Asian business perspectives, rather than to place too much stock on the unique features of either one or the other. Firms from both sides can learn from each other and such international exchanges and interactions can help further enhance their competitiveness.

Each chapter of this book is divided into three sections. The first outlines and explains the strategy theories or models developed by eminent scholars. These are fundamentals which all strategists, whether practitioners or scholars, should be familiar with. The second presents the techniques of analyses, criticisms, modifications, and extensions of these theories. The final section shows how the strategy models described in sections one and two, both original and extended ones, can be applied to explain various cases in the real world, including Western firms in Asia and Asian firms in Western countries.

Although this book covers many important academic theories of global business, it is written from a practical viewpoint and incorporates many important techniques that practitioners will find useful for formulating effective strategies. People working outside the field of pure strategy will also find these tools useful if they understand that the core value of strategy is not in the creation of new ideas, but in the advancement of analytical skills. In respect of academic curriculum, this book is suitable for Business Strategy, Global Marketing, and International Business courses at both the graduate and undergraduate levels.

This book could not have been completed without the high talents and dedication of my assistants. Special thanks go to Dr. Wenyan Yin, who has conducted extensive research in updating theories and cases. She has made extraordinary contributions to this project from start to finish. Further thanks extend to Stephen Ranger who has done a lot more than just editing, by conducting needed research and recommending many valuable suggestions. In addition, I would like to thank Jin Uk Kim, Lorna Geddis, Jimmyn Parc, Wenyan Yin, Ted Moon, Inhyoung Lee, and Euijae Kim, for all their assistance to the first edition of this book. I am also grateful to the brilliant minds who attended my Global Business Strategy course. Their stimulating discussions and ideas, many of which have been incorporated into this book, were a constant source of inspiration. Finally, I would like to thank Pui Yee Lum, Balasubramanian Shanmugam, Anthony Alexander, and other colleagues of World Scientific Publishing Co. for their valuable help in publishing this book.

Hwy-Chang Moon
Beijing Normal University, China
Seoul National University, Korea
The Institute for Policy & Strategy on
National Competitiveness (IPSNC), Korea

About the Author

Hwy-Chang Moon (Ph.D. from University of Washington) is Professor Emeritus and former Dean in the Graduate School of International Studies at Seoul National University. Professor Moon is currently Overseas Professor at Beijing Normal University Business School, the Chairperson of the Institute for Policy and Strategy on National Competitiveness (IPSNC) in Seoul, Korea, a consultant to United Nations Conference on Trade and Development (UNCTAD), and an Honorary Ambassador of Foreign Investment Promotion for South Korea. He has been frequently invited to deliver lectures at several universities including Stockholm University and Helsinki School of Economics (currently Aalto University) in Europe, Keio University and Beijing Normal University in Asia, and The State University of New York at Stony Brook and Stanford University in the United States. He has conducted many consulting/research projects for multinational companies (e.g., Samsung Electronics), international organizations (e.g., UNCTAD), and governments (e.g., Korea, Malaysia, Dubai, Azerbaijan, Guangdong Province of China, and India). For interviews and debates, he has been invited by international newspapers and media, including *The New York Times*, NHK World TV, and Reuters. He has published numerous articles and books, including *The Strategy for Korea's Economic Success* (2016, Oxford University Press) and *The Art of Strategy: Sun Tzu, Michael Porter, and Beyond* (2018, Cambridge University Press).

Contents

CHAPTER 1

The Basics of Strategy

Chapter Guideline

Although many business strategy books deal with Michael Porter's strategy models, few have successfully presented Porter's key points and their true implications in an easily digestible manner. Several studies have also tested the relevance of Porter's competitive strategy in the digital age. While a few studies including Porter argued for the applicability of his strategy in today's business environment, others have suggested for a modification of his models in order to analyze the new business phenomena, such as pure online and platform business. This chapter attempts to cover this issue. It will first explain the different units of strategy analysis, followed by Porter's strategy models and its appropriate levels of analyses. These strategy models will then be applied to some real-world cases in order to demonstrate how they function in today's business environment.

1.1 The Competitiveness of Product, Firm, Industry, and Nation[1]

Competitiveness is often confused with productivity. While productivity refers to the internal capability of an organization, competitiveness refers to the relative position of an organization against its competitors. These two important concepts, however, are often confused and used interchangeably. A firm may enhance its competitiveness by

---

[1] This section is extended from Moon and Peery (1995).

1

simply changing its strategies, for example, a new marketing strategy, while maintaining the same level of productivity. Likewise, a nation can enhance its competitiveness by changing national policies, such as currency devaluation or protectionism, without increasing its domestic productivity. Therefore, we need to distinguish competitiveness from productivity and highlight the relevant strategies for achieving this at various levels of analyses.

The definition of "strategy" remains implicit and open to intuitive interpretation; many scholars such as Ansoff (1965) have avoided giving it a specific definition (Håkansson and Snehota, 2006). Yet, in order to give readers a clearer understanding of strategy, this book refers to it as the efficient way of generating maximum outputs with the minimum input resources. Based upon this approach, some important strategy models can then be integrated and suggested for further development.

The Competitiveness of a Product

A product is competitive if it has a lower price and/or superior differentiation than those of comparable products. Porter's (1980, 1985) generic strategies are thus relevant to the competitiveness of a product, but not always to that of a firm. For this reason, Porter's generic strategies are criticized when they are applied to a firm-level analysis. For example, critics state that the generic model focuses on only the last few hundred yards of what may be a skill-building marathon (Hamel, 1991).

Another point of criticism is that the generic strategies of low cost and differentiation are useful for categorizing competitive strategies, but in themselves do not suggest where costs should be cut or how products should be differentiated (Kogut, 1985). In addition, as the generic strategies model was primarily designed to explain domestic business strategies, it does not adequately describe the complexity of global business strategies. This is mainly because few firms pursue solely a cost or differentiation strategy in global competition; in fact, major competitors frequently adopt both cost and differentiation strategies (Moon, 1993).

The Competitiveness of a Firm

Further criticism of Porter's generic strategies is that it neglects the core competence in formulating firm-level strategies (Prahalad and Hamel, 1990). In this regard, one of the most important perspectives in explaining the competitiveness of a firm is the resource-based view (Barney, 1991). This theory perceives the firm as a bundle of resources and capabilities, which strategically focuses on (a) factor market imperfections, (b) the heterogeneity of firms, (c) varying degrees of specialization, and (d) the limited transferability of corporate resources. According to this view, the competitiveness of a firm depends on the ability to identify and deploy its core competence.

A similar concept has also been developed to explain the theory of multinational corporations (MNCs). This is closely related to owner-ship advantage and the capability to deploy the advantage, which is explained extensively by the internalization theory (Buckley and Casson, 1976; Rugman, 1981) and Ownership-Location-Internalization (OLI) paradigm (or eclectic theory, Dunning, 1977) as found in the foreign direct investment (FDI) literature. Thus, theories related to FDI can provide important insights into firm-level global competitiveness, which are not available in other approaches.

The Competitiveness of an Industry

Most of the existing theories in strategic management are related to the competitiveness of a product or firm. On the contrary, Porter (1990, p. 18) raises an important question regarding the international competitiveness of a nation's industry by asking why firms based in particular nations achieve international success in distinct segments and industries. He defines the international success of a nation's industry as "possessing advantage relative to the best world-wide competitors" (Porter, 1990, p. 25). To explain this further, Porter introduces the diamond model, an analytical framework composed of four determinants — factor conditions, demand conditions, related and supporting industries, and firm strategy, structure, and rivalry.

These four determinants are very similar yet more refined than the variables included in his five forces industry model (Porter, 1980, 1985, 1990). Porter's five forces model stresses the competitive relationship with the key drivers of industrial competition, but neglects the cooperative relationship with the complementary factor. As such, this factor of related and supporting industries was then incorporated as a determinant factor of industrial competitiveness in the diamond model. Despite the far-reaching explanatory power of Porter's diamond model, it is still quite limited when applied to global business. Recognizing this limitation, other scholars extended the original single diamond model to the double diamond model as well as proposed other models to explain the multidimensional nature of global business.[2]

The Competitiveness of a Nation

A nation's competitiveness is different from a firm's competitiveness. For example, the competition between the US and China is not like the zero-sum game between Apple and Samsung. If you buy an Apple phone, it is Samsung's loss, but at the national level, the US and China are not competing over specific products, rather they can both be winners through competition and cooperation. This can occur by using different but often complementing sources of comparative advantages. However, when nations endowed with similar comparative advantages compete in a particular industry, the competition becomes largely a zero-sum game.[3] For example, when China introduced its "Made in China 2025" plan that sets the goal for it to become the dominant player in ten leading high-tech industries, US officials were outraged and sought to contain China by pursuing a trade and technology war. Modeling competitiveness at the national level is thus no easy task.

---

[2]See Rugman and D'Cruz (1993); Moon *et al.* (1995, 1998); Cho (1994), Cho and Moon (2013a); Cho *et al.* (2008, 2009) for the evolution of the diamond model.

[3]There is an interesting debate on this by Krugman, Prestowitz, and Thurow. See Cho and Moon (2000).

Popular models for national competitiveness are international trade theories and foreign exchange theories. Yet, these macro approaches have been criticized for their limitations in dealing with the fundamental sources of national competitiveness. It was out of such a gap in the literature that later theories such as the diamond model and its extended models have been developed to improve the micro foundations of national competitiveness. On the contrary, some scholars argue that if we hope to revitalize the competitive performance of a nation's economy, we must invest in people, not in nationally defined corporations. In the twenty-first century, the education and skills of the workforce may be the dominant competitive weapon.[4]

Where to Start?

I have briefly reviewed competitiveness at different levels of analyses and the relevant strategy models for each level. The conceptual clarity will help portray the vivid institutional reality. Theories for each level are somewhat overlapping, interdependent, and sometimes misused. Among the four different levels of analyses, the firm-level competitiveness is probably the most important unit in understanding our globalized economies because it is not nations but firms that compete in the real world (Porter, 1990). For the purpose of analyzing industry or product competitiveness, the basis of understanding must be at the firm level. I will thus start with the firm's competitive strategy and, when necessary, appropriately incorporate strategy models at other levels.

1.2 Porter's Competitive Strategy

Michael Porter is well known as the guru of strategic management, so I will first review Porter's key points (1980, 1985); then, I will discuss some issues associated with Porter's model and suggest a few extensions in the later chapters.

---

[4]For example, see Reich (1990) and Thurow (1992).

Porter raises two central questions underlying competitive strategy. The first is the attractiveness of industries for long-term profitability and the factors that determine it. Not all industries offer equal opportunities for success and it is important to choose an attractive one. The second relates to the determinants of relative competitive positions within an industry. In most industries, some firms are much more profitable than others, regardless of what the average profitability of the industry may be. A firm can improve or erode its position within an industry through its choice of strategy.

The First Question: Industry Attractiveness (Five Forces Model)

According to Porter, industry structure is what drives competition and profitability, not whether an industry is emerging or mature, high tech or low tech, regulated or unregulated. This is reflected in the fact that some industries such as tobacco and beverages are extremely profitable, while some high-technology industries such as personal computers and cable television are not profitable for many participants.

In any industry, whether it is domestic or international or whether it produces a product or a service, the rules of competition are embodied in five competitive forces: the entry of new competitors, the threat of substitutes, the bargaining power of buyers, the bargaining power of suppliers, and the rivalry among the existing competitors (see Fig. 1).

The collective strength of these five competitive forces determines the ability of firms in an industry to earn, on average, rates of return on investment in excess of the cost of capital. The strength of the five forces varies from industry to industry and can change as an industry evolves. Here, Porter forwards an important argument that a firm is not a prisoner of its industry's structure. Firms, through their strategic choices, are capable of influencing the five forces to their advantage. If a firm can shape the industry structure, it can fundamentally change an industry's attractiveness for better or worse and many

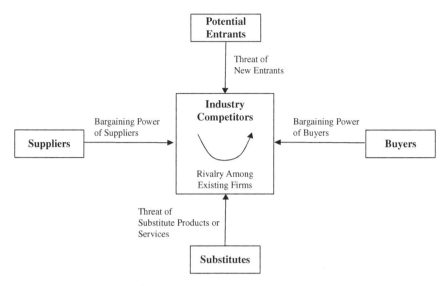

Fig. 1. The five competitive forces that determine industry profitability.
Source: Porter (1980, p. 4).

successful strategies have shifted the rules of competition in this way. Contrary to the critics' assertions, Porter's conception of firm strategy is not that of a passive recipient of unchangeable industry forces, but a proactive entity that has the power to change the very business environment in which it operates.

In an update, Porter (2008) notes that understanding the five forces is not only important for individual firms but also for investors. The five forces can be a powerful tool for investors to distinguish between structural changes and short-term bubbles. Commonly used investment decision tools such as financial projections and trend extrapolations can be misleading as they tend to overemphasize transient factors and industry profitability. From a macro perspective, this leads to a misallocation of resources to unprofitable segments and creates unnecessary volatility. If managers and investors both focus on industry structure, the capital market would not exhibit such inefficiencies that we commonly witness.

The Second Question: Firm Competitiveness (*Generic Strategies*)

The second question in competitive strategy deals with a firm's relative position within its industry. There are two basic types of competitive advantages a firm can possess: cost advantage or differentiation advantage. Cost and differentiation advantages in turn stem from industry structure. In simple terms, they result from a firm's ability to cope with the five forces better than its rivals. Here, again, Porter argues that industry structure and firm strategy are not insulated but are interconnected with each other.

The two basic types of competitive advantage combined with the scope of activities lead to three generic strategies for achieving above-average performance in an industry: cost leadership, differentiation, and focus. This appeared in Porter's early work (Porter, 1980, Fig. 2) and later he divided the focus of strategy further into two variants (Porter, 1985, Fig. 3). In *cost focus,* a firm seeks a cost advantage, while in *differentiation focus,* a firm seeks differentiation in its target segment.

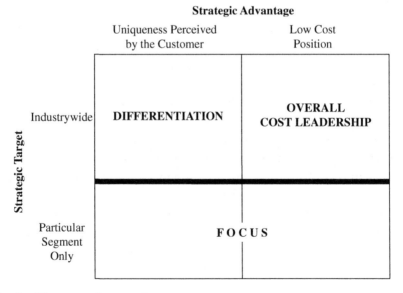

Fig. 2.   Three generic strategies.

Source: Porter (1980, p. 39).

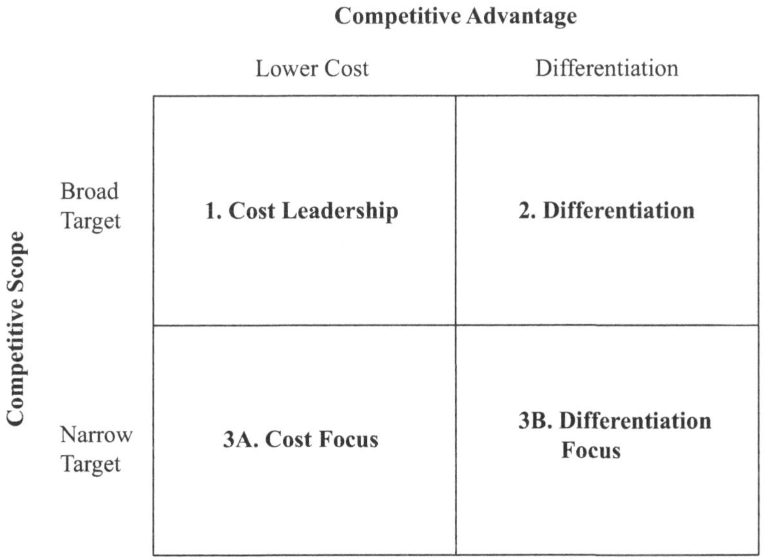

Competitive Advantage

	Lower Cost	Differentiation
Broad Target	1. Cost Leadership	2. Differentiation
Narrow Target	3A. Cost Focus	3B. Differentiation Focus

Competitive Scope

Fig. 3. Four Generic Strategies.
Source: Porter (1985, p. 12).

Stuck in the middle

Each generic strategy takes on a fundamentally different approach toward creating, sustaining, and combining a firm's competitive advantage and deciding the scope of its strategic target. Usually, a firm must make a choice among the four strategies, or it will be stuck in the middle which leads to a competitive disadvantage on all fronts. In most industries, quite a few competitors are in such a situation. These firms will earn attractive profits only if the structure of its industry is highly favorable, or if the firms' competitors are also in a disadvantageous situation.

Stuck in the middle is a very controversial concept that has been criticized by many scholars.[5] However, Porter is more cautious than his critics toward this issue. He asserts that a cost leader cannot ignore the basis of differentiation. If its product is not perceived as comparable or

---

[5] Critics on stuck in the middle will be analyzed further in Chapter 5.

acceptable by buyers, a cost leader will be forced to discount prices well below competitors to gain sales. Therefore, a cost leader must achieve parity or proximity on the basis of differentiation relative to its competitors in order to be an above-average performer, even though it relies on cost leadership for its competitive advantage. Similarly, a differentiator aims at cost *parity* or *proximity* relative to its competitors, by reducing cost in all areas that do not affect differentiation.

The real value of Porter's generic strategy

Porter's critics state that his generic strategies focus too much on competition and therefore his strategic vision is too narrow.[6] However, in many cases, this criticism is unfounded because Porter actually broadens the strategic options since generic strategies provide alternate routes to superior performance. While other strategic planning concepts have been narrowly based on only one route to competitive advantage, most notably cost, generic strategies allow more flexibility in selecting the suitable approach which allows firms to survive and prosper without being locked in a constant state of competition with each other.

1.3 The Value Chain and Competitive Advantage

A firm's competitive advantage stems from the many discrete activities of designing, producing, marketing, delivering, and supporting its product. Each of these activities can contribute to a firm's relative cost position and be the basis of differentiation. Competitive advantage (Porter, 1985) is about how a firm actually puts the generic strategies (Porter, 1980) into practice. How does a firm gain a sustainable cost advantage? How can it differentiate itself from competitors? Competitive advantage grows fundamentally out of the value that a firm creates for its buyers. So, Porter introduces a very useful tool, called the value chain, to disaggregate buyers, suppliers, and firms into the discrete but interrelated activities from which value stems.

---

[6]The various critics of Porter will be explored extensively throughout later chapters.

Potential sources of competitive advantage are everywhere in a firm. As such, all departments, facilities, branch offices, and other organizational units have a role that must be defined and understood.

The Generic Value Chain

The value chain displays total value, and consists of *value activities* and *margin*. Value activities are physically and technologically distinct activities of a firm. Margin is the difference between total value and the collective cost of performing the value activities. Value activities can be divided into two broad types: *primary* activities and *support* activities. Primary activities are those involved in the physical creation of the product, its sales, and its transfer to the buyer as well as after-sales assistance. In any firm, primary activities can be divided into the five generic categories shown in Fig. 4. Support activities assist the primary activities by providing purchased inputs, technology, human

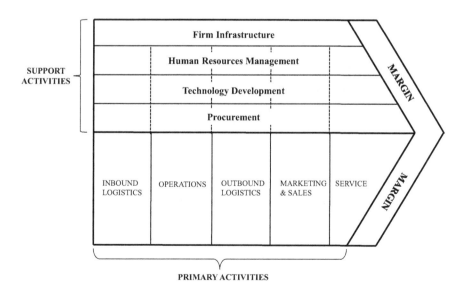

Fig. 4. The generic value chain.

Source: Porter (1985, p. 37).

resources, and firm-wide functions. The dotted lines reflect the fact that procurement, technology development, and human resource management can be associated with specific primary activities as well as supporting the entire chain. Firm infrastructure is not associated with a particular primary activity but supports the entire chain.

Primary activities: Five generic categories

- *Inbound Logistics* — Activities associated with receiving, storing, and disseminating inputs to the product, such as material handling, inventory controlling, vehicle scheduling, and returns to suppliers.

- *Operation* — Activities associated with transforming inputs into the final product form, such as machining, packaging, assembly, equipment maintenance, testing, printing, and facility operations.

- *Outbound Logistics* — Activities associated with collecting, storing, and distributing the product to buyers, such as finished goods warehousing, order processing, and scheduling.

- *Marketing and Sales* — Activities associated with providing a means by which buyers can purchase the product, such as advertisement, promotion, sales force, channel selection, channel relations, and pricing.

- *Services* — Activities associated with providing service to enhance or maintain the value of the product, such as installation, repair, training, parts supply, and product adjustment.

The relative importance of each category depends on the industry. For a distributor, inbound and outbound logistics are the most critical. For a service firm such as a restaurant or retailer, outbound logistics may be largely nonexistent and operations are the vital category. For a bank, marketing and sales are critical toward achieving competitive advantage. For a high-speed copier manufacturer, service represents a key source of competitive advantage. In any firm, all five categories play some role in their competitive advantage.

Support activities: Four generic categories

- *Procurement* — This is the *function* of purchased inputs used in the firm's value chain, not the purchased inputs themselves. Purchased inputs include raw materials, supplies, and other consumable items as well as assets such as machinery, laboratory equipment, office equipment, and buildings. Improved purchasing practices can strongly affect the cost and quality of purchased inputs, and other activities associated with receiving and using the inputs and interacting with suppliers.

- *Technology Development* — This refers to how every value activity embodies technology, be it know-how, procedures, or the technology embodied in the process equipment. Porter terms this category of activities as technology development instead of research and development (R&D) because R&D has a too narrow connotation for most managers. It does not solely apply to technologies directly linked to the end product. Technology development also takes many forms, from basic research and product design to media research, process equipment design, and servicing procedures.

- *Human Resource Management* — A firm performs many activities related to recruiting, hiring, training, developing, and compensating all types of personnel. Human resource management supports both primary and support activities, for example, the hiring of engineers, and the entire value chain, such as labor negotiations. This management affects the competitive advantage for any firm, through its role in determining the skills and motivation of employees and the cost of hiring and training.

- *Firm Infrastructure* — This refers to activities including general management, planning, finance, accounting, legal, government affairs, and quality management. Unlike other support activities, infrastructure usually supports the entire chain and not individual activities. In diversified firms, infrastructure activities are typically split between the business unit and corporate levels; for example, financing is often done at the corporate level, while quality management is undertaken at the business unit level. However, many infrastructure activities occur at both the business unit and corporate levels.

Subdividing the Value Chain

Every activity undertaken by a firm should be captured in a primary or support activity. Therefore, each generic category of the value chain can be further divided into discrete activities, as illustrated by each generic category in Fig. 5. The appropriate degree of disaggregation

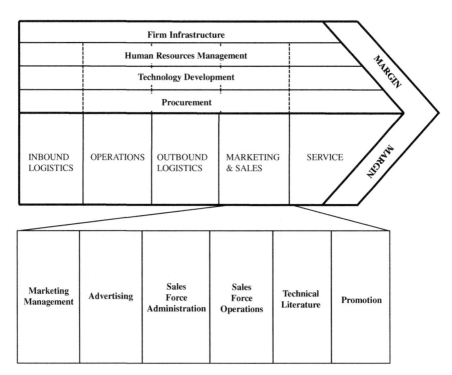

Fig. 5.   Subdividing a generic value chain.

Source: Porter (1985, p. 46).

depends on the economics of the activities and the purposes for the type of value chain that is being analyzed. The basic principle is that activities, which (a) have different economics, (b) have a high potential impact of differentiation, or (c) represent a significant or growing proportion of cost, should be separated.

Linkages within the Value Chain

Although value activities are the building blocks of competitive advantage, the value chain is not a collection of independent activities, but a system of interdependent ones. Value activities are related through linkages within the value chain. These linkages are relationships between the performance of one value activity and the cost or performance of another. Furthermore, they can lead to competitive advantage in two ways: optimization and coordination. Examples of optimization include a more costly product design, more strict materials specifications, and greater in-process inspection which may reduce service costs. A firm must optimize such linkages in order to achieve a competitive advantage. Linkages may also reflect the need to coordinate activities. The ability to coordinate linkages often reduces cost or enhances differentiation. Better coordination, for example, can reduce inventory throughout the firm. Linkages imply that a firm's cost or differentiation is not merely the result of efforts to reduce costs or improve performance in each value activity individually. Much of the achievement is the result of linkages.

1.4 The Relevance of Porter's Strategy in the Digital Age

In the literature of business strategy, Porter's models are very popular among business strategists and industrial economists due to their advantages of well-defined structure, feasibility, clarity, simplicity, and generality (Ormanidhi and Stringa, 2008). Despite this popularity, the applicability of Porter's overall strategy can be questioned as over the past few decades, the global economy has transitioned from mechanized to digital age, which has led to the pace and intensity of change in the global business environment becoming more noticeable, a development which cannot be so easily explained by Porter (Kim *et al.*, 2004; Parnell, 2006; Adner, 2017). Some key features of these changes can be summarized as follows.

Internet-based technologies have influenced the emergence of distinctive products by integrating IT into the product itself. For example, sensors, processors, and software have been embedded into traditional mechanical products. Product-usage data stored in the cloud can be analyzed remotely, while some applications can be operated autonomously. Moreover, advances in platform technologies and modularity have helped the emergence of genuinely new products which integrate multiple tasks using the same infrastructure/platform (Gould and Desjardins, 2015). These products often entail more services in the service/product mix (Vargo and Lusch, 2008). For example, the iPhone offers more than a device capable of making phone calls as it contains cameras, a music player, games platforms, online search tools, contactless payment options, and various other everyday applications. These changes have not only brought additional complexity to the product but have also dramatically improved the functionality and performance of related products (Porter and Heppelmann, 2014).

The emergence of these types of new products has disrupted value chains, and forced firms to reconfigure their activities which used to be performed internally. The growing pressure of innovation and performing the value activities with lower costs and risks has forced firms to pursue new form of value creation, such as platform or ecosystem strategy, by allowing all relevant stakeholders to participate in the firm's activities and co-create values (Nucciarelly *et al.*, 2017). Compared to traditional pipeline business, the focus for firms in the context of platform business is more on resource orchestration than resource control, external interaction for value creation than internal optimization through organizing their internal labor and resources, ecosystem value than customer values in order to maximize the total value of an expanding ecosystem (Van Alstyne *et al.*, 2016).

These new types of products have also altered the industry structure and nature of competition (Porter and Heppelmann, 2014).

The unit of competition shifts from a single firm toward the firm networks or ecosystem-based competition. Moreover, Internet-based technology has allowed for firms to develop a new way of reaching customers and doing business, for example, e-commerce. The creation of a virtual market allows firms to access customers, which has been difficult or impossible with traditional channels due to geographical and market barriers (Koo *et al.*, 2004).

Given such a rapidly changing and complex business environment, managers and scholars are questioning whether traditional business concepts and models, such as Porter's, are still useful or need some modification for firms to gain superior performance in the information and digital age. Porter's five forces model emphasizes the competition relationship within a particular industry, and hence shows limitations in explaining those businesses which require a larger stream of activities across industry boundaries and the complexity in the mix of competition and cooperation relationship among stakeholders.

In this respect, a few scholars have introduced new concepts and models that build upon Porter's original value chain, such as value network, business ecosystem, value grid, and value constellation (Nucciarelly *et al.*, 2017). Alongside this, regarding the generic strategies, some have questioned the completeness of the typology of firms with competitive advantage, with the criticism of the concept of "stuck in the middle," by stressing that the hybrid strategy of combining more than one generic strategy could be more effective in achieving not only the superior advantages but also a better response mechanism to the turbulent and uncertain business environment.

Although preceding studies have sought to modify Porter's strategy models or develop entirely new ones to address these drawbacks when analyzing the current context, this is not the same as dismissing completely his original models or suggesting that they have lost their value. While Porter's models may not be sufficient to understand firms' strategic behaviors and performance, there are still potential interactions between them and new models such as platform or ecosystem strategy. For example, Adner (2017) commented that one can observe interactions between competitive strategy and ecosystem strategy in the case that Apple uses its competitive position in the music players and aligns this business with its network partners involved in its smartphone business. Mekić and Mekić (2014) stated that Porter's models are still viable for a competition-based economy where firms have to produce values in exchange for money, attract consumers, and contain the influences of competitors. In summary, Porter's models are still valid in the current age, but we need to consider other factors for a more comprehensive analysis on the nature of competition as well as the drivers behind firms' competitive advantage.

Case Study 1: Apple and the Mobile Phone Industry[7]

When it first set out, Apple was a leading manufacturer of personal computers and entertainment equipment. However, after experiencing a brief decline, it has since redefined its position to become a major player in the smartphone industry. How did the company successfully enter the mobile phone market without facing severe resistance from existing players? How has Apple's entry changed the industry structure of the pre- and post-smartphone market?

Rivalry among Existing Players. Before the introduction of the smartphone, competition was fierce among existing mobile phone manufacturers. The product life cycle was very short and the tastes among consumers changed frequently. As a result, firms had to invest heavily in R&D as a way to meet the needs of their customer base. This frantic situation changed with the introduction of the iPhone. Since its launch, the number of players in the smartphone industry has dramatically entered a bipolar order with Apple and Samsung as the industry's hegemons. In addition, the smartphone market has changed from a niche to a mass market, and the competition has become fiercer than ever. The intensity of the rivalry is perhaps not as intense or cutthroat as it was during the early 2000s, yet there is still

---

[7]This case study is abstracted and modified from the business case of Chapter 3 of Moon (2018).

a strong rivalry between the two major players, Apple and Samsung. Therefore, the degree of rivalry can be considered to rank medium.

Threat of New Entrants. In the pre-smartphone era, it was easier for firms to enter the market, especially the low-end product markets, due to the homogenization of the hardware involved, the simple technology, and basic design. However, the initial cost of entering this industry was very high in terms of R&D investment and marketing to compete with established companies. In such a context, the threat of new entrants was considered to be medium. Again, the introduction of the iPhone changed this and the threat of new entrants has become lower. Two key factors help explain why there is such a barrier toward entering this market. First, it is difficult for new entrants to convince customers to instantly switch to another brand. Second, it is an immense challenge for a new entrant to produce a better smartphone at a more affordable price than those already in the market.

Threat of Substitutes. In the early 2000s, as Wi-Fi was rolled out, consumers had to rely on multiple devices to perform different tasks, for example, MP3 players for listening to music and personal digital assistants to send emails. The iPhone brought all of these functions into one device therefore negating their use, which has led to the threat of substitutes to become very low. This is perhaps best exemplified by the fact that the cameras in most flagship smartphones are as good as leading digital cameras. With all different everyday functions housed in one phone, it has become unnecessary to purchase and carry a number of different devices at the same time. The only exception is for highly specialized or professional purposes, which tends to be in the minority. In this regard, the threat of substitutes has decreased from medium to low.

Bargaining Power of Suppliers. As there were many suppliers for different parts and components for mobile phones in the early period, they did not have much power to seriously affect the decision-making of mobile phone manufactures. As a result, the bargaining power of suppliers was low, since manufacturers could easily switch to their competitors for desirable price and quality. However, as the platform came to be dominated by a few players providing complex operating systems as the core software system for smartphones, for example, Android or iOS, the device design became increasingly customized for a particular operating system by a specific supplier. In such an environment, it became very expensive to switch suppliers. Here, the bargaining power of suppliers has changed from low to medium since the introduction of the smartphone.

Bargaining Power of Buyers. Customers had high bargaining power because of the wide number of choices in the mobile phone industry. The loyalty of customers was very low, and it was usually determined by quality instead of the brand. As a result, leading manufacturers had to make great efforts to meet customer demands as much as possible in order to retain existing customers and attract new customers. However, the entrance of Apple into the mobile phone market decreased the bargaining power of buyers dramatically by generating an unprecedented fandom for the company's products with the appeal of an eye-catching design, high-quality components, and robust software.

Based on the above analysis, we can see that before the introduction of the iPhone, the overall mobile phone manufacturing industry did not appear very attractive or profitable. Still, the case of Apple shows that an industry's threat of substitutes is subject to changes over time and can sometimes overturn the whole industry structure. However, the entry of Apple revolutionized the industry structure from less attractive to very attractive, as the threats from most of the five forces (except suppliers) have decreased (see Fig. 6). From this analysis, it is clear that the five forces can explain why the iPhone achieved higher profits than mobile makers in the pre-smartphone era by comparing the five forces of the mobile phone and smartphone.

Still, the five forces model does not fully explain why the iPhone was able to so quickly and easily dominate the smartphone market. Its market share in the smartphone sector was only 4% in 2007, but it reached 30% in 2009. Two factors explain iPhone's rapid domination of the market. The first is Apple's coevolution with the involved partners. Upon the introduction of the iPhone, Apple found numerous new business opportunities for the market. In this way, it controlled

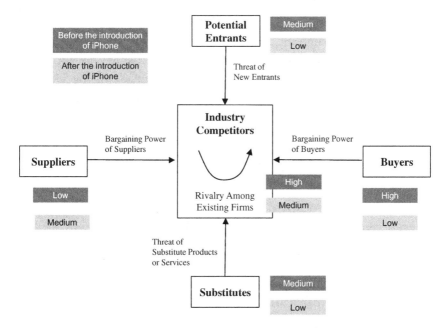

Fig. 6. Five forces of the mobile phone industry.

and coordinated the core portion of the value chain, leaving the other parts to third parties, such as the US network provider AT&T (Laugesen and Yuan, 2010). Moreover, it even cooperated with its major smartphone competitor — Samsung Electronics, the supplier of key iPhone components such as display and memory. Thanks to new sources of profit earning, Apple could enter the market with relatively fewer market obstacles. Its success did not come at the expense of the ecosystem of the industry by abusing its bargaining power, but, on the contrary, it generated more vitality into it by actively cooperating with other firms in Apple's ecosystem.

Case Study 2: Walmart's Challenge in Asia[8]

"The secret of successful retailing is to give your customers what they want." This was how Sam Walton, the founder of the world's largest

---

[8]Some information for this case is abstracted from *International Herald Tribune* (Walmart's overseas push can be lost in translation, August 2, 2006),

retailer Walmart,[9] summed up the key to his company's success in his autobiography. As such, he advocated that one must think about one's business from the customer's point of view. In using this approach, Walmart was able to thrive in many countries outside of the US, particularly in Britain, Canada, and Mexico. However, Walmart failed in India, Japan, and Korea because the company did not understand its Asian customers and just like its French rival, Carrefour, ended up withdrawing from these countries. Walmart's failure in these three countries provides important lessons for Western multinationals that aspire to garner success in these markets.

In contrast to Walmart's failure, the British retailer Tesco has achieved remarkable success in the Korean market. It owns 89% of Samsung Tesco, but has relied heavily on local managers from Samsung to make business decisions. Tesco entered the Korean market in 1999 and by 2006 its profits had grown by 30%. Consequently, this was the same year it became the second largest retailer in South Korea, making South Korea one of Tesco's biggest overseas success stories (Center for Management Research, 2006). If one overseas retailer prospered in Korea, why couldn't Walmart do the same? What went wrong with Walmart? The following illustrates the reasons behind Walmart's failure in India, Korea, and Japan:

- *Cheap Real Estate* — Large stores, vast parking lots, and huge distribution centers have been an integral part of Walmart's success. In this respect, it is understandable to see how Walmart could easily expand to places with cheap real estate (Latin America), but had a hard time expanding to places where real estate was more expensive (South Korea and Japan).

The New York Times (Walmart Selling Stores and Leaving South Korea, May 23, 2006), Walmart's Website (www.walmart.com), *The Economist* (Walmart: Always low prices, February 2, 2008), https://www.1421.consulting/2019/06/walmart-in-china-lessons-to-learn, and others.

[9]Walmart dropped the hyphen from its name in 2019. https://eu.usatoday.com/story/money/2017/12/06/whats-name-walmart-soon-little-less/926828001/.

- *Price* — Walmart's focus has always been on low prices. It provides merchandise in bulk for prices below what its competitors can offer. However, Koreans prefer high quality over price and often equate low price with low quality. Walmart focused on maintaining low prices and selling in bulk, while its local competitors, E-Mart and Lotte Mart, focused on selling the product's quality by creating eye-catching displays and hiring employees who promoted their goods with megaphones.

- *Frequent Visits* — Walmart is an ideal store for consumers who only do their grocery shopping once a week. Most American consumers visit Walmart once a week and buy in bulk because American shoppers rarely shop without their automobiles. By contrast, most consumers in Japan visit stores almost every day, by bicycle and tend not purchase in bulk. With such a stark difference in consumer behavior between the Japanese and the American consumer, Walmart was unable to succeed in Japan.[10]

- *Government Protection* — Walmart was unsuccessful in entering India, where the government was not very flexible as it was concerned about protecting the country's retail sector. Over 90% of Indian retailers were very small, traditional, and unorganized, and there was fear that Walmart could eventually undermine the small retailers who dominated the Indian market.

Walmart's experience in India implies that the company should have planned to buy more local goods, which could help domestic farmers and small manufacturers. More importantly, Walmart should have changed its cost leadership strategy when entering certain Asian countries. The company's "Everyday Low Price" approach backfired in Korea and Japan, where consumers equate low prices with low

---

[10]An interesting example in this case is the UK where consumers have shifted in recent years from a weekly shop to a daily one. However, the COVID-19 pandemic has changed this behavior again as people have gone back to a weekly shop. https://www.theguardian.com/business/2020/apr/28/uk-consumers-big-weekly-shops-lockdown-stores.

quality. The one-size-fits-all approach has to be changed from standardization to localization and cost to differentiation strategy.

In contrast to the failure in Japan, Korea, and India, Walmart achieved a better performance in China where in 1996 it opened its first store in Shenzhen. Since 2008 in particular, it has experienced fast growth of 50% in terms of grocery retail value. As of January 2020, Walmart has 412 retail stores, and recently announced that it plans to open 500 new stores in China over the next five to seven years. How was such success possible? After extensive research and recognizing that it could not compete on pricing with local Chinese competitors, Walmart changed its slogan from "Always Low Prices" as used in the US to the Chinese slogan "Worry Free," which emphasizes quality, assortment of merchandise, and trustworthiness instead of low price. Still, there are some limitations for Walmart to pursue its cost strategy. First, its stores are located in urban areas where the cost of land is very expensive to build large warehouse-type shops. Second, Chinese consumers, even wealthy and middle-class ones, usually do not live in large houses like Americans. Thus, they do not have space to purchase items in bulk and instead just buy a few items per visit. Furthermore, they prefer small neighborhood stores, rather than traveling far.

Since the 2010s, in order to keep up with the growing consumer demand for online shopping, Walmart partnered with a local app JD.com to launch its online shopping and delivery services; it also partnered with Tencent's WeChat Pay to provide a convenient and quality payment service. Moreover, Walmart has committed to developing its own brands, such as Great Value for groceries. Here, it is evident that the competitive strategy for Walmart's online shopping segment is focused on quality and reputation. Such a strategy has been clearly differentiated from local retailers that maintain cost leadership and other foreign retailers such as Costco that pursues a differentiation focus.

Although Walmart is successful in the US, the same competitive advantage may not translate into success in foreign markets. Asian consumers shop at large retailers, not for cheap and bulky items, but for the convenience of a variety of smaller-sized quality products.

Competitive Advantage

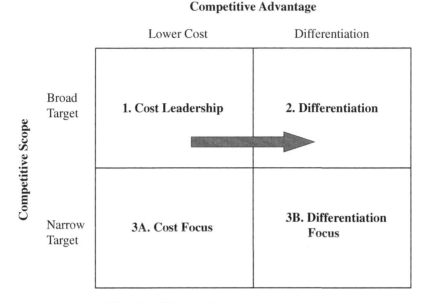

Fig. 7. Walmart's international strategy.

Using the generic strategy model, Walmart's cost leadership strategy in the US should have been changed to a differentiation strategy in Asia. The optimal strategic prescriptions are outlined in Fig. 7.

Case Study 3: Sogo Shosha's Changing Competence[11]

Sogo shosha is a form of industrial organization and is usually a vertically integrated trading company that is found in Japan. The term *sogo shosha* is Japanese for "general trading company," but is often confused with *zaibatzu* or *keiretsu*. The *zaibatsu*[12] commonly consists of a primary enterprise — usually a *sogo shosha* — surrounded by

---

[11] Some of the information for this case has been abstracted from Mitsubishi Corporation Websites (www.mitsubishicorp.com), Innovation 2007 (Mitsubishi Corporation Websites), and others.

[12] *Zaibatsu* refers to those enterprises that existed before World War II, while *Keiretsu* is the modern-day equivalent.

subsidiaries engaged in a wide range of operations such as banking, insurance, shipping, mining, real estate, food processing, and manufacturing.

The seven largest *sogo shosha* are Mitsubishi Corporation, Mitsui & Co., Itochu, Sumitomo Corporation, Marubeni, Toyota Tsusho, and Sojitz. The *sogo shosha* supplies large volumes of raw materials and distributes goods from large manufacturers to smaller distributors and to numerous retailers. What makes them unique is their size, scope, information-gathering capabilities, as well as their functional diversity. They are the Japanese traders that operate at the center of Japan's global economic power and serve as intermediaries for half of their country's exports and two-thirds of their imports.

Other nations have sought to emulate this system to promote a similar kind of economic success. South Korea's large conglomerates, such as LG, Samsung, and Hyundai, have their own version of *sogo shosha* (*Jonghap Sangsa* in Korean), while Chinese firms have begun to launch *sogo shosha*-type companies with assistance from Japanese firms. Even the US attempted to replicate *sogo shosha* in the early 1980s with the signing of the Export Trading Company Act of 1982. Such export companies, however, never developed due to the American tendency to reject government-sponsored programs and a lack of publicity derailed this effort.

In the 1990s and 2000s, *sogo shosha* found itself at a crossroads, adapting to new market conditions and opportunities. This included new business fields in high technology, including biotechnology, computer technology, information technology, and telecommunications. With increasing globalization, *sogo shosha* is faced with both new opportunities and threats.

Facing these new challenges, *sogo shosha* is now changing its business models as follows:

- The activities of *sogo shosha* encompass not only trading but also investments and other business activities. The essence of *sogo shosha* is to provide any needed service to propel the businesses forward.

- *Sogo shosha* is engaged in business with customers around the world in virtually every industry, including energy, metals, machinery, chemicals, food, and general merchandise.

- *Sogo shosha* actively studies market trends and takes the initiative to develop new businesses. Finding a new growing industry and related segments is critically important for *sogo shosha's* sustainable growth.

- The uniqueness of *sogo shosha* is the ability to link and coordinate functions such as logistics, financing, and marketing. *Sogo shosha* thus shares risk with business partners and adds value to the business.

Therefore, the real value or core competence of *sogo shosha* is to find a problem or *imbalance* within a value chain and to fix it. In this way, it can make the value chain more efficient and enhance its productivity. As shown in Fig. 8, this will contribute to the enrichment of society, as well as its business partners in the linking activities of the value chain. As the industry structure becomes more sophisticated

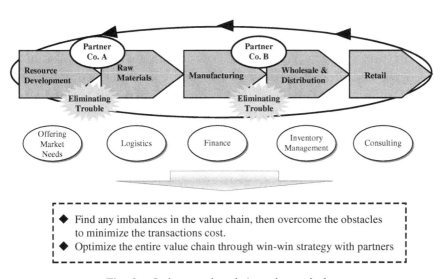

Fig. 8. Industry value chain and *sogo shosha*.

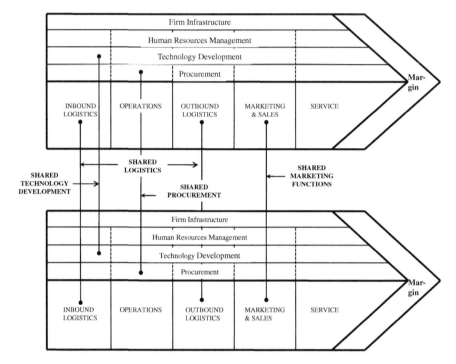

Fig. 9.   Applying Porter's (1985, p. 327) value chain to *sogo shosha*.

and as new industries emerge, *sogo shosha*'s role and scope of business will become greater. When *sogo shosha* leverages its organizational strengths and the networks of its affiliated companies, its power and therefore potential benefits to its business partners will become even greater, as shown in Fig. 8. Leveraging these organizational strengths and linking them to other activities of the industry value chain are the unique advantages of *sogo shosha* that are clearly differentiated from other organizations as depicted in Fig. 9.

Case Study 4: Starbucks in China[13]

Starbucks, perhaps one of the most successful global companies in the world, has had its fair share of problems in China. For this

---

[13]Some information of this case is abstracted from *The New York Times* (Starbucks Aims to Alter China's Taste in Caffeine, May 21, 2005), Seattle Post Intelligencer

multinational company, China is viewed as a must-have market and is a clear priority for growth outside of the US. One key characteristic of Starbucks is the standardization of its stores, which are the same whether one is in New York, London, or Paris. However, the company's formula has not been as well received in China and other Asian countries as it has been in the West.

There are a number of cultural differences that have played a strong role in redefining Starbucks' Asian strategy: (a) Asia is traditionally a continent known for having a tea-drinking culture rather than a coffee-drinking one, (b) Asians tend to view coffee or tea shops as a place to socialize, and (c) Asians prefer enjoy snacks while drinking.

Starbucks is a coffee shop and for the most part keeps its tea menu to a minimum. However, after entering the Chinese market, the company discovered that many customers, while enjoying the Starbucks atmosphere, preferred tea to coffee. The company, therefore, was forced to expand its standardized menu to include a wider variety of tea.

In the West, the revenue of Starbucks is driven by the speed and frequency of its transactions. Customers tend to grab their coffee and a quick pastry before rushing out the door to their next appointment. In Asia though, coffee or tea is more of a social event than a daily necessity. Customers come to meet and chat with their friends and thus Asian customers spend more time in the stores, on average, than their Western counterparts. As a result, Starbucks has had to increase the size of its stores to an average of 2,000 square feet (185.806 m²) to accommodate such customers.

Another change came due to the company's realization that Asians tend to enjoy snacks while having a drink. Starbucks was forced to expand its menu once again to include more foods. For example, Starbucks catered to local tastes by providing snacks such as moon cakes. Although Starbucks has made numerous efforts to

---

(Starbucks adjusts its formula in China, June 16, 2005), *The Economist* (The Forbidden Latte, July 17, 2007), and https://medium.com/swlh/starbucks-20-years-in-china-9fa8e0c33cf1.

adjust its formula to suit the Chinese market, the efforts may not be enough.

On July 13, 2007, Starbucks was forced to close the doors of its branch in the Forbidden City. It was argued that the image of the coffee shop "trampled over Chinese culture" and the outlet was described as "a symbol of low-end US food culture." As a result, Starbucks had to rethink its branding and marketing strategy in order to be fully accepted in China.

Since the closure of the Forbidden City branch, Starbucks has increased its investment in China to win the hearts of customers and the government. For example, Starbucks provides its staff with free coffee, meals, and generous insurance coverage that most local companies do not offer. In 2012, Starbucks invested in a coffee plant in Yunnan province and supported local farmers, and promoted Yunnan coffee alongside its more well-known brands of Columbian and Ethiopian coffee. These series of efforts have contributed to its growth in China, and as of now, it grows at the rate of one new store

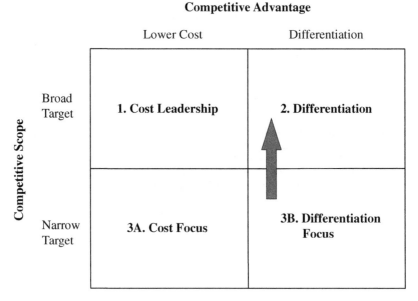

Fig. 10.   Starbucks strategy shift.

per day. The number of Starbucks stores in Shanghai is double that in New York. After gaining success in the first- and second-tier cities in China, Starbucks became more confident and has expanded to the third- and fourth-tier cities.

Despite these efforts, the competition in the Chinese coffee business has recently become more severe. New foreign coffee brands such as Arabica — the most popular coffee shop in Kyoto, Japan — have entered China, and many local brands such as Luckin have emerged. Many brands have also begun to offer a coffee delivery service. Such changes forced Starbucks to consider e-commerce, and it partnered with Alibaba to offer such a coffee delivery service.

In a nutshell, Starbucks used to rely upon a differentiation focus (i.e., the high-end image) strategy; however, facing challenges in China, the company has moved toward a broad differentiation strategy in order to please broader Chinese customers, by including more Chinese menus and thus enlarging its competitive scope, as shown in Fig. 10.

Discussion Questions

1. Why are the ideas of competitiveness and productivity so often confused? What do competitiveness and productivity mean to you? Are they entirely different or interchangeable?

2. Do you agree that there is a need to differentiate among product, firm, industry, and nation when applying frameworks or models of competitiveness?

3. Are there any weaknesses in the five forces model? Would you add, subtract, or alter it in any way in order to improve its analytical power to the current environment?

4. What do you think of the terminology and typology used in the generic strategies? Is it clear enough to comprehend all the competitive firms in the digital age? How would you improve the generic strategies?

5. Do you agree that being "stuck in the middle" is always disadvantageous? Can you think of any examples where this is not the case, particularly with e-business?

6. Do you agree that Porter's strategy models are still relevant in the digital age? Do you think the new models (e.g., platform or ecosystem strategy) complement or substitute Porter's models in the new business environment?

CHAPTER 2

Alternative Business Models

Chapter Guideline

In the previous chapter, Porter's models revealed how they laid the foundation for gaining an overarching view of business strategy. Now, it is time to look at alternative models which provide us with an outlook both complementary and contrary to Porter's views. This chapter will provide a summary of three alternative models from producer, customer, and ecosystem. The three alternative models are applied to case studies of success in order to help the reader gain a better understanding of the models' application in the real business context.

Summary of Previous Models

In the previous chapter, we studied three of Porter's famous strategy models – five forces model, generic strategies, and value chain framework – to explain the sources of firms' competitive advantages. The five forces model determines the industry structure that influences its attractiveness or long-term profitability. Generic strategies then explain alternative routes for firms to gain a competitive position against rivals within an industry. The third model, value chain, helps us understand the sources for firms to achieve cost leadership or differentiation advantage for each of the value-creating activities. We also reviewed the recent debates on the relevance of Porter's strategy models in the digital age, and found that they are still valid but we need to consider other strategic variables that contribute to enhancing the competitiveness of firms. From this perspective, this chapter introduces the alternative well-known strategy models developed by other scholars, to complement Porter's views on the competitive advantage of firms.

2.1 Knowledge-Creating Strategy

When Michael Polanyi first formalized the concept of "tacit knowledge" in 1966, it had profound impact upon all branches of academia. Rather than regarding knowledge creation as a value-free and objective process, Polanyi opened up the possibility that knowledge can be perceived as something derived from a "pre-logical phase of knowing" or, as he describes it, tacit knowledge (Smith, 2003). Business management is no exception to this influence and many scholars in this field have used Polanyi's concept, especially in refining to the notion of knowledge economy.

Nonaka (2007) is a good example of a business scholar who integrated Polanyi's insights into the discipline of business management. Nonaka claims that in an unpredictable economic environment, knowledge is the only true consistent source of competitive advantage for an organization. Those that can create, disperse, and embody "new knowledge" will be the ones that achieve true success because they have the proper framework necessary for continuous innovation. This idea is not entirely novel, of course, as it was first introduced by Drucker's, 1969 book, *The Age of Discontinuity*. Drucker first articulated the term "knowledge society" in which knowledge is identified as the primary source of competitive advantage (Drucker, 1969). Whereas Drucker is considered the father of knowledge management (Makambe, 2015), Nonaka popularized the concept of tacit knowledge in management studies and his theory of knowledge creation is considered "one of the best known and most influential models in the knowledge strategy literature" (Choo and Bontis, 2002).

Nonaka advances Drucker's concept and fuses it with Polanyi's tacit knowledge. By drawing upon Polanyi's (1967) dichotomy of knowledge (explicit and tacit knowledge), Nonaka and Takeuchi (1995) conceptualized it as follows.

- *Explicit Knowledge* — codified knowledge which is transmittable in formal and systematic language, and therefore easily communicated and shared.

- *Tacit Knowledge* — highly personal, context-specific, and therefore hard to formalize and difficult to communicate.

The implication behind distinguishing the two types of knowledge is to underscore the fact that merely processing explicit knowledge does not provide a fertile ground for innovation. Rather, a firm must learn how to tap the tacit knowledge base that exists within the firm and transform it into explicit knowledge which can then be shared and learned by others. Nonaka particularly highlighted the importance of tacit knowledge for continuous innovation and competitive advantage of firms. According to him, Western firms tend to view the company as a machine whose responsibility is to generate quantifiable data and information. On the contrary, some firms in Asia (mostly Japanese in Nonaka's analysis) tend to view the company as a living organism which is in constant flux. In this respect, the success of major Japanese firms in the 1980s and 1990s should be attributed to the advantage held by them in managing tacit knowledge, which fuels creating new knowledge and continuous innovation.

Nonaka (1994) suggested that knowledge is created through the epistemological dimension and the ontological dimension. The former dimension refers to the conversion of knowledge from tacit to the explicit level, and from explicit to the tacit level. The latter dimension refers to knowledge conversion from the individual to groups, and then to the organizational level. Combining the two dimensions in one framework, Nonaka (1994) identifies four patterns for creating knowledge within the firm: tacit to tacit (socialization), tacit to explicit (externalization), explicit to explicit (combination), and explicit to tacit (internalization).

- *From Tacit to Tacit* (Socialization) — This process refers to the transfer of tacit knowledge through social interactions (e.g., face-to-face interaction) between personnel. For example, it is only through years of carefully observing the master that an apprentice will finally begin to learn the tacit side of the art of creation. Tacit cannot be communicated easily as the possessor of the tacit knowledge is usually unaware of his knowledge or cannot systematically convey it to others.

- *From Tacit to Explicit* (Externalization) — This stage is to organize and externalize the internalized knowledge in a manner that can be applicable and understood by others within the organization. For example, a highly experienced staff member organizes his or her internalized knowledge into a format which can be applied to an innovative new product (tacit → explicit). This new information then becomes systemized and distributed to other employees within the firm to foster further innovation.

- *From Explicit to Explicit* (Combination) — This refers to using and systemizing explicit knowledge to create a new form of explicit knowledge, such as utilizing company data to compile a new report. This type of knowledge creation is highly common and is crucial for a firm's basic operation. However, it neither extends the knowledge base of a firm nor provides a fertile plain for groundbreaking innovations.

- *From Explicit to Tacit* (Internalization) — This process internalizes explicit knowledge and transforms it into tacit knowledge. A company worker may acquire explicit information through reports and meetings, and then internalize that knowledge, thus transforming it into tacit knowledge. As learning is achieved by doing in the process of internalization, Nonaka and Takeuchi (1995) suggested that internalization is closely related to organizational learning, which in turn influences organizational performance.

The patterns are not mutually exclusive but rather act in unison to form a "spiral of knowledge" (see Fig. 1), which is referred to as the SECI model (Nonaka, 1994; Nonaka and Takeuchi, 1995).[1]

---

[1] The SECI model includes socialization, externalization, combination, and internalization.

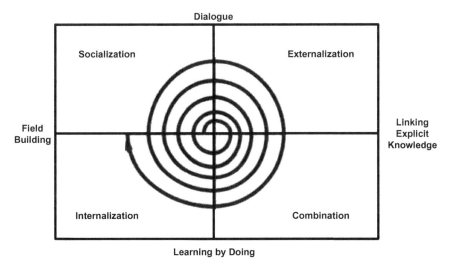

Fig. 1. Knowledge spiral.
Source: Nonaka and Takeuchi (1995, p. 71).

In this model, explicit and tacit knowledge interact with and convert to each other, and individuals' tacit knowledge is the basis of organizational knowledge creation (Kawamura, 2014). This model has been widely acknowledged and adopted for most knowledge management conceptualizations.

Understanding the knowledge spiral is only the first step. One also needs to know how to jumpstart the process of developing new knowledge.

Nonaka identifies three stages in the process: (a) metaphor, (b) analogy, and (c) model. Using this process allows firms to draw from symbolism rather than concrete fixed ideas. The process should begin with the metaphor, which is based on intuitive understanding. The next step is analogy, which provides a structure for the metaphor and connects two disparate concepts together. The final stage is the model. Here, contradictions are resolved and concepts are transferred in a systematic manner, and the transfer of tacit to explicit knowledge is complete.

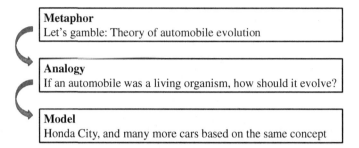

Fig. 2.   Honda's spiral of knowledge.

This abstract concept is easier to understand through actual case examples in which this process has crystallized tangible results. The first one is with Honda. In 1978, one of the top managers of Honda came up with the slogan "Let's Gamble," which expressed the management's desire for a completely new car. The taskforce then refined this slogan and came up with an even more ambiguous slogan, "The Theory of Automobile Evolution." This metaphor, which to a Western manager would seem rather baffling, united the Honda employees in the task of creating a revolutionary new concept car. It was further structured into what Nonaka calls an analogy, which unites two seemingly irreconcilable elements.

In the Honda case, it boiled down to the following question: "If the automobile was an organism, how would it evolve?" This attempt to imagine an inorganic machine as an organism gave Honda employees a fulcrum for innovation and ultimately led to the birth of Honda City, a car which defied many of the conventions of automobile design. After this achievement, Honda systemized this knowledge and spurred a whole series of new cars based on the Honda City, which shares the basic concept of "*automobile evolution*" embodied in the initial model. The final step demonstrates the model phase of Nonaka's spiral of knowledge as Honda successfully transformed what was initially highly tacit knowledge into tangible and reproducible explicit knowledge (see Fig. 2).

Nonaka does, however, caution that in real life it is difficult to clearly distinguish between these stages and often the lines become blurred. Throughout Nonaka's analysis are references, which can be construed as being related to Japanese cultural elements that give Japanese firms a distinct advantage in facilitating this kind of process. Japanese values of harmony (*wa*, 和) and collectivism, noted by eminent Japan specialists such as Benedict (1946), facilitate a collaborative environment in which this knowledge creation process can be disseminated and integrated as a part of the firm's core competency. Thus, Japanese companies are able to build a knowledge-creating company culture, which requires a high level of teamwork, trust, and emphasis on harmony.

On the contrary, the West is characterized by individualism, which when applied to a company setting, encourages personnel to work alone and to build their own personal stores of knowledge in order to develop only themselves. Furthermore, the knowledge creation process in Western firms is more competitive, which means that the high level of collaboration and team work required for Nonaka's model to work would be relatively harder to achieve.

Analysis

In the publication, *Managing Flow: A Process Theory of the Knowledge-Based Firm* (Nonaka *et al.*, 2008), Nonaka extends his spiral of knowledge concept and explores how Japanese companies have continued to develop innovative products based on tacit knowledge management. It is undeniable that Nonaka's insights shed light onto the inner mechanisms of innovation.

At the same time, Nonaka's analysis is static as it does not account for the prior process required to reach this highly evolved phase of knowledge management. Managing tacit knowledge and transferring it to explicit knowledge may be an important source of added value

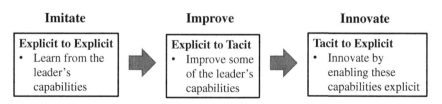

Fig. 3. Three I Model: Evolution of the spiral of knowledge according to stages of economic development.

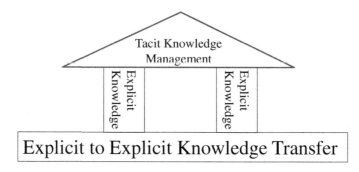

Fig. 4. Explicit to explicit knowledge transfer as a basis for tacit knowledge management.

for advanced firms such as Honda and Canon. However, for less advanced companies, especially those from developing countries, this kind of activity may be too complicated to manage. We can easily imagine that if a firm without extensive industry presence and know-how sought to manage tacit knowledge, it could lead to organizational chaos and inefficiency. Therefore, we can extend Nonaka's static model into a dynamic one and clarify the potential mishaps that Nonaka's model can lead to.

As illustrated in Fig. 3, in the initial factor-driven stage of economic development, explicit to explicit knowledge management should be the primary focus. An appropriate example for this kind of activity would be engineering technology transfers from developed countries' multinational corporations (MNCs) to firms in developing countries. In this phase, if firms of a developing country focus overly on tacit knowledge, it could backfire and create organizational chaos and inefficiency. Therefore, in the initial stage of development, the weight should be placed more on managing explicit to explicit knowledge transfer. Replicating and accumulating hard, quantifiable, and systematic knowledge should be the priority.

Yet, when firms move toward a more innovation-driven phase, they must shift their focus to acquiring tacit knowledge. Since an innovation-driven economy requires constant high-value-added activities for firms to stay competitive, managing the tacit knowledge creation process is highly important. As illustrated in Fig. 4, a solid base of explicit knowledge must support Nonaka's prescription of harnessing the innovative power of tacit knowledge creation.

Therefore, the key is not to take Nonaka's point to the extreme. Of course, managing tacit knowledge is important, but it must rest on a solid foundation of prior explicit knowledge. Even the various Japanese companies that Nonaka discusses are heavily focused on explicit to explicit knowledge transfer during the initial stage of economic development. It is well known that in the post-war era, Japanese companies started out by imitating American and European products and selling their products at lower prices (explicit to explicit). However, after the Japanese economy progressed through the initial stage and moved on to the innovation stage, Japanese firms began to internalize what they had learned from this experience (explicit to tacit) and then created their unique and innovative products (tacit to explicit). If Japanese firms did not accumulate this prior base of hard knowledge over the years through explicit to explicit knowledge transfer, managing tacit knowledge would not have been possible.

Furthermore, even for advanced firms, an excessive focus on managing tacit knowledge could lead to organizational inefficiency. This point is very well illustrated by the case of Microsoft, which is generally considered to be at the forefront of innovation and creativity. Its corporate culture is well known to have a very high degree of individuality and organizational flexibility to facilitate an innovative knowledge creation process. However, the organization was too flexible and overly focused on creativity, so much so that it severely lacked organizational discipline. As Bob Herbold, chief operating officer of Microsoft from 1994 to 2001, noted, the loose organizational structure, which was one of the core strengths of Microsoft's innovations, was also one of its biggest problems. Therefore, Herbold instituted various measures to standardize Microsoft's operational practices and enhanced discipline across this chaotic organization. The result was a more efficient and profitable Microsoft, which saved US$190 million annually on procurement alone (Herbold, 2002).

More recently in 2019, Nonaka and Takeuchi (2019) published a second book, *The Wise Company*, coming some 25 years after the successful last book *The Knowledge-Creating Company*. The authors stated that in the last 25 years, the landscape of knowledge has changed, making the knowledge more abundant, global, complex, deeper, and connected. In such an environment, people need to be more careful about harnessing the right kind of knowledge. The authors argued that depending on explicit knowledge prevents firms from coping with rapid change. Instead, the wisdom, a higher-order tacit knowledge, is necessary to cope with the fast-changing world. To this degree, the new book introduces six unique practices that firms harness to achieve world-changing innovation.

Still, for firms and their leaders, the key message should be that every innovative practice needs to be established on more traditional elements. A simple analogy to this story would be the process of learning martial arts. Regardless of natural athletic ability or reflex, everyone must begin by repeatedly practicing basic kicks and punches in order to learn more advanced moves such as combos and spin kicks. The same is true for knowledge creation and management processes. Without a solid foundation of explicit to explicit knowledge transfer, an excessive emphasis on tacit knowledge will lead to unnecessary organizational chaos and increased operational costs.

2.2 Customer Co-opting Strategy

Traditional economic and business theories took it for granted that the supply and demand sides were strictly segregated. However, this traditional boundary began to change when Toffler (1980) introduced the concept of "prosumer," a portmanteau between producer and consumer. Following this new concept, many scholars increasingly began to adopt this idea in their own analyses. Kotler (1986), for example, used the prosumer idea to present the benefits and challenges which marketers face with the rise of prosumerism. Many experts, especially in the computer programming arena, also commented on this exciting development as a novel way to enhance their product value. This concept of consumers and producers engaging in a collaborative production process has intrigued many observers.

Along similar lines, Prahalad and Ramaswamy (2000) argue that in the new economy, companies must incorporate customer experience into their business models and deal with the many challenges that are involved. As John F. Kennedy famously told the American people in his 1961 inaugural address, "Ask not what your country can do for you — ask what you can do for your country," Prahalad and Ramaswamy assert "ask not what firms can do for the customers — ask what customers can do for the firm."

Previously, businesses and customers have had clearly defined roles, but over time they have shifted and the lines between the two have blurred. The main reasons behind the shift are deregulation, globalization, technological convergence, and the high-speed evolution of the Internet. The emergence of the Internet has allowed consumers to conveniently access almost unlimited information regarding a firm's goods and services. When consumers visit corporate websites, not only can they read up on general company information but can also purchase standardized and customized goods, read shareholder information, check stock prices, access annual reports, and learn about new process and manufacturing techniques. As a result, customers are no longer merely passive recipients but are rapidly becoming co-creators. The current market can be likened to a forum where customers assist in creating and competing for value. In short, the customer is a new source of competence, which in turn can be a new source of competitive advantage.

It is difficult to tap into this new source of competitive advantage, as even accessing internal competence can be challenging, let alone external competence. Furthermore, within a company, there may be a limited number of staff, but the customers or potential customers of a firm can reach far larger numbers. Therefore, the authors provide several steps that a company can take in order to ensure leverage in co-opting customer competence:

- *Encouraging Active Dialogues* — Companies currently have no monopoly or advantage over customers when it comes to information access. Thus, customers must be treated as equals. The firm should also be prepared to learn from customers in order to allow dialogue to progress and evolve, lest the customer becomes uninterested. Nobody wants to have a one-sided conversation where they feel their thoughts and opinions are being ignored or disregarded. If one firm does not listen to its customers, another firm will.

- *Mobilizing Customer Communities* — Online communities can be tightly knit and remarkably sophisticated groups of consumers. Internet chat rooms, for example, are easy to start up and participate in. Yet, chat rooms should not be entirely unstructured and strict rules must be imposed. The benefit of such a customer community is the speed with which it can transfer information or what is known as "viral marketing." Product positioning can often depend on these online communities and their collective personalized experiences.

- *Managing Customer Diversity* — Companies can easily neglect the varying needs among their potential customers. The experience and consequent judgment of a product among customers will vary according to their range of skills and knowledge or their level of sophistication. Based on the customers' level of sophistication, their tolerance of problems or their concerns over privacy and security may vary and thus cannot be ignored.

- *Co-creating Personalized Experiences* — Customization refers to the manufacturer designing products to suit the customer's needs, whereas personalization has the customer involved in the actual creation process. This can be easily understood when one compares picking a meal out of a menu (customization) versus cooking together with the chef in the kitchen (personalization). Many firms have realized that personalization is highly desirable and thus offer opportunities on websites for customers to choose the style, material, and size of their products.

It should be noted though that managing the personalized experience can be even more challenging than developing it. The authors identify some useful ways by which a company can create opportunities for the customers to experiment and select their level of involvement in the process.

First, the firm must be able to manage multiple channels of experience. The Internet is of course a very adaptable and accessible channel for customers; however, it may not be a suitable means for everyone. The firm must take into consideration all types of customers and which channels they would find the most convenient. This means that while a firm's website might be fun and user-friendly, there will still be customers who prefer face-to-face contact or even those who prefer to use the telephone rather than a computer as their main means of contact. Allowing for maximum satisfaction in only one channel of experience alienates a variety of customers from the firm.

Second, the firm must be able to manage variety and evolution. This is different from managing the variety of products available to the customer, and it is the variety of customer's experiences that must be managed effectively. Essentially, the range of customers' experiences will transcend the product itself. Thus, the firm needs products that can shape themselves to customers' needs and evolve alongside those needs. Products, which are static or limited in any way, will have a short selling life and customers will easily lose interest in the firm.

Lastly, the firm should be skilled in shaping the expectations among customers. Consumers are sensitive to "what is next," so companies should play a role in shaping those expectations. It is important to educate the customers as well as being educated by the customer in order to develop future product lines. This refers to encouraging active dialogue and mobilizing customer communities. With that kind of customer input, a firm can learn what the customer expects while simultaneously shaping their next move in the market.

After following the above guidelines, the firm should be in a better position to co-opt competencies among customers. However, the firm must remain vigilant as one of its best assets, the customer, can also become one of its biggest competitors. A shift in power is occurring due to information availability and at this stage companies are no longer mere price-setters but are also price-takers as customers are able to negotiate terms and prices with increased access to information. The companies that do not accommodate these new changes may find themselves pushed out of the market completely as their customers' preferences or loyalties change to suit their own needs.

In order to access all competencies, the firm must be highly flexible and should not be fixed to any specific role within the company. This can only be achieved through constant reconfiguration to optimize the firm toward co-opting customers. The authors acknowledge that this can be traumatic for employees within the firm, but this is where management should step in. It is the manager's responsibility to deal with the traumas that occur and to hire self-motivated staff members who are more responsive to change. The manager is required to maintain a stable center within the firm using organizational values as an anchor so as not to set the firm adrift in a sea of endless competitive possibilities.

Analysis

When Alvin Toffler introduced the term "Prosumer" in his 1980 book *The Third Wave*, it signaled a fundamental shift in the linkage between consumers and producers. Toffler contended that the distinction between the two sides will become increasingly blurred and that value can be created from an active consumer who takes part in the production process. Toffler traces his ideas back to Becker (1976), an American economist who first noted the importance of a "non-money economy." Becker's prediction that the non-working sector (consumers) may generate significant added values for companies was the foundation for Toffler's ideas.

Prahalad and Ramaswamy's true contribution to this long train of thought is that they have presented a practical and focused way in which firms can utilize this concept in their everyday operations. By doing so, the two authors have concretely presented how to manage the prosumer's value-creating activity to the firm's best advantage. This is not to criticize Prahalad and Ramaswamy's lack of originality, but rather to highlight their true contribution. It is important for readers to understand that most, if not all, new ideas are based on a pre-established model or concept, which provides the basic framework for a new idea, and Prahalad and Ramaswamy are no exceptions to this general truth.

Prahalad and Krishnan (2008) have further refined the idea of co-opting customer competence in a book, *The New Age of Innovation*. They assert that co-opting customer competence has assumed increasing importance because of increased globalization and ubiquitous connectivity which are forcing companies to reexamine how they deliver value to customers. The ability to reach out and touch customers anywhere and anytime means that companies must deliver not just competitive products but also unique and real-time customer experiences, shaped by the customer "context."

2.3 Co-creation Strategy Toward Expanded Paradigm of Value Creation

After the seminal work of Prahalad and Ramaswamy (2000) "Co-opting Customer Competence," Ramaswamy continued to explore and expand the research on the co-creation paradigm, by working with other scholars and executives. The development of technology and the emergence of "smart, connected products" have helped firms embrace the power of co-creation strategy, incorporating multiple stakeholders for value creation. According to Ramaswamy (2009), co-creation is defined as "the process by which products, services, and experiences are developed jointly by companies and their stakeholders, opening up a whole new world of value."

For the illustration of the concept, Ramaswamy took an example of NikePlus, *a running experience platform*, launched in 2006. It consists of a smart sensor that collects performance data from one's running experiences. Simply put, when one runs with an Apple iPod, a NikePlus sensor placed inside the running shoe can collect the data being

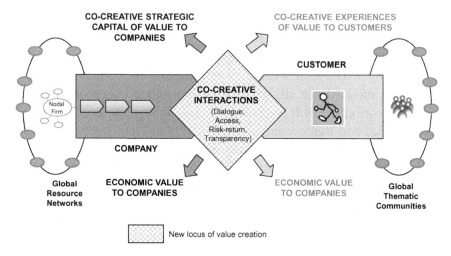

Fig. 5.   Co-creating value through experiences.

Source: Ramaswamy (2008, p. 10).

wirelessly transmitted and stored to the iPod. Furthermore, NikePlus combines collected data with stored music which can help runners enjoy a better running experience, particularly when one's energy starts to dip. In addition, after running, one can visit the NikePlus website and use many functions related to one's running experiences and share them with other people as well. For example, one can track the progress, analyze the performance, share the data with friends, and challenge other runners. Nike extended the collaboration with Apple by integrating NikePlus with Apple's other gadgets, such as iPhone and Apple Watch by taking advantage of new features on its partner's platforms, such as the App Store. For example, by taking advantage of iPhone's built-in GPS, Nike developed its own NikePlus GPS app.

The NikePlus example shows that value creation entails a larger scope of resource networks among partner firms and suppliers as well as individuals both within and outside the firm. As shown in Fig. 5, co-creative interactions are a distinctive strategy for value creation. By involving individuals (runners), group thematic communities (running clubs), and organizations (Nike, Apple), Nike can engage with informed, connected, and networked customers around the world, and offer unique customer experiences and environments to them. Moreover, such interactions attract more individuals, customers, and other stakeholders to become more involved with Nike, and generate more values for both Nike and customers. Hence, co-creative interactions emerge as a new source of value creation.

Compared to the traditional way of value creation, there are two aspects of paradigm changes for co-creation strategy (Ramaswamy, 2008, 2009; Ramaswamy and Ozcan, 2018). First, firms offer more than products and services themselves but experiences through co-creation platforms and interactions among stakeholders. Therefore, value creation does not end up with delivering the products and services to customers, but continues in a joint space of interactions with customers and stakeholders. In this respect, value is thus created not only in exchange or use of resources and process in activities but also in a joint space of interaction. Second, the process of value creation is shifting from a unilateral process within the firm toward the co-creation with various stakeholders. The experiences and interactions among stakeholders affect the experiences of customers, and hence the co-creation approach needs to serve the interests of all stakeholders rather than the interests of customers only. Otherwise, stakeholders will not participate fully or will reduce their engagement in customer co-creation. This then requires competence among firms to manage and orchestrate various stakeholders involved in the ecosystem.

Ramaswamy and Ozcan (2018a, 2018b) referred to the joint place of co-creative interactions as digitalized interactive platform (DIP). DIP is defined as "an evolving digitalized networked arrangement of related artifacts, persons, processes, and interfaces (APPI)."

- Artifacts provide visible and action-oriented interactions, which can be both physical and digitalized things, including data in the form of numbers, text, pictures, audio, and video.

- Persons include customers, employees, partners, and other stakeholders that experience and co-create interactions by leveraging other three APPI components.

- Processes are a sequence of activities and create change, with direction and movement, with one stage clearly leading to the next in a structured sequence of connected events.

- *Interfaces* provide physical and digitalized means through which entities participate and interact with each other.

To better manage the co-creative interactions, Ramaswamy and Gouillart (2010) suggested four basic principles as follows:

- *Consider and produce values for all stakeholders who participate in customer co-creation.* Without any significant values, stakeholders will be less likely to wholeheartedly participate in the interactions.

- *Focus on the experiences of all stakeholders for co-creating values.* The key to improving experiences is to make stakeholders play the central role in designing how they work and interact with each other. However, there should be caution so that co-creation is not a free-for-all, and there should be some rules which the firm sets by providing the overall strategic direction and defining the boundaries. Therefore, stakeholders know what can and cannot be co-created.

- *Interact directly among stakeholders.* The best way for this is to invite all interested parties with a wide range of expertise and perspectives to interact directly and reach out to each other. Such interactions help them hear and see the issues and work on the resolutions together as well.

- *Provide platforms allowing stakeholders to interact and share their experiences.* An effective platform should facilitate participants' awareness of the shortage and understand the concerns of other parties, which are the bases of working together for devising an optimal solution.

Analysis

As products and services become commoditized, forces of globalization and outsourcing flatten the competitive playing fields, and value chains become more fragmented, the co-creation strategy provides a useful approach toward achieving sustainable growth. The co-creation strategy not only offers firms new opportunities for value creation but also reduces risk, time, and capital intensity by leveraging the capabilities and resources of various participants involved in the growing online global networks.

Ramaswamy acknowledged that the idea of co-creation is not entirely new, but has been influenced by the work of C.K. Prahalad on co-opting customer competence. He emphasized how firms had to go beyond dialogue with consumers and also had to recognize that consumers did not want just "finished" products, but meaningful experiences (Ramaswamy, 2009). Nowadays, such a strategy has been widely applied by not only leading industrial companies (Nike, Starbucks, and Apple) but also latecomers (Xiaomi) across various sectors, such as IT, finance, telecommunications, and retail. For example, Xiaomi, a Chinese smartphone manufacturer, generates the bulk of its revenue from lower-margin device sales (two-thirds of the revenue forms the smartphone segment), but a majority of its profits are from online services, such as cloud storage, subscription for TV shows, movies, and games. These physical products function as the platforms for offering various services (Delventhal, 2019).[2]

Considering the growing importance of integrating the various stakeholders for value creation in practice, many other models, concepts, and frameworks have been introduced and discussed in academia, including a two-sided market model (Eisenmann *et al.*, 2006), multi-sided platforms (Boudreau and Hagiu, 2009), smart, connected products (Porter and Heppelmann, 2014), and software-based platform businesses (Parker *et al.*, 2017). Despite the prevalence of value co-creation in practice and growing concerns in recent years, the academic research on this topic is still underdeveloped due to the complexity and difficulty in analyzing the business ecosystem (Lee *et al.*, 2020).

Although there are benefits for all participants in the ecosystem and society as a whole, one of the challenges for firms pursuing

---

[2]For more information, see https://www.investopedia.com/news/how-xiaomi-makes-money/.

the co-creative strategy is the unequal distribution of revenues and profits among participants. A handful of companies such as platform leaders take up almost all of the market or a majority of the profits. In this regard, the four big tech giants, namely, Google, Apple, Facebook, and Amazon (GAFA), have dominated and reasserted their dominance during the Coronavirus pandemic. Given the level of criticism leveled at them for their monopoly of power in their respective business sectors, the CEOs of the four giants were required to testify before the US Congress in 2020.

2.4 Which Model?

Chapters 1 and 2 have provided an overview of a range of business models, which can guide managers, consultants, and scholars toward helping firms achieve their goals. The business models that have been reviewed offer a wide perspective of viewpoints and ways in which one can analyze the firm.

All of the models reviewed have their own unique strengths and weaknesses when compared with one another and all are relevant in their own ways. Chapters 1 and 2 have also offered practical real-life applications of the reviewed models, thus providing a clearer understanding of how they work in the real world.

Our case studies will highlight the fact that there exists a need for firms to develop strategies which are suitable for certain regions. Firms should be flexible enough to realize that one all-encompassing strategy is no longer applicable in the world of global business strategy. A firm must be able to fine-tune certain aspects of its strategy in order to find the best fit according to the area in which it wishes to operate and the customer that it wants to do business with.

Case Study 1: Toyota's IMV Project[3]

Toyota is one of the most successful Japanese companies and is often cited in case studies while its operations are usually benchmarked

---

[3] Information for this case study is abstracted from Toyota Website (www.toyota. co.jp), *The Economist* (Revving Up, October 11, 2007), and Ichijo and

around the world, but not without good reason. In the beginning, Toyota developed and produced cars in Japan and exported cars abroad. As its popularity and success grew, Toyota began to produce cars where its markets were located, such as in North America and Western Europe. Later, the company identified major business opportunities in newly industrialized economies (Korea, Taiwan, Hong Kong, and Singapore) and then developing regions, most notably the BRICs countries (Brazil, Russia, India, and China). However, Toyota quickly realized that its model could not adapt to the tastes and needs among developing countries due to its lack of local knowledge.

To solve this problem, Toyota moved onto its next stage of development. The company developed a global production and supply network to solve the problems of local production. In particular, it launched the project entitled "Innovative International Multi-Purpose Vehicles" (hereby known as the IMV project), which was designed to learn about how to understand and pay attention to local needs.

As part of the project, Toyota upgraded and expanded its plants in Argentina, Indonesia, South Africa, and Thailand as part of its efforts to extend outreach to Asia, Oceania, Africa, and Latin America. The success of the IMV project was very much dependent on local engineers working together with Japanese engineers along with close collaborative efforts between headquarters, subsidiaries, and affiliates. To further ensure success, Toyota set up joint training centers where Japanese and local personnel in key markets trained together.

Instead of performing simple manufacturing operations in the target countries, Toyota began planning and developing with local engineers and designers. By doing so, Toyota has fundamentally changed how knowledge is created and disseminated within its organization. Previously, new knowledge was created in the Japan HQ and unilaterally transferred to subsidiaries, as illustrated on the left side of Fig. 6. However, after undergoing structural changes, new knowledge was also created in foreign markets and transferred to Japan. Joint training centers for all employees offer opportunities for

Kohlbacher (Global Knowledge Creation-The Toyota Way, 2006) (www.toyota-supplier.com).

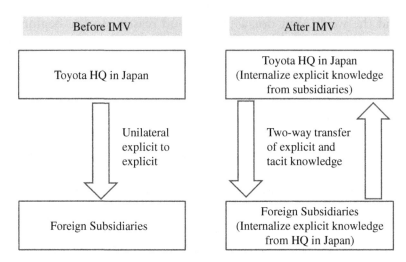

Fig. 6.   Comparison of knowledge flow before and after IMV.

knowledge transfer between employees and instructors, regardless of nationality or the base of operation, as well as tacit to explicit knowledge transfers regarding new technologies and designs, as represented on the right side of Fig. 6.

Such a knowledge creation process also occurs within the domestic sphere. Toyota is well known for cultivating deep and long-term relationships with affiliated companies, sub-contractors, and suppliers. In particular, Toyota's support system provides high-level access to tacit knowledge, which can then be transferred into explicit knowledge. If any of Toyota's affiliates experience problems in generating new knowledge, the company sends in teams of experts to work together with the affiliated company's personnel. Working together facilitates the transfer of knowledge, which in turn improves the affiliates' competitiveness. Such cooperative and collaborative activities lead to positive results such as lower production costs, creation of appropriate technologies, and better understanding of consumer needs. Furthermore, the transfer of knowledge allows the firms to cultivate long-term relationships as they learn to understand and respect each other's operational methods. As the relationship continues, these feelings will grow and the transfer of knowledge becomes more significant as trust between the two parties increases.

This case shows the operational effectiveness of the collaborative knowledge-creating process between various parties. In Toyota, knowledge is created through cooperation between foreign branches and the Japanese home base as well as among Toyota's affiliates and subsidiaries. Furthermore, this case illustrates cultural aspects, which Nonaka touched upon. As we can see from Toyota's case, collaboration and cooperation among the different parties involved is crucial for this knowledge creation process to work. Particularly, Japanese cultural values, which place a high level of emphasis on collectivism and harmony, explain why this kind of knowledge creation process is better developed in Japanese firms than in Western firms.

Case Study 2: Renault Targets Asia[4]

While the main focus of Nonaka's article is on Japanese firms, Western firms such as Renault have taken a similar approach. As of 2019, Renault was the ninth largest automaker in the world, in terms of global sales volume (WheelsJoint, 2020). Over many decades, the company has come to be well known for numerous revolutionary designs, security technologies, and motor racing. While it is wildly popular across Europe, it has not made much headway in Asia, until recently.

Renault has historically maintained all of its R&D, production, and manufacturing facilities within or around France. This has enabled it to become an expert regarding its European customer's needs and desires. However, upon going global, Renault has had difficulty in gauging the needs and desires of the Asian consumer, mainly due to a lack of tacit knowledge about this new market.

When entering the Japanese market, Renault made a move to form an alliance with one the major Japanese automakers Nissan. The two auto giants combined their production facilities, allowing Renault and Nissan engineers to work side by side. In this way, Renault was

---

[4]Information for this case is abstracted from the Renault Website (www.renault.com), *The Economist* (Charge! May 8, 2008), and *The New York Times* (Renault Rolls the Dice on Two Auto Projects Abroad, August 29, 2002).

able to integrate many of Nissan's manufacturing operations and technologies into its other production sites. Not only did the two firms work together in the production side but also put their heads together in the design department. From this aspect, the alliance was mutually beneficial. As the design teams worked together, there was a two-way transfer of knowledge. Nissan began to build cars which were more suited to the European market, and thus it improved its market share in Europe, while Renault produced cars which were suited to the Asian market.

The two companies were able to transfer a high level of tacit knowledge between each other. Following this experience, Renault then decided to form a joint venture with the Korean automaker Samsung Motors in order to continue its successful foray into East Asia. The two began to actively produce cars together and have managed to maintain a fairly large market share within Korea (fourth in the market with a 5% share in 2019). Renault has successfully introduced the French brand into Korea and is now seeking to extend this success to other Asian countries.

As a result of its successes in Asia, the Renault group has come to realize the benefits of knowledge creation and transfer. Its R&D centers were traditionally maintained in France and operated by local designers and engineers. However, since its experiences in Asia, the firm has opened up international design centers, employing 20 different nationalities, which are aimed at (a) developing creativity, (b) stimulating innovation, and (c) supporting Renault's international operations.

One of these international design centers is based just outside of Seoul, Korea. Besides the main activities mentioned above, this design center is also expected to work with other design centers across Asia and track design trends within the region. Merely having the different nationalities working together creates an environment suitable to the transfer of explicit knowledge, but by working so closely together and through observation of each other's methods, tacit knowledge is more efficiently transferred.

Renault's experience with knowledge creation and transfers has been very successful, partly because of a suitable choice in whom it has partnered with. Partners must be willing to transfer their knowledge, which requires a high level of trust, particularly when the partners are not only collaborators but also competitors. Renault's case illustrates how a non-Asian company can be engaged in a highly collaborative process with Asian firms to facilitate a two-way transfer of tacit and explicit knowledge. Renault could potentially be a model for other firms from outside the region to follow in terms of engaging in a highly cooperative alliance with Asian firms for mutual gains.

Case Study 3: Apple's Customer Co-opting Strategy[5]

As one of the leading tech giants, Apple has established a unique reputation in the consumer electronics industry, which is based on its devoted and loyal customers. Although this customer base exists largely in the US, Apple is beginning to make headway in Asia, in particular with its range of portable electronic devices, such as iPads and the highly desirable iPhone. China in particular has become Apple's second largest market after the US in terms of iPhone sales. One way that Apple is improving its market share in Asia is through leveraging customer competence.

- *Encouraging Active Dialogue* — Apple operates Apple Stores throughout Asia, which allow customers to try and test out a variety of new Apple products while trained staff members stand on the sidelines waiting to assist those with questions or problems. Furthermore, in-store technicians are normally available to deal with queries and device problems. Customers, therefore, have an interactive space, which they can readily access in order to discuss the products on sale with trained representatives and other customers. A further step could be to open Apple cafés, which are beginning to

---

[5]Information for this case is abstracted from the Apple Asia Website (www.asia.apple.com) and *The New York Times* (My Son the Blogger — An M.D. Trades Medicine for Apple Rumors, July 21, 2008).

appear in the US. With the café culture that already exists in Asia, the Apple café would be expected to be popular with Asian consumers.

- *Mobilizing Customer Communities* — Online communities are particularly important in Asia where the Internet is far-reaching and social barriers prevent people from having open conversations with strangers in an offline setting. Therefore, Apple offers discussion forums on all of its Asian websites in local languages. The discussion forums exist for users of Apple products as well as technicians and computer experts. One of the best-known Apple forums, www.macrumors.com, is owned and operated by a former Korean doctor, Dr. Kim. He infamously gave up his career in medicine to blog full time on his widely successful website. Large varieties of sites exist throughout Asia and are creating a cult following similar to that of the US.

- *Managing Customer Diversity* — Apple manages customer diversity in two ways. The first is by providing a wide range of products within a particular product range. This allows the company to offer something to everyone within one product range. Second, Apple offers a number of channels through which the customer is able to communicate with the company. The most impressive and speedy channel is the Apple website which can be accessed in almost any language and country where it is present. Manuals and downloads are available online, as is technical support. The company also offers call center services which customers can access for any reason ranging from technical problems to complaints or ordering new products. Products can be purchased through any of the channels available.

- *Co-creating Personalized Experiences* — Apple now accepts software developments from users, which can be distributed among other users and downloaded for free. This allows customers to personalize their Apple products in their own way. Still, the company is often criticized for being too protective of new designs and concepts until the day that they are launched. Were Apple to become more open during the design process, customer feedback could benefit the company greatly and increase overall customer satisfaction.

In general, Apple has made significant achievements in terms of co-opting customer competence, particularly in the areas of managing customer diversity and mobilizing customer communities where it has excelled. However, Apple would benefit more from further encouragement of active dialogues and co-creating personalized experiences. Both of these aspects require development for a closer customer relationship, which Apple until now has avoided due to its secretive product development process. Opening up this aspect to its devoted customers and co-opting their competence will bring significant added value to the firm.

Case Study 4: Xiaomi's Unprecedented Rebound with Co-creation Strategy[6]

The Chinese tech giant Xiaomi has often been referred to as "the Apple of China." This company was established in 2010 in Beijing and its first entry into a foreign market was Singapore in 2014. Since then, Xiaomi has expanded to more than 80 markets and has more than 1,000 retail outlets worldwide. The extent of this overseas drive is that more than 40% of its total revenue comes from foreign markets. Its smartphone is the most popular model in India. The company itself was also, in 2019, included for the first time in the Fortune Global 500 list and was the youngest company among these listed companies.

Despite its current success, Xiaomi has also faced numerous challenges. In 2016, Xiaomi struggled in both domestic and international markets. Its smartphone sales dropped by around 18% in 2016. Some problems have been identified to explain the sales decline, such as the supply chain and organizational difficulties that are associated with the firm's rapid growth. Some studies also pointed out the exclusive

---

[6]Information for this case study is abstracted from https://www.wired.com/story/behind-the-fall-and-rise-of-china-xiaomi/, https://blog.mi.com/en/2019/10/25/xiaomi-makes-future-50-list-for-the-first-time/ and https://www.livemint.com/industry/telecom/xiaomi-has-world-s-largest-iot-platform-manu-jain-155430 5616765.html.

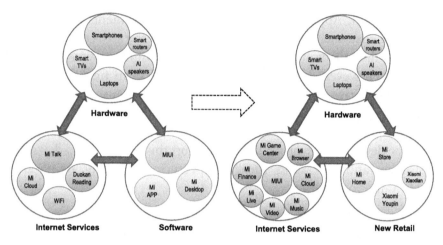

Fig. 7.   Xiaomi's evolving Triathlon business model.
Source: Lam and Leung (2018).

reliance on online sales, which made it difficult to acquire for millions of potential customers in China's smaller cities and rural areas who are less tech-savvy.

In the wake of this setback, the Xiaomi CEO concluded that they needed a third leg to their business model, offline retail stores. In 2017, Xiaomi incorporated a "new retail" strategy, which emphasized the integration of its online and offline channels into its "Triathlon business model." Originally, Xiaomi comprised three modules — hardware, software, and Internet services. Since 2017, Xiaomi has upgraded its business model by incorporating the "software" section into "Internet service," and adding the "new retail" section. Xiaomi's Triathlon model now includes three components — hardware, internet service, and new retail (see Fig. 7).

Xiaomi went beyond selling phones to develop sustainable connections with customers. It has developed an ecosystem which comprises core products — smartphones including accessories such as chargers, earphones, and power banks; smart devices (or internet-connected devices) such as robots, rice cookers, and televisions; and lifestyle products such as backpacks, suitcases, pillows, and other daily

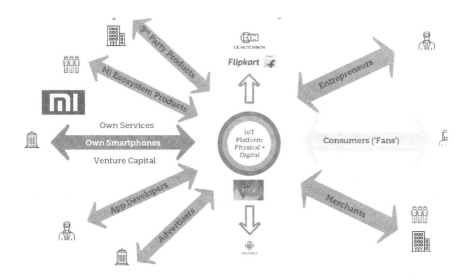

Fig. 8. Xiaomi's business model portfolio.[7]

necessities. By March 2018, the ecosystem incorporated more than 210 partner firms to provide Xiaomi with internet-connected home and tech products that draw customers to its stores. Among them, more than 90 firms were focused on R&D of smart hardware and consumer lifestyle products. Xiaomi supported these start-ups in terms of branding, capital, supply chain, product design, management, and access to Xiaomi's online and offline retail channels. Its ecosystem strove to provide "killer products," which are featured as inexpensive but with high-quality features, top performance, and impressive design.

The offline store of Xiaomi — Mi Home — has played an important role in allowing consumers to experience these killer products. These stores provide a more rewarding shopping experience, help strengthen the brand image, increase purchase rate for interrelated products, and help to integrate with online channels.[8] The interactions

---

[7] http://www.simon-torrance.com/blog/xiaomi-businessmodel.

[8] On the contrary, Xiaomi's online channels include the online retail store — Mi Store — which is available on both the mobile app and the Mi.com website; Xiaomi's

between offline and online channels have extended the customer reach and enhanced their experiences. This has become a critical driver for Xiaomi's growth. In fact, it has actually won more than 100 international design awards for its products and has built the world's largest IoT platform, connecting more than 190 million devices under its ecosystem (see Fig. 8).

All of these smart devices (IoT products) are connected to Xiaomi's app MiUI, which enables users to control all their appliances with their phone. Its popularity has led to Mi Fans and even "Mi Fans Clubs" emerging around the world who provide feedback and ideas on product development, testing, advertising, and marketing. Mi Fans are very active in exchanging product ideas and creating new features for smartphones and operating systems through online forums, Xiaomi BBS, and the MiUI forum. As a result of this close following, Xiaomi consistently updates MiUI every Friday at 5 pm Beijing time. Such activities make customers feel invested in Xiaomi, and makes them more bonded and loyal to Xiaomi.

As with many other businesses, Xiaomi initially relied on selling hardware products and online services. However, as smartphones have become more commoditized at an impressive speed, the battle is fierce among these manufacturers, which makes it difficult to maintain margins from the hardware productions. On the contrary, its online services such as software content remain a very small percentage of its overall revenues. Xiaomi's new retail strategy has acted as the new growth engine for developing its IoT ecosystem. The development of retail stores has also encouraged the growth of shipments of smartphone and the consumption of Xiaomi's other online services. Considering the growing importance of the IoT ecosystem, in January 2019, Xiaomi announced its dual-engine strategy of "Smartphone + AIoT" with an investment of RMB10 million over five years.

---

self-operated boutique style e-commerce marketplace — Xiaomi Youpin; and its flagship store Tmall.

Discussion Questions

1. Do you agree that Japanese companies are more innovative than others, in particular Western companies? Why or why not?

2. Is one type of knowledge ever better than another? When is explicit knowledge better than tacit knowledge or vice versa?

3. Do you believe that firms are really co-opting customer competence? What are your experiences as a consumer?

4. Do you agree with the steps recommended for co-opting customer competence? Would you add anything?

5. Do you agree that co-creative strategy for value creation is superior to the conventional firm-centric value creation strategy?

6. How would you evaluate the dominant position of the four tech giants (Google, Apple, Facebook, and Amazon)? Does their presence promote or hinder market competition? Should they maintain their current dominant power or do they need to be broken up for the sake of market efficiency?

7. How would you define strategy? Which elements are important in creating a strategy?

8. Do you believe that a firm can really become more competitive by following any of the models introduced in this chapter? Will following these models always have positive effects on the outcome?

CHAPTER 3

Applications of Business Models to Non-Business Areas

Chapter Guideline

This chapter revisits Porter's models, but under a different context. In each section, Porter analyzes the most recent developments in technology, society, and business through the lens of his analytical frameworks. The first section discusses the impact of the fourth industrial revolution and newly emerging technologies on the business environment and proposes several guidelines toward using such technologies to the firm's competitive advantage. The next section explains how philanthropic institutions can enhance their performance through a more strategic approach. The last section introduces the concepts of CSR and CSV, and proposes strategic directions for firms to maximize societal and firm benefits simultaneously in both normal and urgent situations.

Summary of Previous Models

In the previous chapter, I looked at three alternative perspectives and business models presented by leading scholars. Nonaka's article revealed a new framework for knowledge management, while Prahalad and Ramaswamy discussed very practical ways in which firms can utilize their customers to increase their value. Ramaswamy further developed the concept of co-creation by incorporating all the related stakeholders including customers in an era of increasing interconnectedness. I have also identified several problems and possible extensions that could enhance the efficiency of each model. Now, I come back to Porter and analyze three hot topics through the lens of his analytical frameworks.

3.1 Strategy and Technology

The Internet is regarded as one of the most powerful forces shaping business strategy along with globalization. Yip (2000) asserted that the Internet is a globalization driver that expands the geographic scope of opportunities due to the transformative effect this technology has on the business landscape. However, doubts began to emerge when the dot-com bubble burst in 2001. Following this event, many began to believe that the Internet was not a miracle invention that would somehow propel business strategy into a completely new world.

Following the dot com burst, there was a reevaluation of the relationship between the Internet and business strategy as many investors were left wondering how this madness had occurred. In commenting on this, Warren Buffett shrewdly noted in an interview with the BBC (2001) that it was largely the result of "irrational exuberance." For their part, Rangan and Adner (2001) analyzed the relationship between the Internet and business strategy and debunked seven common myths surrounding the Internet. Their conclusion was that rather than regarding the Internet as a completely revolutionary technology, it should be regarded as an additional tool that can be utilized for a firm's benefit. Their analysis is largely correct, but leaves us without a clear prescription.

Porter (2001) offers a comprehensive diagnosis and prescription to the "irrational exuberance" generated by the advent of the Internet in the 1990s. He begins by describing the focus on the Internet among business as a form of general and widespread fervor. During the 1990s, many businesses overestimated and misunderstood this new technology and assumed that the Internet would bring about a revolutionary change to the business environment. Companies rushed to embrace this new technological innovation and hastily claimed that the world of business entered a completely new phase in history. New concepts and terminologies emerged such as "e-business strategies" and "new economy." These became part of everyday language and were thrown around by many business leaders and scholars, reflecting the overly optimistic mood at the turn of the new millennium. However, Porter debunked this myth at the time and claimed that the Internet is simply an enabling technology, albeit a powerful one. At the time, most people were too fixated on what the Internet can do for their business. They pointed to features such as high switching costs and network effect, which can provide huge advantages to those who move first. While it is true that most businesses must embrace the new technology to sustain a competitive edge, Porter was keen to emphasize the view that the Internet should not be adopted at the cost of existing competitive advantages.

This observation still holds true in the digital age of the fourth industrial revolution.[1] This term was first introduced by Klaus Schwab, the Founder and Executive Chairman of the World Economic Forum, at the Davos annual summit in 2016. Schwab argued that a range of new technologies is fusing the physical, digital, and biological spheres, and that these technologies are drastically changing how individuals, firms, and governments operate, thereby leading to a transformation of society as a whole. Digital technology, in particular, is regarded as the fundamental driving force for the fourth industrial revolution. Nearly all revolutions and development are made possible through digital technologies, such as artificial intelligence, big data, cloud computing, and the Internet of Things (Schwab, 2016).

---

[1] Schwab (2016) said the fourth industrial revolution is building on the third industrial revolution, but it is not merely a prolongation of the third one. Based on Schwab's description, I further summarized the features of fourth industrial revolution from the four aspects. First, *fast changing* — the fourth revolution evolves in a nonlinear way at unprecedented speed. Second, *high uncertainty* — there are many new standards in almost every industry, and thus firms should be very careful and flexible in adapting to shifting industrial standards. Third, *broad connectivity* — it integrates a wide range of technologies and disciplines, and thus firms need multiple competences for achieving the market success. Fourth, *unlimited potential* — it provides high potential for great success for all players including latecomers and young start-ups.

Porter and Heppelmann (2014) stated that technologies before have mainly contributed to the huge productivity gains and growth across individual activities, but the products themselves were largely unaffected. However, they see that emerging technologies in the current age are embedded in and become an integral part of the products, therefore changing the nature of products. For example, sensors, processors, and software are put inside products, and this enables firms to monitor and analyze the product-usage data, connect with other products, and trigger more innovation with new and better functions, products, and services. Therefore, emerging technology breakthroughs can drive a radical change in the fundamental dynamics of competition (Siebel, 2017).

John Chambers, former executive chairman and CEO of Cisco Systems, predicted that 40% of today's businesses will fail in the next decade; 70% will attempt to transform their businesses digitally, but only 30% will succeed (Siebel, 2017). The recent Big Data Executive 2018 Survey by NewVantage Partners that is aimed at senior Fortune 1,000 executives showed that an overwhelming 97.2% of executives reported their companies are investing in building or launching big data and AI initiatives. However, only over one-fourth (27.3%) of executives reported success, which shows they still have a long way toward commercializing their big data and AI investments (Bean, 2018).

The most successful companies are not those that rush into fully integrating themselves with the technology, but those that use the technology as a tool to complement and bolster their previous sources of competitive advantage. What most of these optimists forgot is that sustainable profitability does not come from simply adopting a technology that everyone else can easily replicate. A standardized technology cannot be a source of uniqueness. Rather, what is truly important is how to differentiate, specialize, and provide unique services to the customers, utilizing the technology as a means to an end. A standardized technology can be utilized by everyone and everywhere, which quickly diminishes the potential for early movers to continuously exploit it as a source of sustainable competitive advantage. Simply put, if you can do it, soon everyone else can too.

So, what should be done to correct this misunderstanding among firms? Porter's suggestion is simple yet powerful: return to the fundamentals. He makes an important distinction between the use of the Internet and Internet technology itself. This is important because while the Internet as a technology itself is standardized (which means anyone can use it in the business operation), the use of the Internet is what truly creates economic value. This logic is also applicable to the use of new emerging technologies in the fourth industrial revolution. What we should care about is how the new technologies can be utilized properly in the strategic context. Porter asserts that businesses must look at two fundamental factors in profitability: (a) industry structure and (b) sustainable competitive advantage. These two factors, which have been extensively analyzed in Porter's previous works, transcend all technological innovations and types of businesses. At this point, Fig. 1 takes the example of the Internet of Things (IoT) and illustrates its impact on the industrial structure driven by five competitive forces as based on the analysis of Porter and Heppelmann (2014).

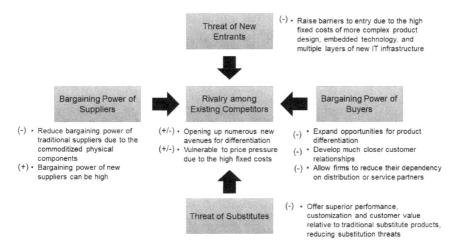

Fig. 1. Impacts of IoT on industry structure.
Source: Porter (2001).

Porter and Heppelmann (2014) described IoT as the "smart, connected products" which is composed of three core elements — physical components, "smart" components, and connectivity components. Physical components refer to the mechanical and electrical parts. Smart components include sensors, microprocessors, data storage, software, operating systems, and user interface. Connectivity components comprise ports, antennas, and protocols which enable wired or wireless connections with products. The three components are interdependent. Smart components expand the capabilities and value of physical ones, while connectivity amplifies the capabilities and value of smart components. Hence, the emergence of IoT shifts the basis of competition from traditional *discrete products* to *product systems* composed of closely related products, and to *systems of systems*, that is, a set of product systems.

In this regard, IoT technology creates new competitors, new bases for competition, and requires firms to equip entirely new and broader capabilities. Porter and Heppelmann suggested four key capabilities for IoT — monitoring, control, optimization, and autonomy. By adopting IoT technology, some firms seek to broaden and redefine their industries, whereas other firms, which could be threatened by such developments, may find that their traditional products become commoditized and lose competitiveness. Although the degree of net effects could be different across industries, Fig. 1 suggests that many industries may undergo the improved profitability, particularly because of the rising barriers to entry and the first-mover advantages stemming from the early accumulation and analysis of product usage data.

Porter stated that IoT will offer a lot of new value creation and growth opportunities, although this does not mean that all firms will have the same opportunities to enhance their potential. In this case, the truly successful firms are those that are able to reshape the industry structure to their utmost advantage, for which IoT can provide a very useful conduit. Porter implies that depending on how firms fuse their traditional advantages with new technologies, they can fundamentally alter the structure to create new economic value and unique services for their customers. In order to ground out the basic principles for firms to follow in achieving this, Porter returns to the two basic fundamentals of all successful businesses:

- *Operational Effectiveness* — This refers to performing the same actions as your competitors, but in a more efficient manner. As IoT not only redefines the standard for operational effectiveness but also substantially raises the bar of best practices, firms have to continuously incorporate new methods and maintain efficiency in order to not fall behind rivals in terms of costs and quality. Over time, the best practices will soon become the standardized ones which all firms can utilize to enhance their operations. Therefore, any innovation can be replicated quickly and will unlikely be a continued source of competitive advantage for firms.

- *Strategic Positioning* — How a firm decides to implement this concept is crucial as strategic positioning is where the winners and losers differ. Rather than simply trying to differentiate through the new technologies, firms must be able decide how to integrate new smart and connected capabilities into their existing value systems in order to bolster their core competence and provide something unique to their customers. Porter stated that the entire set of choices will reinforce one another, which will then define the firm's distinctive strategic positioning. Specifically, Porter suggests the following ten areas for enhancing a firm's competitive advantage (see Table 1).

Some may argue that the IoT will change everything. However, Porter counterargued by stating "that is a dangerous oversimplification," as the rules of competition and competitive advantages still apply. Companies must utilize the new technology, but cannot expect to distinguish themselves solely based on utilizing them since everyone will be able to utilize this standardized feature. Instead, firms must look to more traditional sources of strengths, complemented and enhanced by the power of technologies. Only then can firms create true economic value and specialized services for the customers, which will then lead to a sustainable, long-term competitive advantage.

Table 1.   Firms' strategic concerns for competitive advantage.

1	Which set of smart, connected product capabilities and features should the company pursue?
2	How much functionality should be embedded in the product and how much in the cloud?
3	Should the company pursue an open or closed system?
4	Should the company develop the full set of smart, connected product capabilities and infrastructure internally or outsource to vendors and partners?
5	What data must the company capture, secure, and analyze to maximize the value of its offering?
6	How does the company manage ownership and access rights to its product data?
7	Should the company fully or partially disintermediate distribution channels or service networks?
8	Should the company change its business model?
9	Should the company enter new businesses by monetizing its product data through selling it to outside parties?
10	Should the company expand its scope of operations?

Analysis

A wide range of new emerging technologies can transform various aspects of business, but they must be integrated effectively into the firm strategy and value chain or they may actually compromise the firm's strategic fit. Such an outcome would also further lead to destructive competition for the industry as a whole. Many firms and investors alike, swept away by the overhyped prospect of this new technology, often forget the fundamentals of competitive advantage. This aspect is a unique positioning and a value proposition that enables firms to differentiate themselves from competitors and provide unique economic value to the customers. Although technologies enable firms to enhance operational effectiveness or differentiate from rivals at the early stage, they may become a standardized feature in itself sooner or later. Therefore, a firm that relies on technology to distinguish itself from the rest of the pack has made a critical error by forgetting what the fundamental sources of competitiveness are.

Furthermore, Porter correctly points out how firms, in their hasty drive to achieve an early-mover advantage, have engaged themselves in destructive competition based on low price. Firms are then forced to run faster to maintain the same pace and eventually all firms participating in the industry must suffer decreased profit margins and cutthroat competition. Currently, firms have been hasty in spending vast sums of money for research and development (R&D), but such spending and innovation capabilities or competitive advantages do not always evolve in a linear way.

According to PwC's 2018 Global Innovation 1000 Study, the two most successful firms in the digital world, Tesla and Netflix, were selected for the top 10 most innovative companies in the world. Both companies are relatively new to the scene. However, both firms ranked lower in terms of R&D expenditures. Tesla ranked 113th and Netflix 157th, respectively, among the 1,000 listed companies. In contrast, Volkswagen and Samsung Electronics ranked 3rd and 4th in terms of R&D spending, respectively, but both firms failed to be recognized as the world's most innovative companies in their fields. Therefore, the path to competitive advantage should ultimately rely on the strategy, but not technology itself or the amount of investment in technologies.

3.2 Strategy and Philanthropic Organizations

Weber (1930) once stated that profit, when ethically generated and used for the greater good of society, can be the fundamental building block for a healthy capitalist society. Weber's extensive analysis on the relationship between the traditional Puritan emphasis on thrift, hard work, and ethical profit and the normative fabric of a modern capitalist society can be regarded as the original conception of philanthropy through private foundations.

As Weber's grand reconciliation between profit and ethics prescribed, wealthy Americans went on to find various philanthropic foundations that tackle many social issues. From Andrew Carnegie to modern figures such as Bill Gates and Warren Buffett, the most successful individuals of the American (and perhaps global) capitalist system have altruistically given away billions of dollars for greater societal causes. However, the normative nature of these foundations has somewhat prevented an objective and precise strategic analysis of the activities they perform.

Porter and Kramer (1999) boldly defy such a taboo and identify several problems associated with the current state of practice in philanthropic foundations and give several suggestions to fix the current problems and enhance their performance. Their central question asks whether society is efficiently maximizing the full benefit of philanthropic foundations. The simple answer is "not quite" and the authors begin to present their case as to why the current practices are problematic.

Foundations or charities exist because they can channel funds to solve social problems more effectively than individuals or governments. Since foundations are subject to tax exemptions and other benefits, society expects foundations to achieve more social impact than if the same amount of resources was channeled through governments or individuals. For example, if a donor gives away US$100 to a foundation, society as a whole loses about US$40 in tax revenue. It is expected that this US$40 must be better utilized to serve society than if it would have been given to the government. However, this is under the assumption that all of the US$100 is effectively used by the foundation. In reality, this may not be always true.

Furthermore, by holding so much money (US$330 billion) and not spending it for charitable purposes, society is incurring a substantial cost in terms of deferred social benefits. Since donations receive tax exemptions and foundations are not taxed for the appreciation of their financial assets, the amount of tax revenue that would have been collected by the government accumulates substantially over time. In addition, one must consider the fact that these foundations have substantial administrative costs such as staffing and screening appropriate candidates. From these discussions, one can easily see that foundations are actually a very expensive way to allocate capital for social services.

Foundations, by withholding the money, have an obligation to provide social benefit which exceeds the withheld purchasing power.

How can they achieve this aim? The key to this answer is "strategy." Just as businesses set up strategies to achieve their goals, foundations must do the same. The authors suggest four specific areas that foundations must focus on.

- *Selecting the Best Grantees* — This process must start out based on a unique position where the foundation can best utilize its expertise to generate the most social value. Instead of trying to provide funds for all disadvantaged students, foundations must focus on a certain segment of the population. Also, instead of focusing on a vague goal, foundations must set up a specific goal such as "we will reduce high-school dropout rates in a certain area." In essence, foundations must develop their unique capability to specialize in creating societal services. Furthermore, foundations must be able to critically examine their own performance, not just their recipients. Only through constant self-assessment can foundations innovate in order to create more value for less input. Foundations, just like firms, cannot be all things to all people. They must choose their battleground and must make decisions regarding the tradeoff they will face in terms of the scarce resources they have.

- *Signaling Other Funders* — Just like how a corporation markets itself to potential investors, a foundation must do exactly the same to its potential donors. By promoting the foundation as a specialized and effective organization in providing societal services, donors will have more confidence in the money that they donate, knowing that it will be spent most effectively.

- *Improving the Performance of Grant Recipients* — Instead of simply giving away money, foundations should also monitor and help recipients in enhancing their performance. If the money is simply given away, there is no guarantee that it will be spent for the intended purposes. Through engaging and monitoring the recipients on a long-term scale, a foundation can ensure that it achieves its fundamental purpose, which is to create more societal value from every dollar spent. This is linked to the above two activities as monitoring and engaging the recipient will further improve the foundation's self-assessment as well as its ability to signal to other donors.

- *Advancing the State of Knowledge and Practice* — Since foundations are uniquely positioned to be active in achieving a certain societal goal over the long term, they can fund research and support a systematic progression of projects. The knowledge and experience accumulated through this process can then be transmitted to other organizations such as the government and philanthropic organizations to further enhance the impact of the entire system.

In essence, just like successful firms, foundations must also be highly specialized, systematic, and focused in their approach to create social services. In order to achieve this, the foundation's staff, methods, and activities must be tailored to best fit the target segment and societal service that it wishes to provide. However, the reality is that the operations of most foundations are far from their prescriptions. According to the available data, foundations are spread too thin in terms of money and staff. This is a major problem because foundations cannot focus or take a unique position without concentrating their resources into specific target areas.

Porter and Kramer (1999) also discussed the problems in the foundations' self-assessment methods in detail. Foundations rarely assess themselves properly because of a tendency to favor more performance criteria as the way to measure their achievements. Such an approach is not effective as it only focuses on whether the money was spent as intended rather than whether the money has actually generated the desired societal impact. Furthermore, recipients themselves also do evaluations, which raises questions over objectivity. Lastly, most evaluations are done in a very limited scope where individual grantees are interviewed. This is highly problematic and a more comprehensive and general self-assessment approach would enhance the effectiveness of foundations.

Porter and Kramer (1999) concluded that the current foundation practices not only diminish effectiveness but they inevitably reduce the satisfaction that donors, staff, and trustees derive from their work. Unless foundations accept the fact that they must enhance their accountability, expertise, and productivity, they cannot truly perform their intended functions.

Analysis

To some people, applying an analytical business framework to a philanthropic foundation may seem rather inappropriate. The idea of fusing the cold and calculating nature of business strategy to the warm and altruistic purpose of philanthropic foundations may not sit comfortably. However, as one can see from the article by Porter and Kramer, they were able to clearly identify the true strengths and weaknesses of philanthropic foundations and make valuable suggestions to enhance their performance through a business framework. Just as a successful business must generate more value with every penny that it spends, a philanthropic foundation must generate more social value for every dollar that comes from its donors. The general lesson that can be learned from this analysis is that productivity, positioning, innovation, and specialization are key for both business and non-business entities alike.

3.3 Strategy and Society

Corporate Social Responsibility (CSR) has been receiving increasing attention from various segments of academia, managers, and policy makers. International organizations such as the United Nations, for example, have taken proactive measures to promote and implement CSR as a measure to fight global poverty, especially in the context of its ambitious "Sustainable Development Goals." This reflects the recognition that spurring a healthy and responsible entrepreneurial environment is one of the most powerful drivers of economic, social, and political development. Therefore, it is no surprise that much research has been conducted and many works have been published on this important issue. Furthermore, many scholars have identified and analyzed various dimensions of CSR, such as the relationship between

CSR and business ethics (Balmer *et al.*, 2007; Balmer *et al.*, 2011; Schaltegger and Burritt, 2018), CSR and finance (Cochran and Wood, 1984; Cheng *et al.*, 2014; Cumming *et al.*, 2016), and CSR and politics (Jeurissen, 2004; Vallentin and Murillo, 2012; Giuli and Kostovetsky, 2014).

More systematically, Porter and Kramer (2002, 2006, 2011) look at the relationship between CSR and business strategy. The starting point of the authors' analysis points out two major problems with the current state of CSR. The first problem is that many view the relationship between society and businesses as inherently conflictive. CSR is perceived as an obligation that firms must begrudgingly perform in order to appease people's concerns that corporations negatively affect society. The second problem is that because of this erroneous perception, firms promote CSR in generic terms, as if it is a chore that must be done rather a cause they believe in. It is largely done carelessly and without much effort. Therefore, it is not surprising that the current state of practicing CSR is both inefficient and insincere at the same time.

Porter and Kramer suggest that it is time for firms to take a different approach to CSR and firms should regard CSR as a fertile ground for opportunity, innovation, and competitive advantage. Fundamentally, the relationship between firms and society is not a zero-sum relationship, but a mutually beneficial one in which both society and firms can enhance each other through CSR. How can this be achieved? The starting point in answering this question is for firms to start looking at CSR in the same strategic mindset in which they operate their day-to-day business. Currently, most CSR ranking systems focus solely upon superficial data such as number of hours, amount of money, and number of volunteers mobilized for CSR activities. These are rather meaningless as the true measure of effective CSR should be the impact of CSR not the input.

At this point, Porter and Kramer analyze the four prevailing justifications for CSR:

- *Moral Obligation* — This is the most common and traditional dimension which describes the normative obligation that induces individuals to be good citizens and perform positive citizenry. Commercial success therefore must be achieved without breaking societal moral codes of conduct and without harming the environment.

- *Sustainability* — Companies are obliged to operate in ways that will not harm society's long-term economic potential. For example, using hazardous materials to enhance short-term profit should be avoided since it can contaminate the environment and harm the local community.

- *License to Operate* — A firm consists of various stakeholders whose interests must be protected. Traditionally, this obligation was merely confined to the shareholders' profit maximization, but now the concept has been expanded to incorporate a wider range of groups. For example, if a company is to operate in a certain area, it must be aware of the concerns that the residents of that area have.

- *Reputation* — The corporate image is crucial, especially with the rise of environmental and political awareness in society. In this regard, sophisticated consumers will prefer companies with a good CSR track record and will be more sensitive to any controversial issues on such matters. This is important for firms because it translates into corporate image, which affects sales and profitability.

The underlying premise for the above four categories is that firms must sacrifice a certain degree of their profitability in order to achieve socially beneficial outcomes. In other words, the prevailing notion of CSR regards firms and society as locked in a zero-sum battle between profit and CSR. Porter and Kramer (2006), however, assert that not only is this view outdated but also socially inefficient. Firms are not separate from society as firms have a tremendous capability to enrich it by providing various resources to increase social capital. Society, in turn, can help firms become more profitable and competitive through providing better human resources and business environments. The two entities can engage in a positive-sum game instead of a zero-sum one. In order to help refine this concept better, Porter and Kramer suggest two types of CSR:

- *Responsive CSR* — Every corporate activity has some kind of impact (both positive and negative) on the society in which it operates. Responsive CSR is a corporate measure designed to mitigate adverse effects from business activities. For example, companies which deal with hazardous materials can allocate additional resources to make sure that these materials do not harm society. It should be noted that responsive CSR may stop adverse effects, but does not generate any additional benefit to the firm or the society.

- *Strategic CSR* — Contrary to responsive CSR, strategic CSR is a more proactive and evolved way of performing CSR. In other words, CSR activities not only prevent adverse effects but also generate positive externalities which benefit both firms and societies. For example, Microsoft works with the American Association of Community Colleges (AACC) to provide better equipment, human resources, and other aid to enhance the quality of IT programs in these colleges. As a result, more students are able to obtain better jobs (societal benefits), while Microsoft is more easily able to recruit IT specialists suitable for its operations (firm benefits).

Porter and Kramer have reflected upon the examples of Marriott and Nestle that illustrate how the positive effects on both firms and society could be expanded by performing CSR in a strategic context. In the case of Marriott, it provides paid on-the-job training for unemployed job candidates. Ninety percent of those in this training program end up taking jobs with Marriott. In this way, society benefits with more employed constituents, while Marriott can reduce the administrative cost in screening potential candidates.

For Nestle, they required a stable and fresh source of milk in Moga, India, in order to establish their business in this lucrative market. However, the situation in Moga was not good as local farmers were suffering from low calf-survival rates, poor logistics, lack of infrastructure, and overall poverty. Nestle achieved a remarkable task by establishing refrigerated collection points for local dairy farmers and then used those points as a fulcrum for strategic CSR. From these collection points, Nestle deployed trained veterinarians and other experts to local farmers to transfer knowledge, technology, and the equipment necessary to enhance the calf-survival rate and set up better farm infrastructure. Through these efforts, the once poverty-stricken area of Moga transformed into a bustling dairy industry hub of India, while Nestle was able to reap immense profit from the fresh dairy that local farmers produced.

These examples show that in contrast to the traditional CSR (or responsive CSR), strategic CSR enables a firm to move on from simply addressing social problems to making CSR profitable for firms. In other words, strategic CSR not only helps society but also the firm itself. Yet, when addressing social issues, Porter repeatedly asserted that no firm can be everything to everyone. Firms must therefore pick and choose their most advantageous battleground in order to succeed. The same principle can be applied for CSR. Firms must concern themselves with social issues which they are most capable of solving and additionally focus on those that will help enhance their competitiveness and profitability. Depending on the firm, the same social issue may be categorized differently.

For example, carbon emissions and pollution are a general social issue, but for Honda, it has both a value chain impact and a social dimension. Furthermore, even within the same industry, different companies may have a different sense of priority on the same social issue. Porter and Kramer provide the example of automobile safety in which Volvo has clearly made it its priority, while for Toyota, environmental friendliness is more of a priority than safety. The point here is that a firm must perform CSR in areas where it is most affected and will be the most effective. All social issues are important, but certain firms are better equipped and motivated to tackle specific challenges. For example, General Electric is better equipped to perform CSR in healthcare than Honda, while Honda is more willing to allocate its resources in CSR related to tackling carbon emissions.

In conclusion, Porter and Kramer urge firms and social constituents to stop looking at CSR as a burden but more as an opportunity. At the same time, society must also stop regarding firms as immoral entities that will sacrifice social benefits for the sake of profits; rather, they should see them as an integral part of society which can generate immense economic and social value. Instead of regarding CSR as a "responsibility," the concept should evolve to "Corporate Social Integration." There are plenty of dimensions and arenas in which both firms and society can harmoniously interact to create beneficial social value. The key step is for both parties to realize this outcome and thus transform their mindsets toward a more positive and proactive approach.

Porter and Kramer (2011) further developed strategic CSR and introduced a new concept known as creating shared value (CSV). By drawing the basic idea of strategic CSR, Porter and Kramer defined "shared value" as "policies and operating practices that enhance the competitiveness of a company while simultaneously advancing the economic and social conditions in the communities in which it operates." They further clarified the traits of *shared value* across the following three aspects. First, it extends the definition of the market by incorporating social needs into the conventional economic needs. Second, addressing the social harms or weaknesses does not necessarily raise the costs for firms, but can actually help them increase their productivity and enlarge their market through innovative technologies, operational and managerial methods, and approaches. Third, the shared value is neither about personal values nor about sharing the value already created by firms, rather it is about newly created value and an expanded share of the total economic and social value.

Accordingly, CSR mainly aims to do a good duty in response to external pressure. Hence, these social activities are usually separated from firms' core business activities and profit maximization. As the main beneficiary is society, the impact of CSR is often limited by the corporate budget assigned for these activities. When firms are in financial difficulties, it is natural to expect that they would then cut back on their CSR budget in order to free up resources for their core business. On the contrary, CSV stresses creating new economic and societal values relative to costs. Firms integrate social activities into their value chain and strategy for competitiveness. Thus, CSV is integral to profit maximization and positioned at the center of corporate agenda. As not just society but also firms benefit from CSV activities significantly, firms will be less vulnerable to the environmental changes and will commit long-term and sustainable investments in their communities. Porter and Kramer suggested three distinct ways for creating shared value:

- *Reconceiving Products and Markets* — This refers to developing appropriate products for the unmet social needs of the global economy, such as health, better housing, improved nutrition, help for the elderly, greater financial security, and stronger environmental protection. For example, food companies that used to concentrate on taste and quantity to encourage consumption have refocused their product development by addressing better nutrition as a way to enhance healthier lifestyles within the community. Firms can also adjust their product lines to suit the markets from lower-income and disadvantaged communities in both advanced countries and developing countries, which are often defined as the bottom of the pyramid.

- *Reconfiguring Productivity in the Value Chain* — A firm's value chain activities are often affected by various social issues, such as the availability of natural resources and water supplies, health and safety, working conditions, and equal treatment among employees. It is evident that these social problems incur internal costs on the firm, and thus addressing these social problems will not only contribute to the social progress but also boost corporate productivity. Porter and Kramer stated that although few companies have fully exploited productivity enhancement in these social areas, there is growing consensus that such problems can be addressed by better technology at nominal incremental costs, and achieve net cost savings through improvement in resource utilization, processing, and quality. For example, Walmart reduced its packaging and realigned its delivery routes as a way to reduce its carbon footprint while at the same time saving the company US$200 million in costs.

- *Employing Local Cluster Development* — Corporate resources are often limited and thus the success of CSV activities is often affected by the availability of supporting companies and the surrounding infrastructure. Porter named it "clusters," which is a concept defined as geographic concentrations of suppliers, related businesses, other firms, service providers, logistic infrastructure, and institutions such as schools and universities. Building clusters for addressing social problems will not only improve the firms' productivity but also has a higher potential of sharing benefits with more involved partners, thereby generating higher spillover effects. Porter and Kramer suggested that it is critical to building open and transparent markets, which leads to the positive cycle of economic and social development results.

Analysis

Strategic CSR presents a new paradigm in understanding and executing the original concept of CSR. It is true that for many years the general public has held a skeptical view regarding the true motivations of firms and promoted CSR as a way to keep business entities in check. However, firms are not only an integral part of society but are also entities that can generate immense social capital and value through their vast resources and capabilities. Strategic CSR and CSV are very similar conceptually in terms of motivation, relation to business, beneficiary, and the overall effects (Moon and Parc, 2019).

Moon (2012) argued that although Porter and Kramer proposed a new concept of CSV to make a distinction with (responsive) CSR, CSV stresses the *process* of achieving both shared value between firms and society (Moon and Parc, 2019). This highlights the need for another terminology that can act as the antithesis: to (responsive) CSR. In this case, Moon (2012) suggested *Corporate Social Opportunity* (CSO) which considers addressing social issues as new opportunities for creating profits and competitiveness. This stands in

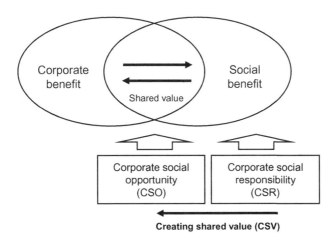

Fig. 2. CSR, CSV, and CSO.

Source: Moon and Parc (2019).

contrast to the concept of conventional CSR which considers social activities as the responsibility of firms which should be met by their own internal costs. On the contrary, CSV is the tool of shifting CSR to CSO by identifying the shared value which leads to further benefits for both firms and society (see Fig. 2).

One possible extension would be to expand Porter and Kramer's studies into analyzing the multiplying effects that the positive externalities generated by corporations can have on society as a whole. The authors mainly focus on redefining the relationship and interaction between firms and society in terms of CSR. In other words, the focus is limited to the two-way transfer between the two sectors. However, as the authors emphasize toward the end of the article, the concept of CSR must change from responsibility to integration. In order to depict this idea more aptly, one must also be aware that the CSR performed according to this article will have a more far-reaching consequence than that described by the authors. As Fig. 3 depicts, what Porter and Kramer propose can be extended to a more comprehensive mechanism for generating positive externality: a situation in which all social constituents can enjoy. While the authors have described well the dynamics that should occur between the targeted segments of

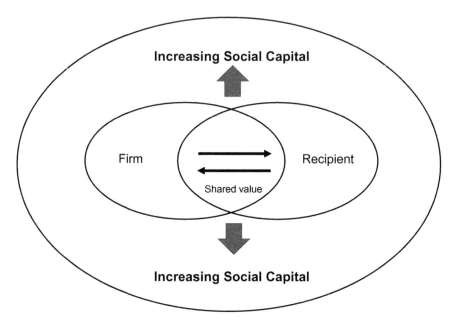

Fig. 3.   Extended view of strategic CSR.

society and firms, they did not mention how this will emanate throughout society.

Consider the example of Microsoft-AACC mentioned in the previous section as a way to explain strategic CSR. As Microsoft allocates its human and financial resources to various community colleges around the US, the recipients benefit from increased employability and job stability, while Microsoft benefits from an enhanced pool of human resources. However, this increased pool of human resource not only benefits Microsoft and the recipients but other firms as well. Furthermore, since community colleges generally cater to more underprivileged students, this CSR activity also generates additional social capital by reducing the wealth divide and enhancing livelihoods in the poorer areas of America. Thus, what we can see is not just a two-way interaction between the firm and the target segment of society but a creation of immense social capital that benefits others that are not directly involved in this CSR, as shown in Fig. 3.

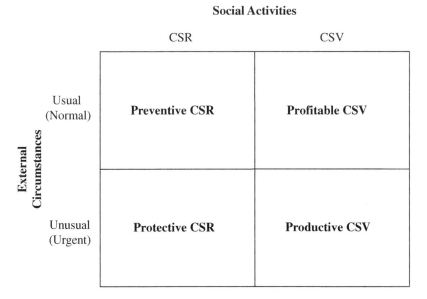

Fig. 4. CSR and CSO for usual or unusual conditions.

Another extension of Porter and Kramer's study is to distinguish how CSR or CSV operates under usual or unusual conditions. Here, unusual conditions refer to national emergencies such as natural or man-made disasters. Throughout history, the response to national emergencies has usually been the responsibility of governments (Wilson and Oyola-Yemaiel, 2001). These days though firms, large firms in particular, are playing a larger role in providing various forms of assistance for disaster relief (Johnson *et al.*, 2011). Based on these two dimensions, a new framework with four distinctive types of CSR or CSV is displayed in Fig. 4. Porter's distinction between CSR and CSV is mainly related to the social activities under normal conditions.

• Preventive CSR: Under normal conditions, firms' CSR activities are conducted in response to external pressure or to avoid unexpected costs because of unethical behavior or neglecting social activities. This implies that firms do a good duty not because they are ethical in essence, but often because they will suffer more if they do not conduct such activities. Thus, firms are encouraged to engage in CSR activities in a more active manner.

- Profitable CSV: Under normal conditions, profit maximization is always the ultimate goal. Therefore, even when firms address the social problems in their business, they consider both corporate and social benefits when pursuing such activities. This implies that firms are always concerned more about the overall productivity of their value chain in the long run than just their contributions to society.

- Protective CSR: Under emergency conditions such as natural disasters, terror attacks, or global pandemics like COVID-19, there is more need for assistance. The corporations should then help society more than they normally would, particularly in the case of those sectors that have been severely affected. Yet, even in this case, it is more efficient for firms to help society with their particular expertise or competitive advantage than just providing general financial donations.

- Productive CSV: Instead of emphasizing profit maximization for firms' normal CSV activities, under emergency conditions, firms have to supply their products to meet the needed demands of society. In such an urgent situation, the government and firms often work together to produce the needed products to help the country. For example, the American firms 3M and GM produced face masks and ventilators during the Coronavirus pandemic, although these products were not within their existing business areas.

Case Study 1: Giordano of Hong Kong[2]

Giordano is one of the Asia-Pacific's leading apparel brands. It was established in 1981 by Jimmy Lai who was based in Hong Kong. From its humble origins, it has grown to a global retailer with 2,187 stores in over 30 countries worldwide as of June 2020. A majority of

---

[2]Information for this case is abstracted from Giordano Homepage (www.giordano.com/hk), Giordano Online Shopping Homepage (http://hk.e-giordano.com), Hong Kong Trader — www.hktdc.com (Clothing Retailer Presses Ahead with Global Expansion, May 1, 2001), and Inside Retail, https://insideretail.asia/2020/03/11/giordano-to-focus-on-global-expansion-as-sales-fall-in-greater-china/.

its stores are located in the Asia region, including Greater China, South Korea, Southeast Asia, and the Middle East. Since the mid-2000s, Giordano has made notable progress in its online strategy and like many other retailers has hedged its bets on expanding its business and consumer market through the Internet. In 2006, in China alone, Giordano was able to hit online sales of RMB40 million (US$5.5 million) with only two IT employees assigned to the task of website maintenance and no further investments made.

Using the five forces model, we can analyze just how attractive the apparel retail industry is and then compare that analysis with another post-Internet strategy implementation. Below is the pre-Internet industry analysis:

As we can see from Fig. 5, the apparel retail industry is not very attractive: competition is stiff, barriers to entry are low, and buyers hold strong bargaining power. Giordano has suffered due to the high level of industry competition in the region from other retailers such

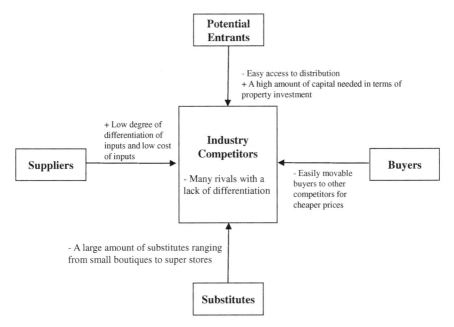

Fig. 5. Five forces analysis of the apparel industry (before the Internet).

as Uniqlo and California WHO.A.U. However, if a particular firm were to extend its brand recognition to the Internet, it can potentially increase its sphere of influence over competitors and grab a larger share of the market. Giordano has done this and has become one of the few garment retailers in Asia to offer online shopping through its website. Still, if we apply the same model but include factors related to the Internet, we can see a difference in industry attractiveness.

As illustrated in Fig. 6, we can see that the Internet has enhanced the level of industry attractiveness. However, the Internet should not be solely considered in explaining the enhanced level of the firm's competitive advantage, but should be used in conjunction with the firm's existing strategies and business plans. Giordano started with manufacturing, but moved into retailing and is now reaching more customers than ever by taking advantage of the opportunities offered by the Internet.

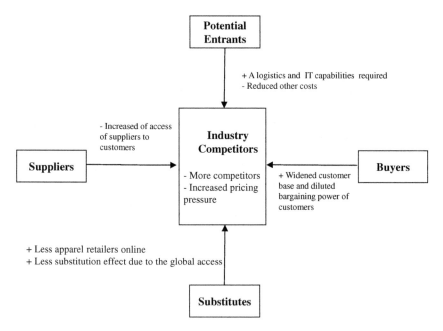

Fig. 6. Five forces analysis of the apparel industry (after the Internet).

At the same time, this online strategy has been widely adopted by other apparel retailers and with the fast growth of online platforms, Giordano can no longer exploit the advantages it had with the online business. In 2019, despite the strong growth of e-commerce in other regions, Giordano's overall sales in this sector declined by 15% mainly due to the unsatisfactory performance in mainland China, which is the company's largest market for such business. The sales fall in China was brought on by the strong competition from local established third-party platforms, for example, Taobao. The company is also responsible for failing to understand the particular market on the basis of consumers' tastes and preferences about the products and promotional activities.

In order to develop further its e-commerce business in all regions, Giordano said it will improve its product mix and collaboration with other online platforms. The experiences of Giordano showed that technology alone will be unlikely to sustain a firm's competitive advantage. A single piece of technology can easily be caught and improved upon by a rival sooner or later. Accordingly, technology should be complemented with an effective strategy that is designed to maintain its core competence and unique positioning against rivals.

Case Study 2: Temasek Trust of Singapore[3]

Temasek Holdings in Singapore established the Temasek Trust in 2007 with an initial budget of S$500 million to provide financial oversight to and governance of Temasek's endowment gifts. To date, it has managed over S$2 billion. The foundation was launched to focus on programs which contribute to the development of people in Asia, including Singapore. The Trust's philosophy has been to both benefit from and contribute to the growth and development in Asia. Temasek Holdings sees its long-term future as anchored in a thriving and peaceful Asia; thus, it is in the company's best interests to

---

[3]Information for this case is abstracted from Temasek Holdings Webpage: www. temasekholdings.com/sg, www.temasektrust.org.sg.

cultivate various communities across Asia. It does accept gifts from third parties, but it does not actively solicit donations.

The Trust supports non-profit philanthropic organizations, including Temasek Family of Foundations and Stewardship Asia Centre (SAC), which provide impactful programs for their communities. The programs of Temasek Family of Foundations aim to strengthen social resilience, foster international exchange, enhance regional capabilities, and advance science and nature for a sustainable world. SAC is a thought leadership center which aims to promote effective stewardship and governance across Asia.

Given these goals, does Temasek Trust actually have a specific strategy? Is it creating the maximum value with the resources it is holding back from society? The answer is no. The main problem is its purported goal of contributing to long-term growth in Asia. There can be hundreds if not thousands of milestones to be reached in order to fulfill this goal. Therefore, Temasek must reduce the scope of its aim and focus on a specific area along the following guidelines.

- *Strategy Depends on Choosing a Unique Positioning* — The Trust must decide which social challenge it wishes to address and focus on it.

- *Strategy Rests on Unique Activities* — Every other aspect of the foundation must then follow and be geared toward the position it has chosen for itself.

- *Positioning Requires Trade-offs* — The Trust has to be willing to forego other opportunities and just say "no."

- *Goal is Superior Performance in a Chosen Arena* — The Trust has to begin monitoring its performance in its chosen arena and consistently improve upon them.

With a well-defined strategy in place, the Trust must then create value, which means that its activities will lead to social benefit. This can be achieved in four ways: (a) selecting the best grantees, (b) signaling to other funders, (c) improving the performance of grant recipients, and (d) advancing the state of knowledge and practice.

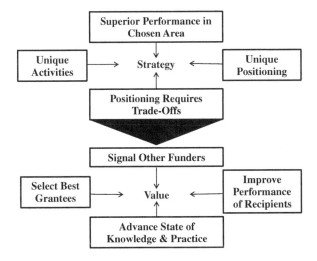

Fig. 7.   Creating value.

Using the framework below, the Trust can provide a much greater social benefit overall (see Fig. 7).

The Trust therefore, after selecting a focus such as higher education, would act to ensure that only the best applicants secure scholarships, thereby increasing the likelihood of a successful graduation. Further, the Trust should ensure that it is able to improve the performance of recipients in order to improve the returns on the money it has spent. Signaling to other funders would increase the amount of capital available to aid the project, and so a Trust must be willing to act interdependently with other funders. Lastly, the Trust should continuously advance its knowledge and practice by investing in research projects related to its area of expertise, and transmit its experiences to other foundations to enhance the role of the entire philanthropic system.

Case Study 3: Yuhan Kimberly Goes Green[4]

Yuhan Kimberly is an example of a company that has truly leveraged itself on the basis of CSR. Its reputation precedes itself and it is

---

[4]Information for this case is abstracted from Yuhan Kimberly Homepage-www.yuhan.co.kr, Chosun Ilbo-www.chosun.com (Moon Kook-hyun, CEO of

flooded with inquiries from other firms and various governments year after year regarding the secrets of its success. At Yuhan Kimberly, the CEO title holds a different meaning. He is not known as the Chief Executive Officer but rather the Chief Environmental Officer.

Kook-hyun Moon, the former CEO of Yuhan Kimberly, led the company from success to greater success with his self-created concept of "environmental management." He began his career at Yuhan Kimberly in 1983 after spending a year in the US developing new management concepts. Upon his return, he implemented a number of reforms within Yuhan Kimberly based upon two principles: (a) clean production/conserve resources and (b) efficient and transparent management.

The company, a paper manufacturing company, imports only enough pulp to cover approximately 5% of its production, while 95% comes from recycled paper. Reforms were not only instigated within the company but soon spread nationwide. Furthermore, Moon launched the forest for life initiative in 1984 with the slogan "Keep Korea Green" (*Uri Kangsan Purugae Purugae*). During its first stage of existence (1984–2014), the company planted 50 million trees in Korea and in other countries, such as North Korea and Mongolia. For the second stage (2015–2025), the company has carried out various practices with a new vision under the slogan of "A Better Life through Coexistence of Forest and Human." Over 20 years later, people in Korea are beginning to feel the positive impact of this program and its benefits as their mountains have been reforested and their rivers cleaned after a period of rapid industrial expansion which ravaged the natural beauty of Korea.

Moon realized early on that most companies only operated at about 34% of their equipment's capacity, as they did not run machines during the night or on holidays. By not operating at full capacity, many companies see their debt ratio grow, while their profitability remains low. Great facilities do not always equate to improved

Yuhan-Kimberly January 19, 2001), Korea Herald www.koreaherald.co.kr (Time to Talk to Yuhan Kimberly September 21, 2004), https://news.mt.co.kr/mtview.php?no=2020030616214450234, and Yuhan-Kimberly CSR Report 2017.

efficiency; thus, he implemented a flexible work program, which allowed his factories to run for 24 hours per day. Workers would just come in for four days of 12-hour shifts, but then rest for four days (three rest days and one education and training day). As a result, the company began to experience one of the lowest staff turnover rates in the world and did not have to resort to layoffs during the financial crisis of 1997 that affected many companies in Korea.

When it comes to CSR, many companies shy away from this concept due to a fear that it will result in an obligation that will eat away at their profits. However, since 1970, Yuhan Kimberly has challenged this perception by maintaining a high level of profitability. By focusing on environmental protection as well as employee protection and training, the company has managed to streamline its business practices. In this way, the company has been able to save money, increase efficiency, and enhance brand recognition. This has led it to an increase its competitive advantage to a level previously unseen, which is now the benchmark for companies wishing to develop their CSR operations.

Still, if a company were to apply the CSR strategy proposed by Porter and Kramer, the effects would be further reaching and more beneficial within and outside the firm. Yuhan Kimberley's CSR thus far has been more of the responsive-type, which helps protect society as a whole and improves the company's image, but by moving to more strategic CSR or CSV, it can create more benefits for both the firm and society.

Yuhan Kimberley is obviously toying with the concept of strategic CSR by the way it has altered its factory practices, but this impacts only one part of the value chain. Despite the limited application, the benefits of Yuhan Kimberly's strategic CSR or CSV have been profound. It will be interesting to see whether the company further integrates strategic CSR into its value chain and what kind of impact this will have on its operations and broader business environment.

Recently, during the Coronavirus pandemic, the Korean government requested local companies including Yuhan Kimberley to produce medical masks at the price of 120 Korean Won (about US$0.1) per mask. Despite the significant production gaps, Yuhan Kimberley along with other Korean firms agreed to make contracts with the government and provided the required number of masks during the pandemic. These social activities are driven by necessity rather than efficiency, and are therefore more in line with *Productive CSV* under unusual conditions as illustrated in Fig. 4.

Discussion Questions

1. Do you agree with Porter's summation that new technology can be more damaging than improving the industry attractiveness?

2. Can you think of a business type that could make healthy, sustainable profits solely from emerging technology? Explain your case.

3. Can a pure business strategy really be applied to other institutions such as philanthropic or charitable foundations? Explain.

4. What problems can be foreseen when applying the steps recommended by Porter and Kramer to a foundation-type organization? How can these be overcome?

5. Corporate Social Responsibility — useful strategy or merely an image booster? Discuss.

6. Do you think strategic CSR and CSV are conceptually similar? If so, how?

7. Do you think firms should always focus on seeking CSV rather than CSR from an efficiency perspective? If not, how should firms integrate both CSR and CSV? And, under what condition should firms pursue CSR or CSV?

8. Using Porter and Kramer's framework, how could we improve either Temasek Trust or Yuhan Kimberley's strategy? Discuss.

CHAPTER 4

Extension of Generic Strategy

Chapter Guideline

Now that we have a clear understanding of the far-reaching analytical power of Porter's frameworks, it is time to take a more detailed look into his methods. This chapter will extend Porter's discussion and will take a more in-depth and updated look into Porter's insights. How did Porter come up with his approach? What is Porter's definition of strategy? How are other prominent figures in business affected by Porter and how do they assess him? This chapter will provide answers to these questions in order to present the reader with a more clear and comprehensive view toward understanding Michael Porter's true contribution.

Summary of Previous Models

In the previous chapter, we witnessed the flexibility and far-reaching explanatory power of Porter's analytical framework. Furthermore, the previous chapter succinctly presented the most cutting-edge issues in business such as new technology, philanthropy, and corporate social responsibility (CSR). The common theme that flows throughout these works is that these issues must be approached within the context of a broader strategy. For example, technology must be interwoven into a broader strategic context, while philanthropic activity must also be targeted and executed based on a strategy to maximize the value of every dollar spent. CSR needs to be further dealt with in a strategic manner. It is evident that Porter's various frameworks have had enormous staying power in a field in which short-lived fads are the norm. Therefore, this chapter will attempt to present the reader with materials that provide a more in-depth understanding of the impact and origins of Porter's various frameworks.

4.1 Operational Effectiveness versus Strategic Positioning

In understanding business strategy, one common error is to apply the military conception of strategy to the world of business (Moon, 2018). While many of the ideas conveyed in military strategic thinking are highly applicable to business, it is important to bear in mind that the ultimate objectives for military strategy differs from that of business. As the eminent Prussian military strategist, Clausewitz (1982 [1832], p. 101) asserted, "War is an act of violence intended to compel our opponent to fulfill our will.... physical force is therefore the means; the compulsory submission of the enemy to our will is the ultimate object." It is clear then that war is inevitably a zero-sum struggle because the winner must inevitably subdue the loser. Business strategy, however, is far from a zero-sum game unless firms erroneously engage in destructive competition. Porter (1996) lucidly explains how an appropriate application of business strategy can lead to a positive-sum game, which further maximizes the value created by individual firms.

Porter (1996) begins by lamenting the current trends among business practices that usually neglect positioning (which is at the heart of strategy). Managers, in their attempt to cope with a dynamic and volatile environment have engaged in destructive hyper-competition that is purely based on productivity, quality, and speed. These are, in Porter's terms, operational effectiveness aspects and are clearly necessary but not sufficient in order to gain a real sustaining competitive advantage.

It is important to distinguish the terms operational effectiveness (OE) and strategic positioning (SP) because the two are often confused and misused. OE, in essence, is executing similar activities more efficiently than rivals, while SP means performing different activities from rivals or performing similar activities in different ways. OE is the basic condition, while strategy is what gives the firm its true source of competitive advantage.

Examples of OE include organizational efficiency, advanced technology, and better managing practices. These are all areas where Japanese firms were able to excel during the 1980s. Through this advantage in OE, Japanese firms were able to offer superior quality at a lower cost. However, the problem with this kind of advantage is that other firms will soon catch up with these best practices and move closer to the productivity frontier, which leads to destructive hyper-competition. The gains from this competition benefit the consumers and suppliers at the expense of the firms' profit as they increasingly face diminishing returns on their enhanced OE. Therefore, the consistent source of long-term competitive advantage comes from occupying a unique strategic position and shifting the productivity frontier outward, as illustrated in Fig. 1.

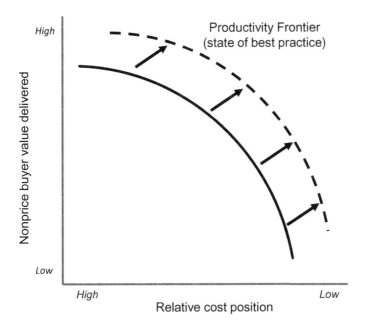

Fig. 1. Operational effectiveness vs. strategic positioning.
Source: Porter (1996).

How can firms achieve such an outcome? Porter suggests three ways in which firms can develop their true competitive advantages:

- *Variety-Based Positioning* — This positioning serves a wide variety of customers, but a very specific set of their needs. For example, the automotive lubricant company Jiffy Lube does not offer any other service or products. The company's intense focus on lubricants gives customers a unique value proposition which rivals cannot match.

- *Needs-Based Positioning* — This is based on targeting a particular customer segment and servicing its needs through a set of activities. It is crucial to understand that differences in needs will not translate into meaningful positions unless the best set of activities to satisfy them also differs. IKEA, for example, seeks to satisfy all the needs of a specific segment of customers — young and price-sensitive customers. It provides various home furnishing options, but specifically caters mostly for newlyweds or younger couples.

- *Access-Based Positioning* — Customer needs may be similar across segments, but the best configuration of activities to reach them is different. These include geography, customer scale, or any kind of differences in access channel. Access-based positioning derives its strength from segmenting customers who are accessible through different ways or channels. For example, Carmike Cinemas, a movie theater operator, established theaters all across rural America. The company specifically targets towns with a population lower than 200,000 and customizes all of its operations accordingly. Standardized, low-cost theaters suit the rural Americans' taste and create a competitive advantage that is very difficult for competitors to replicate.

The common theme behind all three types of positioning is the presence of a unique set of activities which are optimized to serve the firm's target customers. This differentiating feature, according to Porter, is what sets successful firms apart from mediocre ones.

However, just picking a position is not enough as other firms will look to take over that position through various maneuvers. This can happen when rivals either reposition themselves to the valuable position or by straddling, which refers to a rival providing the same benefits in that position.

Does this mean that finding a unique position is futile? Not entirely. Porter asserts that occupying these unique and valuable positions for the long term requires trade-offs. For example, a firm can choose to tailor all its activities to serve the lower-end of an industry, thereby occupying a unique position. This firm can then focus all its resources to consolidate its position in a particular part of the industry.

Only when a firm makes trade-offs to occupy these positions, can it truly obtain strategic positioning. By making a trade-off, the firm pushes potential imitators to make their own trade-offs, thus creating a situation in which it is costly for them to compete. But, how do these trade-offs occur? The first source is inconsistency in image. For example, if a company, which used to provide luxury products, suddenly tries to reposition or straddle itself into the lower-end, it will suffer from image inconsistency. This is a significant risk for the potential imitator. The second source is the required changes in firm activity. Again, a former luxury product provider must reorganize certain parts of its organization and reallocate its resources to move into the lower-end segment. This increases additional costs and thus creates a barrier which protects the firm that already occupies a unique position in the lower-end market.

In this respect, a firm already occupying a unique position must strive to make the magnitude of this trade-off as large as possible in order to fend off potential competitors. This can be achieved by what Porter describes as choosing the best "fit," which refers to combining various individual activities into a cohesive and unique system. When a firm creates a robust "fit," different activities create a synergistic effect that reinforces the entire system. As such, this fit is difficult for competitors to replicate and overcome.

More specifically, Porter presents three types of fits which are most common among successful firms.

- *First-Order Fit* — It is important for a firm's overall strategy and its individual activities to be consistent. This brings cohesion to the position as all activities are geared toward achieving a single goal.

- *Second-Order Fit* — After consistency is achieved, a firm can arrange its activities so that they reinforce each other to generate synergies. Then, the whole business becomes larger than the sum of the parts as all the activities are not only being focused but also creating a plus-alpha to bolster the entire system.

- *Third-Order Fit* — The most sophisticated fit involves those who are not directly participating in the firm's activities. In a third-order fit, outside players such as customers and suppliers magnify the synergy through their interactions with the firm.

The higher the order of fit, the higher the magnitude of the trade-off that potential imitators have to suffer. This effectively enables firms to capture unique positioning and long-term sustainable competitive advantage.

In this respect, why do firms fail to achieve this advantage? One of the main reasons is what Porter calls the "growth trap," which refers to a situation where a firm's desire to promote increased growth comes at the expense of the firm's strategic position. For example, when a firm having been successful in one market segment determines that this particular segment is saturated, it is pressured to seek new fields to grow further. This in itself is not a bad maneuver, but the problem is that many firms sacrifice their original "strategic fit" to pursue new endeavors. Therefore, firms that wish to gain long-term competitive advantage must look to maintain profitable growth by deepening their original strategic position rather than trying to broaden it. This does not mean that firms should limit themselves to certain areas. Rather, firms must broaden their scope of operation only under the condition that the expansion does not compromise the fit.

In conclusion, successful firms must keep pushing the productivity frontier while at the same time deepening their strategic position by upgrading the order of their fits. Without such commitment, firms will end up broadening at the expense of their unique positioning while also damaging the entire industry structure by promoting hyper-competition based solely on superior OE.

Analysis

Porter's valuable insights identify well the problems with current business practices and offer a clear-cut remedy. Additionally, even in a dynamic, ever-changing business environment, there are still certain core conventional principles that firms can hold onto along with the ability to use them as their blueprint for success. Lastly, Porter's analysis on "fits" shows readers why truly successful companies with long-term competitive advantages are not those that are most efficient in terms of doing the same activities better than others, but rather those that focus on differentiating themselves from the rest of the pack by creating a unique "fit." This concept also shows why competitors who focus solely on OE will have a very difficult time emulating and competing against firms that have made trade-offs and distinguished themselves from the rest.

However, there are several issues that need to be raised with this perspective. The first is the elusive relationship between OE/SP and Cost Leadership/Differentiation. According to Porter's logic, cost advantage is derived from more efficient performances of certain activities, while differentiation is generated from the choice of activities and method of conducting activities. This logic is represented as the bold, straight arrows in Fig. 2.

It is important to note that the examples that Porter uses, such as Southwest Airlines and IKEA, achieved their cost leadership advantage through SP. Similarly, the two fashion brands of H&M and Zara have also gained cost advantage by pursing strong SP by targeting fashionable but price-sensitive young women. Therefore, the question arises as to whether SP can actually be a source of cost leadership as well as differentiation. Conversely, even OE can lead to cost leadership and differentiation as pursuing a unique fit can lead to differentiation. In other words, Porter's logic which seems to equate operational

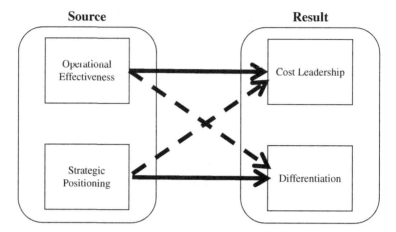

Fig. 2.   Sources of competitive advantages and results.

effectiveness and cost leadership (and strategic positioning with differentiation) does not hold in reality. As the dotted arrows in Fig. 2 represent, each source of competitive advantage can lead to cost leadership, differentiation, or even both.

To make this point clearer, consider the example of three automobiles — BMW X3, Toyota Camry, and Hyundai Sonata — in the context of Porter's productivity frontier (see Fig. 3). The Camry is a cost leader that has achieved that position through enhancing OE. The BMW X3, on the contrary, is a luxury brand which has obtained its unique position through differentiation. Both are on the forefront of the productivity frontier, but have achieved their positions in vastly different ways. Now, Hyundai, which is lagging behind BMW and Toyota from either perspective, has a choice to either catch up with Toyota through enhancing its cost leadership or follow BMW into the luxury market through differentiation. Either way, Hyundai must improve its OE in order to do so.

The dotted line shows the potential trajectory that Hyundai might take in order to reach the productivity frontier. At this point, it should be asked whether it is making the mistake of becoming stuck in the middle. In this case, no. It is simply pursuing its path and catching up with the leaders by enhancing its OE. Even Porter, who has

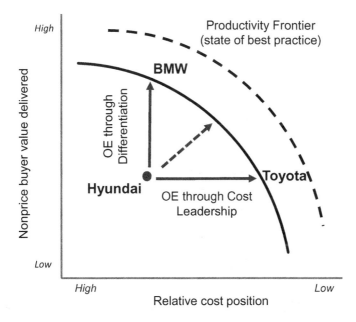

Fig. 3. Strategies of BMW, Toyota, and Hyundai.

been critical of the stuck-in-the-middle approach, implicitly acknowledged this point by stating that improvement of both cost and differentiation is possible when a company is behind the productivity frontier. Thus, Hyundai's strategy is valid, although it appears to be stuck in the middle.

This example shows that OE by improving both cost and differentiation can lead to a viable strategy. Unlike Porter's assertion that cutting costs and enhancing OE are not long-term strategy options, Japanese companies are doing just that and are still being successful. Lexus, which is a high-end car, achieved its leadership within the luxury car market through cost leadership. Lexus is in essence a cost leader within the high-end car market.

Another problem with Porter's logic is the relationship between generic strategies (cost leadership and differentiation) and the three strategic positions (Needs-based, Variety-based, and Access-based). Needs-based refers to serving a specific segment of customers; variety-based is to serve a wide array of customers through a subset of an industry's products or services; and access-based refers to differentiation by serving specific customers for specific needs. However, these three strategic positions clearly overlap with Porter's original two generic strategies of cost leadership and differentiation, and the distinction between these two sets of strategic options is unclear.[1]

This is not to discredit Porter's original work, but to point out that there are certain inconsistencies between this article and his previous approaches. Pointing out these gaps in Porter's work may offer some opportunities to expand and enhance his original framework. Therefore, it is always important to clarify these problems by first gaining a thorough understanding of Porter's framework and then improving it through an augmented or simplified analytical framework. It is clear from this analysis that one major recurring problem in Porter's discussion is the concept of stuck in the middle. Although Porter criticized the stuck-in-the-middle approach, many firms have actually diversified and achieved success through this approach. Reconciling these apparent contradictions in Porter's model should provide us with a more comprehensive and accurate picture of the appropriate firm strategy.

4.2 Why Do Good Managers Set Bad Strategies?

During a special lecture at the Wharton Business School in 2006, Michael Porter raised a key question on why most strategic errors come from within the firm. In addressing this question, he pointed to three aspects:[2]

- *Destructive Competition* — As described before, firms can collectively engage in destructive competition by adopting the wrong approach. Managers often think of competition in terms of being the best in the industry and this notion in itself is harmless. However, the problem arises when managers attempt to be the

---

[1] This issue will be further discussed in the next chapter.
[2] See Knowledge@Wharton (2006).

best in all parts of the industry. Just like no one person can be the best in everything, no single company can become the best in all aspects of an industry. Rather, a company can be the best in a specific segment of an industry or a specific target. The current practice though has been extremely destructive as firms have defined their goals purely in terms of advancing the interests and profit of shareholders. This leads to what Porter terms the "Bermuda Triangle of Strategy" in which firms sacrifice their uniqueness in order to achieve unprofitable growth just to increase shareholder value.

- *Confusing Strategy and Operational Effectiveness* — The appropriate corporate goal, therefore, should be to think of ways to deliver unique value to customers through a set of differentiated fit of activities. Strategy then means devising ways to differentiate oneself from the rest of the competitors by conducting activities through alternative ways. As such, managers must constantly distinguish between whether the measures they are implanting go under strategy or operational effectiveness. Without this distinction, companies will end up sacrificing their strategic objectives for the sake of operational effectiveness which may generate short-term advantages but compromise the unique strategic position.

- *Capital Market Biases and Leadership* — This is a problem associated with a firm's valuation by financial analysts. Typically, they point to one firm in an industry which creates the largest value for shareholders and places pressure on other firms to emulate. This leads to homogenization of firm practices and hence leads to a no-win situation. Therefore, it is increasingly important for leaders and CEOs to communicate the firm's overall strategy, which is differentiated from those of its competitors, throughout the organizational chain. Because all individual activity must be aligned with the overarching strategy, it is not just the top managers that should have knowledge of a firm's strategy but also those that are at the bottom.

Analysis

This section introduced Porter's (2006) lecture on strategy, but there is nothing new with his perspective. The lecture was just based on his previous article (Porter, 1996), i.e., strategic positioning versus operational effectiveness. Again, however, this does not mean Porter's approach is outdated; in fact, it has truly revolutionized the discipline of strategic management. Ever since Porter first devised his frameworks in the early 1980s, his insights have remained highly valid.

Porter remained consistent in his view and has been more accurate than any other scholar. Despite several inconsistencies and criticisms about his research, this view once again shows that his timeless validity proves that Porter is the undisputed leader in the field of strategic management. In a more recent interview with Porter during his visit to India in May 2017, he said that the substantial technological development has raised the bar on rigor and discipline with which people make strategic choices. He further stressed that despite the constantly changing technology and business landscape, he found that the same fundamental framework applies and companies must still seek to achieve competitive advantage (Doshi, 2017).

4.3 Retrospective: An Interview with Michael Porter and Related Articles

In the next few sections, an interview with Michael Porter is included along with several articles written by people in various fields of business and academia who have been profoundly affected by Porter's insights.

Michael Porter's Competitive Strategy

Argyres *et al.* (2002) analyze and present the impact that Porter's theory has had on the field of business strategy. They highlight two main points about his work. One is the profound influence of Porter's analytical framework on various academic disciplines and subject areas. For example, it is extensively utilized not only for management strategy and policy but also in education, healthcare, environmental protection, and urban revitalization. Despite its broad application, one overarching theme is his belief in healthy and rigorous competition as the primary source of societal advancement. The second point is that Porter's ideas have had unusual staying power in a field where fads are the norm and most theories are effectively refuted after a short while.

An Interview with Michael Porter

In his interview with Argyres and McGahan in Argyres *et al.* (2002), Porter begins by illustrating the process in which he came to devise his analytical frameworks. During the 1960s and 1970s, when Porter entered the world of business academia, the connection between industrial organization and strategy had not been clearly established. Both sides had strengths as well as weaknesses. On the industrial side, frameworks existed, but there were too many exceptions to the rule, while on the business side the traditional economic mode of the *ceteris paribus* (the practice of fixing all other independent variables and then looking at one variable's impact on the dependent variable) mode of thought was unrealistic. Therefore, all cases were taken individually and every case study required separate Strengths, Weaknesses, Opportunities, and Threats (SWOT) analysis which did not really have a general applicability. This explains why Porter decided to take the strongest points of both worlds and adopt an approach which led to the Five Forces framework and the Generic Strategies. These were both attempts to encompass the most important independent variables into a comprehensive and readily applicable analytical framework.

This approach was first met with skeptics doubting whether these frameworks can generalize all the complex and intricate inner workings of competition and strategy, especially with the advent of new technologies and ever-volatile market conditions, which led many to discredit Porter's attempt. However, contrary to this skepticism, Porter's analytical frameworks have displayed a significant amount of staying power and can be applied to a vast array of social phenomena.

In the latter portion of the interview, Porter discusses some interesting possible extensions to his framework and theories that could be pursued in the future. One of the most prominent is the question of the evolution of industry structure. Although Porter's model has appropriately dissected the existing industry structure, it does not show how the structure itself evolves. How do the five forces change and due to what variables? How does firm behavior change over time depending on the industry structure? These are questions that are also left open to explore.

Strategic Management: From Informed Conversation to Academic Discipline

Barney in Argyes *et al.* (2002) evaluates Porter's contribution as transforming the study of strategic management from "mere academic conversation" to a "rigorous academic discipline." It is interesting to note that the resource-based view, for which Barney (2002) is a leading proponent, has been one of the major critics of Porter's frameworks. Yet, even the leading critics acknowledge that Porter has transformed the field of strategic management into a proper discipline. This is especially true as there was no consensus even on the purpose of strategic management before Porter. Yet, he was able to aggregate all of the relevant points and visualize them into a cohesive framework and concept.

Of course, Porter's approach is not without problems as it defines strategic management largely in terms of economic theory. Other psychological and sociological phenomena are also recognized as being important in the field. However, he was the first one to comprehensively link strategic management with another field thereby enhancing the validity of both in terms of applicability, conceptualization, and theoretical rigor. Another contribution has been choosing the right unit of analysis in strategic management, which is the industry structure. By focusing on the right level, Porter was able to uncover most of the main determinants of a firm's performance and choice of entry or exit.

Porter's Added Value: High Indeed!

Brandenburger in Agryes *et al.* (2002) points out that Porter's most important contribution is that his frameworks have been able to give a clear and visual representation of the most important variables that affect business performance and industry structure. Furthermore, they also give a more realistic picture than the diagrams and graphs in economic theory. Compare the supply and demand graph, which depicts a large number of small buyers and small sellers, to the Five Forces. The problem with supply and demand is that it makes unrealistic assumptions, as in real life there are many small buyers but only a few big sellers. Business is not about small buyers and sellers, but about a few highly active and significant players and the Five Forces model captures the reality of this situation.

Competitive Strategy: It's OK to be Different

Bachman (2002), who is a managing partner of the prominent investment firm Edward Jones, wrote the last article of this Retrospective. It is interesting to see how Bachman employed Porter's theory (unintentionally) in creating his highly successful financial enterprise. Bachman explains that in the early days of Edward Jones, the company suffered from a lack of capital compared to its more established competitors. Therefore, Bachman decided to tailor his firm's activities to serve the needs of a very specific market segment, that being rural America.

Since the firm had so little capital, it could not afford to serve major investors or provide flashy and risky financial instruments. Instead, they took a more conservative approach and decided to add a personal touch to financial investment. Since the customers were mostly looking for stable, long-term financial instruments and wanted to have close and personal relationships with their investment manager, the firm's activities became customized to this segment. Without realizing it, Edward Jones was creating a robust fit, which Porter described as essential toward achieving long-term competitive advantage. As Bachman highlights, the key contribution is Porter's affirmation that it is not only okay to be different but also desirable. By making a trade off, which is to not serve the major investors and offer elaborate financial instruments, Edward Jones widened the gap between itself and potential imitators and has been able to survive and prosper in the volatile world of investment firms.

Analysis

What distinguishes the greatest academics from the other brilliant minds is their ability to build a system of thoughts. Many intellectuals throughout history have been able to advance a discipline through their insights, but only a select few have been able to actually synthesize and build an entirely new system. In economics, for example, despite the numerous stellar minds that have advanced the discipline, no one has been able to surpass Adam Smith in terms of staying power. This is because Smith's seminal work, *The Wealth of Nations*, built a whole system which transformed the entire *mode of thinking* in economics. He established the foundations of classical value theory and provided a revolutionary blueprint for understanding human progress in terms of economic growth. Furthermore, he founded a novel philosophy based on the doctrine of utility in an era when many people still thought the optimum end of economic activities was accumulating a state stockpile of gold bullion (Ekelund and Hebert, 1997, p. 124).

Just like Adam Smith established a new system in his own times, Michael Porter also built an entirely new school of thought which transformed the *mode of thinking* in the discipline of strategic management. More specifically, when one looks at how Porter began by realizing the missing link between economic theory and industrial organization, one can clearly see how his approach is a fusion of the two. If we summarize this process through an example, it is as follows:

One can formulate a basic econometric equation as

$$Y = \beta_0 + \beta_1 X_1 + \beta_2 X_2 + \beta_3 X_3 + \beta_4 X_4 + \beta_5 X_5, \ldots, \beta_i X_i \ldots$$

What economic theory tends to do is to fix all X variables except for example X_3 which represents barriers to entry. In this fashion, one can determine the impact that this single variable has on the dependent variable (Υ). While this model is useful in determining the precise impact of individual variables on the dependent one, it ignores the dynamic nature of real business contexts in which all these independent X variables simultaneously affect the dependent one.

In contrast, the traditional SWOT analysis (Fig. 4) is highly tailored for individual cases and gives a realistic view as to how all variables affect a particular situation. By analyzing the strengths, weaknesses, opportunities, and threats, firms are able to analyze their plan of action in order to gain their objective. However, it is not clear which variables should be included in each cell of the SWOT framework.

In this respect, through numerous case studies and empirical analyses, Porter selected the most important X variables out of the hundreds that emerged from his research. By picking out the independent variables that mattered the most in a large number of case studies, he then visualized them as a framework which is readily applicable and captures most of the important determinants of the dependent variable. Porter's frameworks, in essence, are a healthy balance between the economic approach and the SWOT analysis.

Still, this is not to say that Porter's approach is without criticism. Barney (1991) and many other proponents for a resource-based view point out that by overfocusing on industry attractiveness, Porter

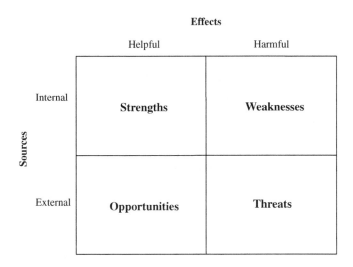

Fig. 4. SWOT framework.

neglects the fact that the attractiveness of an industry is not independent of the firm's resources. Firms have resources and capabilities that
are not affected by outside determinants and can even overcome the
difficulty imposed on them by inherently unattractive industry structures. Furthermore, while Porter rightfully points out that cost and
differentiation are the two main modes of strategic positioning, he
does not properly identify the sources of these advantages. Adding to
this criticism, some have noted that the threat of substitutability does
not apply to highly sophisticated industries.

These points may be constructive criticism yet many are based on
a misinterpretation of Porter's work. In response to the criticism that
Porter neglects the inelasticity of a firm's resources and capabilities,
he clearly mentioned that firms not only participate in the industry
but also have the power to change the industry structure itself. As a
matter of fact, Porter asserted that the most successful firms in any
industry are those that have been able to change the industry structure to suit their advantages.

The resource-based view perceives the firm as a bundle of
resources that, in order to be competitive, must be immobile and
unique in nature. These resources are, in essence, gained through the
various administrative decisions and strategic choices that a firm
makes across its value chain, as depicted in Fig. 5. Therefore, these
aspects are comprehensively captured by Porter's value chain and his
discussion on creating a unique fit of activities. The resource-based
view is a very detailed and thoughtful extension of the dynamics of
Porter's value chain analysis and this view shows how these individual
elements interact to generate unique advantages for firms. This view
though is still largely within the frameworks that Porter has devised
in the past. Furthermore, one prominent criticism of the resource-
based view is that it largely ignores external factors and concentrates
too much on endogenous variables that firms can control. Porter
presents a comprehensive view of the external forces that affect industry structure and attractiveness through his five forces model.

Joan Magretta has also stressed in her book *Understanding Michael
Porter* (Magretta, 2011) that while strategy has become even more
important — not less so — in the turbulent and uncertain period,

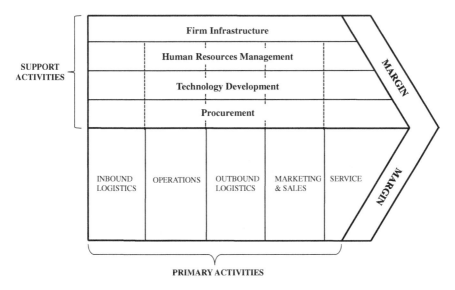

Fig. 5.   Porter's value chain analysis.

Porter's frameworks have become the foundation of the field of strategy. She further described Porter's important contribution as follows:

> Porter has steadfastly focused on timeless principles. His is the general theory that applies in all cases. If you enter Porter's world, you will have to do without the catchy metaphors: no blue oceans, no dancing elephants, no moving cheeses. What you will get, instead, is a rigorous and clear mapping between your strategy and your organization's financial performance... Among academics, he is the most cited scholar in economics and business. At the same time, his ideas are the most widely used in practice by business and government leaders around the world.

Hence, what we can see from these analyses is the far-reaching impact Porter has had over the years and how his view has consistently been proven valid despite the passage of time. This is particularly remarkable when we consider the fact that strategic management is a field in which ideas tend to come and go in a very short space of time. Lastly, we can see that even Porter's many critics largely acknowledge the sweeping and immense explanatory power that his various frameworks possess. At the same time, this does not mean that we cannot improve Porter's model and devise an enhanced framework that can reconcile the various inconsistencies among Porter's frameworks. This is a point that we will discuss further in the next chapter.

Case Study 1: How Samsung Beat Sony and Is Catching up with Apple[3]

The Samsung Group is South Korea's largest conglomerate by revenue (2019, US$272 billion) leading in several industries around the world. It is composed of numerous international businesses which are all united under the Samsung brand, including the following:

- *Samsung Electronics* — one of the world's largest electronics company

- *Samsung Heavy Industries* — one of the world's largest shipbuilders

- *Samsung C&T* — a major global construction company

This case study will focus on the strategy of Samsung Electronics. The Samsung brand is perhaps one of the best-known South Korean brands in the world and in 2005, Samsung (20th) overtook its Japanese rival Sony (28th) as the world's leading consumer electronics brand. In 2019, it was ranked 6th compared to Sony's 56th by

---

[3]Information for this case study is abstracted from the Samsung Website (www.samsung.com), Management & Accounting Website (http://maww.info), *The New York Times* (Bits, December 17, 2007), Wired (The Civil War Inside Sony, February 11, 2002), *The New York Times* (Sony Sets a New Course to Bolster Electronics, June 27, 2008, Infighting Left Sony Behind, April 19, 2004), Woman Consumer, June 11, 2020, http://www.womancs.co.kr/news/articleView.html?idxno=60812, Interbrand's Best Global Brands, https://www.rankingthebrands.com/The-Brand-Rankings.aspx?rankingID=37&year=1273, https://www.vneconomictimes.com/article/business/samsung-vietnam-celebrates-10th-anniversary-of-samsung-electronics-vietnam, and https://www.nippon.com/en/in-depth/d00493/sony%E2%80%99s-strategy-for-taking-on-the-gafa-giants.html.

Interbrand's Top 100 Best Global Brands survey. Samsung has now come close to Apple, which was ranked 1st place in the Top 100 Best Global Brands in 2019. Alongside this, Samsung Electronics' profit in 2018 was twice that of the combined profits of all of Japan's top 10 electronics companies including Sony. The case study below analyzes how Porter's concepts of positioning, trade-off, and fit apply to Samsung's growth strategies.

Positioning

As previously mentioned, Porter stated that there is a succinct difference between OE and SP, which if confused can cause problems in the sustainability of competitiveness. Therefore, positioning can be subdivided into these two subsections: OE and SP.

Operational effectiveness

According to Porter, OE is the act of performing similar activities to rivals, but in a better way that results in improved competitiveness. OE is not merely limited to efficiency, but refers to the many practices that allow a company to better utilize its inputs.

This can be demonstrated more clearly by using the value chain model. The value chain categorizes the generic value-adding activities of an organization. The "primary" activities include inbound logistics, operations (production), outbound logistics, marketing, and sales and services. The "support" activities include infrastructure, human resource management, technology development, and procurement. Improving any one of the primary or support activities over competitors allows Samsung to perform similar activities but in a superior way to its rivals.

Samsung has indeed managed to improve multiple activities within the value chain, thus putting it a step ahead of its rivals, such as Sony, in the same market. Figure 6 highlights the areas where Samsung has made integral changes to its activities. It has improved upon infrastructure, technology development, and operations in order to gain a degree of advantage over its competitors.

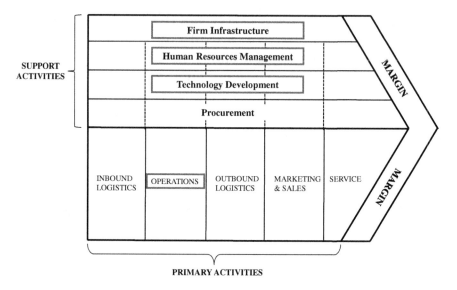

Fig. 6.   Samsung's value chain alterations.

Infrastructure, in particular, has transformed dramatically over the years. When CEO Jong-Yong Yun took over in 1997, he drastically cut 24,000 workers and sold US$2 billion in non-core businesses. Furthermore, Samsung's top-down management is particularly noteworthy, because the company only provides general direction, while individual teams determine the specifications according to their situation. Such a system allows the company to respond to the fast-changing environment in a speedy and flexible manner (Moon, 2016). Samsung managers who have worked for other big competitors claim that at Samsung they go through far fewer layers of bureaucracy to win approval for new products, budgets, and marketing plans. Overall, this streamlining has improved the company's ability to seize opportunities. The Sony Chairman noted in a speech regarding Samsung's aggressive restructuring, "to survive as a global player, we too have to change."

With regard to technology development, Samsung is investing heavily in R&D and new factories across all product lines. According to PwC's The Global Innovation 1000 study, Samsung was the fourth largest corporate R&D spender worth US$15.3 in 2018, behind Amazon (1st), Alphabet (2nd), and Volkswagen (3rd). Samsung has realized that to stay on top it must be willing to provide consumers with a constant stream of well-timed hits, and this means staying one step ahead of the pack in terms of technology development.

Operations are perhaps the most unusual segment for Samsung and where it differs almost completely from its competitors. While most competitors in the high-tech industry are developing proprietary software and content, Samsung has refused to enter the software business. Instead, it is focused on developing only the necessary hardware, and while most competitors outsource their hardware segments, Samsung refuses to do this. Rather, it has invested billions of dollars in large-scale cutting-edge factories at home and abroad. Since 2008, Samsung has actively expanded its investment in Vietnam to turn it into Samsung's global manufacturing hub. Over the last decade, Samsung's total investment in Vietnam amounted to 26 times the amount invested 10 years ago up to over US$17.3 billion. CEO Yun was quoted as saying that "if we get out of manufacturing, we will lose." Thus, its diversification and vertical integration in manufacturing creates a negative aspect for competitors, which then acts as a boom for Samsung.

As we have learned, while OE is necessary for a firm, it is not by itself sufficient to maintain sustainability of competitiveness. Therefore, we now need to look at the second subsection of positioning.

Strategic positioning

SP refers to performing different activities from rivals or performing similar activities, but in different ways. Porter states that a company can outperform rivals only if it can establish a difference that it can preserve. While changes in OE can be easily copied and benchmarked, changes in SP are not as easily imitated. Furthermore, Porter argues that competitive strategy is about being different and thus strategy is the creation of a unique and valuable position, involving a different set of activities. SP, Porter claims, emerges from three sources: variety-, needs-, and access-based positioning (see Fig. 7).

From this strategic point, Samsung has positioned itself in a variety-based position as well as a needs-based position. Samsung's variety-based positioning refers to its restraint toward entering the software market, and its commitment to hardware. By manufacturing and selling only hardware, it is producing only a subset of the industry's products, thus customers are forced to look elsewhere for their software needs. However, this works to Samsung's advantage, as it has been able to position itself as an absolute leader in the high-tech hardware industry, even above Sony in terms of revenue. Such a strategy also works well for Samsung's competition with Apple in the smartphone business. For example, after the initial failure in developing its own operating system, Samsung quickly turned to Google's Android system while concentrating its resources toward strengthening its hardware competitiveness. Until 2010, Samsung lagged far behind Apple in its share of the smartphone market, but since 2011 it has managed to achieve a leading position.

As for needs-based positioning, Samsung, through its pricing structure, has targeted mid-level consumers. While a majority of its competitors fight it out over the lower-end of the hardware spectrum, Samsung is raising the stakes by providing superior design and quality for all kinds of mid-range products while remaining within its price

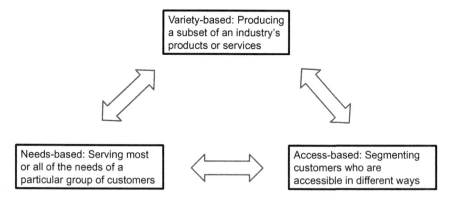

Fig. 7.   Variety-, needs-, and access-based positioning.

bracket. Thus, through two different yet complementary positions, Samsung is managing to stay ahead of the pack. Combining its alterations to OE alongside the company's SP makes it ultimately more difficult for rivals to benchmark its unique fit of activities. However, for Samsung to further safeguard its position, the company must focus more on trade-offs.

Trade-offs

According to Porter, a sustainable advantage cannot be guaranteed by simply choosing a unique position as competitors will imitate such an approach in two ways. A competitor can choose to reposition itself to match the superior performer, or a competitor can seek to match the benefits of a successful position while maintaining its original position (known as straddling). Thus, in order for a strategic position to be sustainable, there must be trade-offs with other positions. Trade-offs occur when activities are incompatible and arise for three reasons:

(1) *Inconsistency in Value Delivery* — This refers to how a company known for delivering one kind of value may confuse its primary customers and undermine its own reputation by attempting to deliver two inconsistent values simultaneously.

(2) *Trade-offs from Activities* — This inevitably arises from firm activities if they are over- or under-designed.

(3) *Coordination and Control* — These variables are lacking if a firm tries to serve all things to all customers, thereby confusing the firm's efficient operations.

In this case, strategy can also be defined as making trade-offs in competing and choosing what not to do. Samsung has chosen what not to do quite clearly. As previously mentioned, it has remained distant from the software market, so customers have now come to expect excellence in the hardware. If Samsung had moved into software, it may have ended up undermining its own reputation. The trade-off may not have been worth the risk. While software development could potentially be complementary to the hardware product line, Samsung would have been forced to spend vast sums on developing the new product line in terms of product configuration as well as different equipment, employee behavior, skills, and management systems. The company would then dilute the funds and efforts funneled into new hardware development.

As Samsung was determined to focus on hardware, its management was making its organizational priorities very clear. This undoubtedly filtered down to the employees, who were then provided with a very clear framework to make operational decisions. This contributed to the smooth everyday running of the firm and has translated into the perception among customers of Samsung as a well-organized, trustworthy, and focused firm. Still, as hardware becomes increasingly commoditized and higher values are created in software and contents, and services provided in the hardware, Samsung may need to rethink its trade-offs when upgrading its position along the value chain.

Fit

Lastly, to ensure a lockout of imitators, fit is required to create a configuration that maximizes the synergies among the various value chain activities. Fit among activities is generic and applies to many companies, but the fit that Porter refers to is more strategy specific because it has the capability to enhance a position's uniqueness and amplify trade-offs. There are three types of fit: consistency between each activity and the overall strategy; reinforcing of activities; and optimization of efforts.

In essence, the whole matters more than any individual part when discussing ideas of fit. For Samsung, as it has a clear strategy with one overall goal, there exists a consistency among its different activities. This can be identified when one looks at the company's main production locations. As Samsung is not attempting to be a low-cost provider in the market place, it is able to avoid low-wage countries where production quality might also be compromised. Therefore, Samsung tends to base its manufacturing and R&D facilities in more developed countries such as the US and Japan. Of course, it cannot afford to stay out of developing economies altogether, but it is important for Samsung to have customers see that the company has a strong presence in developed countries.

Furthermore, Samsung's improvements in overall company infrastructure are allowing it to optimize the company's efforts. It currently has four independent business divisions, including consumer electronics, information technology & mobile communications, device solutions, and Harman, which produces electronics components. The continued growth of Samsung should also be attributed to the synergies generated from the integration among divisions. As a result, rollout periods have become much shorter. It used to take more than a year for the company to go from a new product concept to rollout, but now it only takes a few months. As such, faster rollouts mean rapidly renewed product lines. Samsung renews its flagship product lines about every 6 months now compared with Apple that refreshes its product line every year. As Samsung is ensuring that none of the company's efforts are wasted, fit is essential for its strategy. Therefore, with its improvements in OE, Samsung is able to perform similar activities better than its competitors; with its SP firmly targeted, the company increases its competitive advantages, and with a strong fit configured among its overall value chain activities, it is able to lock out competitors that are tempted to imitate the "Samsung Way."

Although seemingly simple, management should target a consistent SP for the long term. Continuity is an important concept here as it helps reinforce a company's identity. Frequent shifts in strategy may not only be costly but also cause organizational dissonance. Samsung, however, seems to have dug itself in for the long haul and as one of Korea's main players, and is slowly taking over the world of high-tech hardware.

Why Not the "Sony Way?"

We have expounded fully on the "Samsung Way," but it was not so long ago that Sony Electronics was the undisputed leader in consumer electronics. Over the last decade, it has lost ground to

Samsung, and this begs the following question: Just what is Sony doing wrong? Currently, Sony's market capitalization is now 30% of Samsung and 5% of Apple. Exactly where have the two companies diverged? In many ways, Samsung and Sony are similar. They are both producing upper- to mid-range consumer electronics at reasonable prices, but unlike Samsung, Sony has become heavily involved in the movies, music, and video games markets. A strong conflict among this new business segment, consumer electronics branch, and the digital media sector has hampered the company's operations. Sony is the only conglomerate to be in both consumer electronics and entertainment.

With regard to OE, Sony has made few significant changes over the years, but the only significant change that the company has made is in the area of "technology development" (see Fig. 8). This has indeed been modified in that Sony has most significantly expanded its scope from hardware to software. In hardware, Sony continues to stay ahead of or equal to its competitors, and recently the company has moved into the digital media segment. Acting within a digital media segment has altered its value chain, but has not essentially altered its OE for the better.

In fact, the point of altering the value chain is to perform similar activities to rivals, but in a better or more effective way. Yet, many of Sony's rivals are already performing a similar type of activity within their value chains. Companies such as the Korean firm Iriver have already hedged their bets on both hardware and software products. After purchasing an Iriver media device, one can download software to supplement and support the hardware.

By contrast, after purchasing a similar hardware product from Sony, one might find the software slightly less accommodating. The problem is that, in a bid to increase profits, Sony has begun to spread itself thinly over a number of markets, which Porter would refer to as having "no uniqueness," and to make matters worse there is a distinct lack of "fit" among these businesses. The digital media segment requires the hardware produced by the consumer electronics segment to function. However, the hardware division does not yet feel reliant on the digital

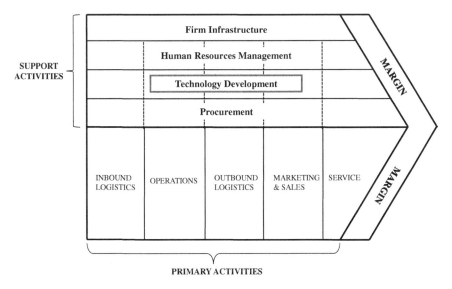

Fig. 8. Sony's value chain alterations.

media segment. As Sony has been frozen by its fear of piracy, it has not been able to find a resolution to this ongoing "civil war."

Sony's digital Walkman device is a good example as its users were hampered by the excessive procedures designed to block illegal file sharing.[4] Furthermore, the Walkman was built without hard drives, as Sony's copy protection mechanism does not allow music to be transferred from one hard drive to another. Yet, when we look at hardware products such as Apple's iPod touch, we witness an almost flawless integration with other Mac software such as iTunes, iPhoto, and the App store, which creates an interactive experience among photos, movies, games, and music.

Essentially, the conflict is that Sony's electronics division needs to let customers move files around effortlessly and create synergies, but

---

[4] "File-sharing" is more related to the MP3 era than the cassette tape era. There was though a strong "home taping is killing music" movement during this period, although it could be argued it had little effect. https://www.theguardian.com/music/2008/jun/17/popandrock.

the entertainment side wants to maintain barriers as it sees every customer as a potential thief rather than a "prosumer" as Apple or Iriver does. Ironically, Sony's electronics division showed support for Napster, the file-sharing website, against the legal battles from Sony's entertainment divisions. Sony Entertainment has also led the fight against companies that manufacture CD burners, and Sony Electronics joined in on a lawsuit against Launch Media, an Internet radio service that is partially owned by Sony Entertainment.

It seems that Sony has attempted to expand outward in OE while failing to do so in SP. This has essentially created a conflict between the OE aspect of its business and the SP aspect as well as a conflict within the SP aspects of its business. If there is to be a complementary coexistence among both OE and SP, Sony has to go back to the drawing board and take a closer look at its OE and develop it beyond merely the technology development sphere. More importantly, the company has to reevaluate its SP by selecting aspects of its business that are going to correlate with specific types of SP.

Sony's strategic movement over the last decade has proven such a strategic analysis as it has suffered consolidated net losses between 2008 and 2011. Since then, it has initiated a recovery to bring back its historical glory. This was done by reducing its reliance on computers, televisions, and mobile phones, while focusing on small-scale products such as camera sensors, consoles, and video games. A breakthrough came in 2017 when the positive results of its restructuring first began to emerge and the company experienced profitability led by its game and network services business. More recently, in early 2020, Sony announced that it will promote another restructuring effort by merging Sony Mobile Communications, Imaging Products and Solutions, and Home Entertainment & Sound into one division, which will be named Sony Electronics Corporation. This represents efforts to optimize the company's organizational structure by reducing operational costs and generate synergies among these businesses. At the same time, Sony hopes to venture into financial services and other sectors, and to make these businesses equal to its electronics business.

Discussion Questions

1. Porter claims that only strategic positioning can lead to a real sustainable competitive advantage, not operational effectiveness. Do you agree? Why or why not?

2. Do you think that some aspects of operational effectiveness can lead to sustainable competitive advantage? If so, which aspects and why?

3. Porter highlights the need for top-level management to convey strategy to all levels of the firm. Why do you think this is so? How can this best be achieved in large firms?

4. Is the resource-based view of the firm more pertinent than Porter's views and frameworks? Do you agree or disagree? Discuss.

5. It is argued that Porter is undoubtedly the guru of strategic management. Do you agree? Which aspect of his work do you most respect and agree with and why?

6. What would you prescribe Sony to do in the future in order to enhance its competitiveness further?

CHAPTER 5

New Models for Business Strategy

Chapter Guideline

Porter's model has provided a firm foundation for many fields in the discipline of strategic management. However, as evident from the various analyses done so far, Porter's model suffers from some inconsistencies. There are also many avenues for improvement in order to present a more comprehensive view on strategy as seen with other concepts and theories. This chapter will show attempts by various scholars to reconcile and complement Porter's models to advance the state of knowledge in the field of strategic management.

Summary of Previous Models

In the previous chapter, we saw the profound impact Porter's theory has had on many aspects of management strategy. His seminal 1996 article entitled "What is Strategy" redefined strategic management and demonstrated Porter's penetrating insight into the fundamental concepts of this field. These insights have had enormous staying power as evident from his interviews, which remain consistent and highly valid even after the phenomenal changes in the international business environment over the past decades. Furthermore, we have read about business leaders, scholars, and even critics who praise Porter's massive contribution to the field. Despite this praise, scholars always leave some avenue for criticism and extension. Now, it is time to look at the scholars who have tried to reconcile some inconsistencies in Porter's model and present new frameworks in order to advance the state-of-the-art knowledge in strategic management.

5.1 Blue versus Red Ocean: A Critique of Porter?

It is without a doubt that Michael Porter's definition of strategy has had a profound impact on business studies. However, like any other academic landmark, many counterpoints and new approaches have followed Porter's seminal works. The most common criticism regarding Porter is that his strategic prescription of becoming either a low-cost provider or a differentiated player seems too limited to fully convey the complexity of the real world. For example, Ridderstrale and Nordstrom (1999) recommended that readers forget the old world order and make a difference in a new world order which they dub "Funky Business." According to them, the old notion of competitive strategy that repeatedly takes the same beaten path does not lead to success in the new world order. Indeed, the idea of creating uncontested and "funky" new dimensions sounds very alluring in a world swept up in an exponential tidal wave of economic, technological, societal, and political change.

The dichotomy of funky and non-funky gained an even wider audience after Kim and Mauborgne (2005) introduced the catchy metaphoric dichotomy between Red Ocean Strategy and Blue Ocean Strategy, which describes the difference between a saturated unprofitable market space and a profitable untapped market space. Industrial organization economics thus far has emphasized the importance of competing within a pre-established structure. Therefore, competition, in essence, has been regarded as a zero-sum game in which a relative gain by one competitor leads to a loss for the other. Previous frameworks focused on how the industry space was divided among the various competitors within the industry. Kim and Mauborgne, on the contrary, assert that this overlooks a much more profitable potential of creating industry spaces outside of the preexisting structure. This untapped space is dubbed the Blue Ocean and is a market-creating strategy that makes competition irrelevant. By comparison, Red Ocean is a market-competing strategy, stressing the competition within existing markets (Kim and Mauborgne, 2017).

Kim and Mauborgne identified that 14% of firms which invested in Blue Ocean generated 38% of total revenues and 61% of total profits in their empirical study. The reasons behind these statistics are various, but the most important one is destructive competition. Production methods and technology have become increasingly standardized and easily replicable. Therefore, the best way to increase revenue is not by constantly struggling and edging ahead in the Red Ocean, but rather to find a new Blue Ocean in which firms can reap immense profits. The implication behind this theory is profound. For decades, strategy gurus have preached that the two viable strategic options are differentiation and cost. However, according to the authors of the Blue Ocean Strategy, firms have the opportunity to break from the pre-established value/cost trade-off and set completely new rules for the game. The firm can create this Blue Ocean through a focus on the demand side rather than the production side that is achieved by reducing costs while driving up buyer value.

How does one achieve such a feat? The authors offer several concrete steps that firms can adopt from the example of the US wine market. The strategy canvas in Fig. 1 shows the seven elements that determine the US wine market. Price, use of enological terminology,

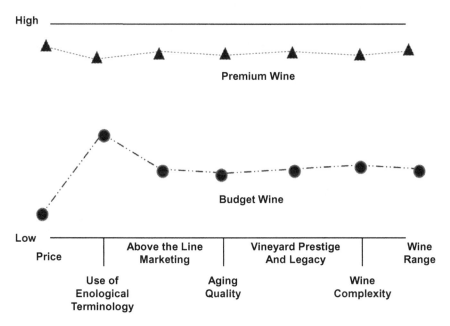

Fig. 1. Strategy canvas of U.S wine industry in the late 1990s.

Source: Kim and Mauborgne (2005).

above-the-line marketing to enhance consumer awareness, aging quality of the wine, prestige attributed to the vineyard, complex determination of wine taste, and a wide range of wines depending on consumer preference. The remarkable feature here is that there is a convergence between premium and budget wines. Although they are very different, they have identical strategic profiles based on the same seven elements on the canvas. In other words, despite claiming to be different, both budget and premium wines compete in the same criteria for a similar group of consumers.

The Blue Ocean Strategy, on the contrary, requires a firm to compete based on *different criteria*. This is precisely what Yellow Tail, an Australian wine company, did in the US wine market. Instead of trying to compete based on the same seven elements, Yellow Tail deleted all the enological terminologies and prestige from its labeling, and focused on creating a fun, easily approachable wine at a competitive price. Yellow Tail's strategy canvas is depicted through the square spotted lines in Fig. 2.

The remarkable aspect to note about this new canvas is the creation of three additional criteria (far right of Fig. 2), which are represented at the right edge of the bottom axis. These three

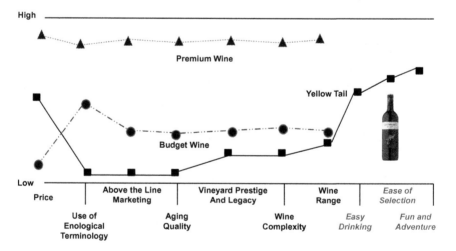

Fig. 2.   Yellow tail's strategy canvas.

Source: Kim and Mauborgne (2005).

additional criteria represent the essence of a Blue Ocean Strategy that seeks to alter the preexisting structure and reap immense profits by doing so.

The authors further present a readily applicable framework that can be used to envision and implement their ideas (see Fig. 3). With this, we can see that creating a Blue Ocean requires eliminating and reducing preexisting elements while creating and raising ones that did not exist or only had a weak presence in the industry. For instance, Yellow Tail eliminated enological terminology, aging quality, and above-the-line marketing. The company also reduced wine complexity, wine range, and vineyard prestige. The new wine brand raised the retail store involvement and created an easy drinking experience, ease of selection, and a sense of adventure in the wine industry.

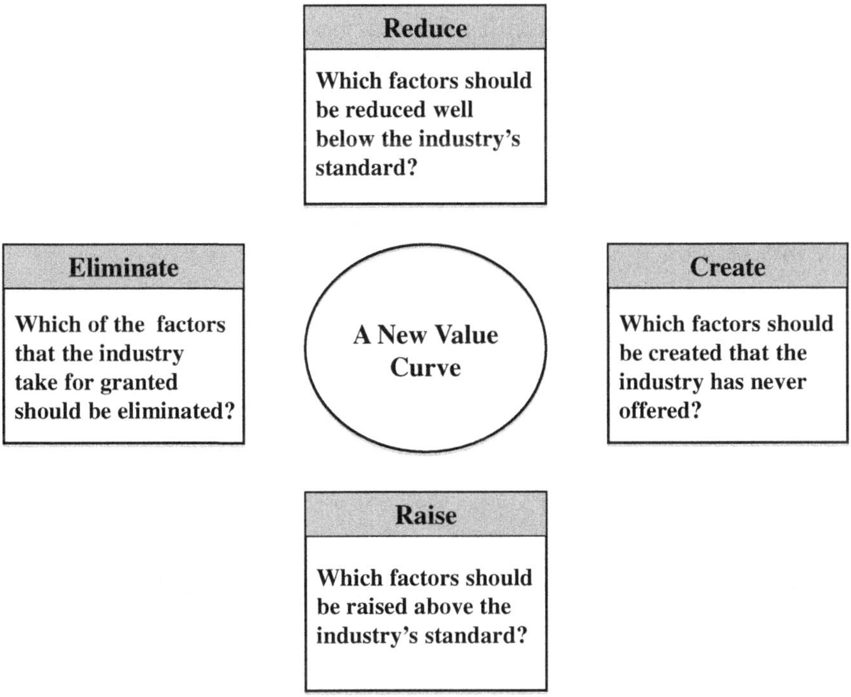

Reduce

Which factors should be reduced well below the industry's standard?

Eliminate

Which of the factors that the industry take for granted should be eliminated?

A New Value Curve

Create

Which factors should be created that the industry has never offered?

Raise

Which factors should be raised above the industry's standard?

Fig. 3.   The four actions framework.

Source: Kim and Mauborgne (2005).

This induced a formerly neglected customer base (those who were reluctant to consume wine due to the complexity involved with wine drinking) to become Yellow Tail customers.

The authors conclude that the Blue Ocean Strategy has always been present, but has never been systematically analyzed. Therefore, they attempted through their article to provide a comprehensive and analytical framework to create and analyze Blue Ocean and present a quantitative analysis of this exciting new concept. Kim and Mauborgne further published the updated and expanded version of *Blue Ocean Strategy* in 2015, and more recently in 2017 they published a follow-up, *Blue Ocean Shift: Beyond Competing, Proven Steps to Inspire Confidence and Seize New Growth*. Their first book focuses on the conceptual development of "what is" Blue Ocean thinking for new business ventures, while *Blue Ocean Shift* presents "how to" shift from red to blue oceans with a step-by-step process to identifying untapped growth opportunities. In their book, they introduced three components of making a successful Blue Ocean shift:

- *Adopting a Blue Ocean perspective* — A shift in mindset from Red Ocean to Blue Ocean strategic thinking, so that firms can expand their horizons and adjust their understanding of where opportunity resides.

- *Having a set of market-creating tools* — Practical tools for market creation with proper guidance on how to apply them to turn the Blue Ocean perspective into a reality. Although Kim and Mauborgne's 2005 book also introduced these tools, the 2017 book delves more deeply into them with concrete processes at the operational level.

- *Having a humanistic process* — Instead of treating execution as something that automatically occurs after the strategy is set, firms need to stress the emotions and psychology of people. This process then inspires and builds people's confidence to own and drive the new strategy for effective execution, thereby being committed to seeing changes and overcoming the constraints they face.

In addition, Kim and Mauborgne (2017, 2019) stressed the importance and substantial benefits of *nondisruptive creation* for creating new markets, which means creation without disrupting or destroying existing businesses or markets. Microfinance, life coaching, and more recently, online dating, crowdfunding, and smartphone accessories are all good examples. This concept is contrary to Joseph Schumpeter's "creative destruction," which he says occurs when an innovation creates a new market that displaces earlier technology or an existing product or service (Kim and Mauborgne, 2019). Schumpeter argued that creative destruction is at the core of economic growth. Yet, Kim and Mauborgne suggest that the nondisruptive strategy is a positive-sum approach to innovation, as opposed to the zero-sum nature of disruption (Kim and Mauborgne, 2019).

Such a strategy is particularly attractive as it helps avoid head-to-head clashes with established companies and reduce conflicts with social interest groups and government agencies. Furthermore, in the era of the fourth industrial revolution where smart devices are replacing jobs, this strategy plays a key role by allowing firms to pursue growth without painful adjustment costs upon society.

Analysis

The Blue Ocean concept has been a sensational hit in many ways because of the message it entails. Simply, firms do not have to be prisoners of the preexisting industry structure, but rather they can reformulate and even find new territory outside of the industry structure to reap high profits. This refreshing message was like a godsent oasis to many managers who were struggling to find new ways to operate within the dried-up and barren landscapes of established industry structures. However, as sensational as this concept may sound, we must be very careful to accept the novelty of the Blue Ocean.

Kim and Mauborgne criticized that organizational leaders often accept market boundaries as given, and hence firms have to develop their strategies, such as cost and differentiation, within the environmental constraints. The first scholar to systematically analyze and present a framework for industry structure was Michael Porter. In his seminal 1980 book *Competitive Strategy*, he emphasized the importance of industry structure in determining firm profitability and competitiveness. Porter further discussed how industry structures are not static but dynamic and that firms can alter the structure to their own advantage. Therefore, we can see that the Blue Ocean and the nondisruptive creation strategies actually already existed, yet were not articulated to the extent that they have been in this article. The Blue Ocean can also be regarded as one type of strategic positioning (SP) of Porter (1996).

In this regard, we can conclude that the Blue Ocean is not a completely revolutionary concept. Rather it is a refinement and articulation of a preexisting concept that Porter had devised in his previous studies. To be more precise, we can incorporate the Blue Ocean concept into the productivity frontier curve (Porter, 1996). As shown in Fig. 4, the Blue Ocean can be seen as the act of pushing the productivity frontier outward by altering the industry structure.

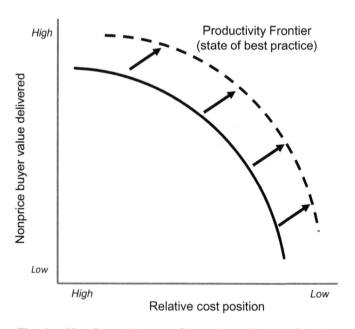

Fig. 4. Blue Ocean in terms of Porter's productivity frontier.

Kim and Mauborgne's contribution to this thought is to formalize and refine the preexisting concept into a readily digestible manner. While the Blue Ocean shows us a very precise and detailed analysis of how to alter the industry structure and create profitable business opportunities, the entire concept itself is not entirely novel. In practice, rather than tilting toward the Blue Ocean Strategy, firms should consider both types. In fact, Kim and Mauborgne (2015) stressed the necessity of creating a balanced portfolio across businesses of Red and Blue Oceans. Furthermore, in the Red Ocean, firms can find ways to avoid or minimize the competition among rivals while gaining superior profits.

5.2 Another Critique

As the analysis part of the above section demonstrates, a thorough understanding of Porter's work is necessary before making truly valid criticisms. The Blue Ocean concept is a refinement rather than a criticism of Porter's conception of strategy. Therefore, the next article by Moon (1993) starts off with a thorough review of Porter's generic strategies to provide the readers with a better understanding of Porter's view and relevant critiques. Moon points out several issues with Porter's framework and then presents a new and enhanced framework, which attempts to reconcile these inconsistencies.

The starting point is Porter's ever-famous Generic Strategies (see Fig. 5). This simple yet powerful model succinctly summarizes his argument that successful firms must make a choice in order to acquire true competitive advantage. Firms cannot be all things to all people; therefore, they must make trade-offs in order to formulate unique fits. This provides the firm long-term and sustained competitive advantage. As such, those firms that are unable to make their choices and necessary trade-offs are dubbed as "stuck in the middle" and will eventually lose out to more competent competitors who have achieved their unique fits.

There is though one problem with Porter's Generic Strategies model. It is the concept of "stuck in the middle" which views all strategies as mutually exclusive. To put it simply, is it not possible for firms

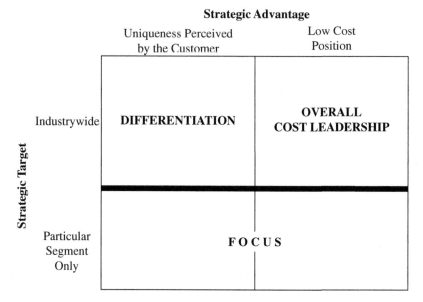

Fig. 5. Porter's generic strategies.
Source: Porter (1980, p. 34).

to shift their strategies depending on the stage of development they are in? Firms cannot simply start with a unique fit. There must be some kind of intermediate process or unique fit that must be preceded in order to reach this advanced level of firm development. Therefore, the evolutionary nature of strategies, depicted in Fig. 6, can significantly enhance the generic strategy model.

Consider a typical new entrant to the international market. In general, such a firm would not be able to compete with its more established competitors based on technology, capital, or experience. While there are exceptions, such as high-tech start-ups and consulting firms, most new firms gain their entry through advantages in basic factor conditions such as low labor cost. This is what Porter termed cost focus. As the new entrant accumulates additional experience (capital and resources), it will move on to either a differentiation focus or cost leadership, depending on which of these two it will base its advantage on. After this stage, the firm will naturally gravitate to its final

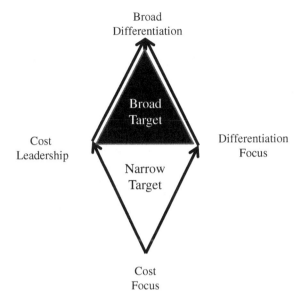

Fig. 6. Dynamic model of Porter's generic strategies.
Source: Moon (1993).

destination, that is, broad differentiation where a firm will compete based on its unique fit but serving a broad competitive scope.

The evolutionary path among a number of Korean Multinational Corporations (MNCs) aptly illustrates this dynamic concept. Hyundai, for example, started out with a typical cost focus strategy in the 1970s by producing small cars with cheap labor. As Hyundai accumulated experience, technology, and brand value, the company then moved on to cost leadership in the late 1980s and throughout the 1990s when it began to produce a wider range of automobiles but still at a significantly lower cost than its competitors. Note that even in this intermediate stage, cost leadership and differentiation coexisted in the Hyundai case. This, according to Porter, would be a classic "stuck-in-the-middle" situation in which firms will not be able to gain a sustainable competitive advantage. However, Hyundai incrementally increased its brand value, technology, and scope of competition through this strategy and it is currently looking to move tentatively into the final stage of firm evolution, which is broad differentiation. This is evident when looking at Hyundai's focus in the last few years on luxury models such as Genesis. Did Hyundai fail? Hardly! Hyundai has been designated as a "compulsory success story" for study at prestigious MBA schools such as Harvard and Stanford (Sa, 2008).

This evolutionary path also shows how important it is to distinguish the upper shaded triangle depicting the "major league" (consisting of top global firms) from the lower triangle representing the "minor league" (consisting of new entrants) in Fig. 6. This is useful as it aptly describes two different spheres of competition that exist in global business and the strategies that firms will take depending on the "league" in which they compete.

Another major problem with Porter's framework is its unilateral focus on competition. While this factor is the most important force dictating global business strategies, it does not represent the whole picture. Two alternative strategies that are frequently adopted by emerging MNCs must be taken into account in order to present a comprehensive framework. The first is the shelter strategy in which firms seek protection from market (or competitive) forces as a way to gain an initial foothold. Of course, this type of protective strategy is not sustainable in the long run, but many firms do indeed choose this strategy, at least in the initial stage. Second is the use of a cooperative strategy or as it is more commonly known, the strategic alliance. Many firms choose to cooperate rather than compete as frequently noted by many prominent scholars such as Ohmae (1989). In particular, considering the complexity and broadening scope of global business, cooperation among firms will continue to increase in the future.[1]

Figure 7 incorporates all the points that have been made above. Global strategy can be divided into three broad categories: (a) protectionist, (b) competitive, and (c) cooperative. Under these choices, firms can pursue a combination of various strategies according to the developmental stage and arena in which they wish to be.

---

[1]This point will be further discussed in Chapter 7.

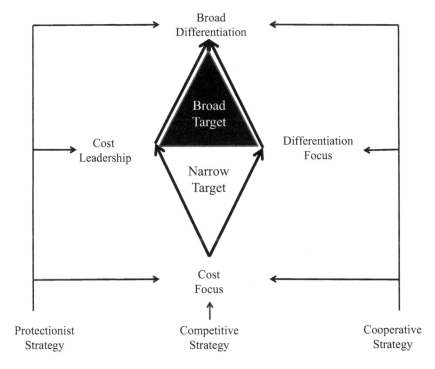

Fig. 7. Comprehensive global strategy.
Source: Moon (1993).

In sum, the new model reconciles two problems Porter's model had. First, the static nature of Porter's model is transformed into a more dynamic one. Most firms do not just stay with one strategy as such choices evolve continuously depending on the stages of development. Second, although important, competitive strategy is not the only type available. Many firms pursue various other approaches including the protectionist and cooperative strategy.

The core message behind of all these discussions is that many of the strategies that Porter believed mutually exclusive are not actually so. Stuck in the middle is not a product of incorrect strategic choice, but rather a phase of evolutionary development. Lastly, although the path that individual global players have taken may differ, the ultimate destination for all of them is broad differentiation.

Analysis

The comprehensive global strategy presented above attempts to reconcile some of Porter's inconsistencies and adds other dimensions by incorporating the concepts of shelter, competitive, and cooperative strategies. Although Porter always preaches that firms cannot be all things to all people and that rigorous competition is the name of the game, the reality is quite different as many firms simultaneously engage in various types of strategies and cooperate with other firms.

What we can derive from Moon's model is that Porter's concept of trade-offs and creating fits describes the path taken from cost focus to cost leadership or cost focus to differentiation focus. After firms have reached these two points, regardless of how they reached the tip of the narrow target, they will all attempt to move on to the final destination that is broad differentiation.

Consider Toyota and BMW. Toyota started out with a cost focus and then eventually moved on to a cost leadership position through its high-quality yet reasonably priced cars. According to Porter, Toyota should stay in that position, make trade-offs, and create its own unique fit of activities for a sustainable competitive advantage. However, Toyota did not follow this path and rather forged new paths by introducing the Lexus and other high-end models to cater to a much wider range of customers. Did Toyota lose its competitiveness and get stuck in the middle? Not at all! Toyota is evolving to achieve the final stage of development that is broad differentiation. The same could be said about BMW, which is a very well-known luxury carmaker. According to Moon's model, BMW was at the differentiation focus stage where it used to sell to a limited, high-end customer segment. However, rather than dwelling in and solidifying its competitive advantage in that position, BMW has introduced the 1 Series as an entry-level vehicle for consumers.

Moon's study shows one overarching problem with Porter's approach, which is the overfocus on firms from advanced countries. Porter's research is based on his observations of firms which are active in developed markets where the conditions are more stable and consequently more static. This is perhaps why in some cases scholars from developing or newly developed countries are in a better position to make observations that Porter might have missed. In Asia, global MNCs with worldwide brand recognition coexist with many other firms and rely greatly upon the traditional factor of cost advantage. This is very rare in the US and other developed countries where the level of economic development simply makes it difficult to observe both types of firms simultaneously. Therefore, scholars from developing countries are in a better position to observe and ameliorate the problems found in Porter's static model. Figure 8 presents visually the differences between Porter and Moon.

Since Porter mostly analyzes established firms operating primarily in developed nations, a majority of his observations are clustered around the productivity frontier. Firms already on the productivity frontier may show the end product of what a successful firm should be, but this does not offer much in terms of achieving the evolutionary path that a firm can take in order to achieve the state of best practices. On the contrary, Moon bases his theory on a wider scope

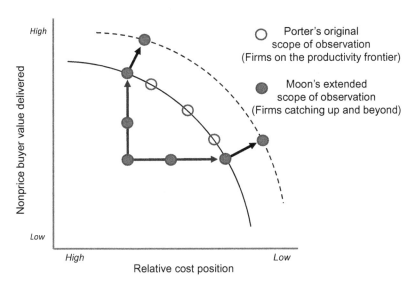

Fig. 8. Differences in scope of analysis between Porter and Moon.

as he observes the firms of catch-up, as well as the firms on the productivity frontier.

5.3 Dynamics of How to Sell What to Whom

Moon *et al.* (2014) continue the critical evaluation of Porter's framework. While the previous article resolved only one problem, namely, the static nature of Porter's framework, this article attempts to enhance the model on a more comprehensive scale.

At this point, it is important to look at the evolution of Porter's generic strategies as they have undergone significant changes since their inception in the 1980s (see Fig. 5). The three generic strategies neatly organize the most commonly used competitive strategies into a readily applicable framework. The key concept introduced through this framework is the question of scope (industry-wide or a particular segment) and the type of advantage (differentiation or overall cost leadership). Porter further enhanced this version in 1985 by introducing an additional dimension in the Focus arena (see Fig. 9).

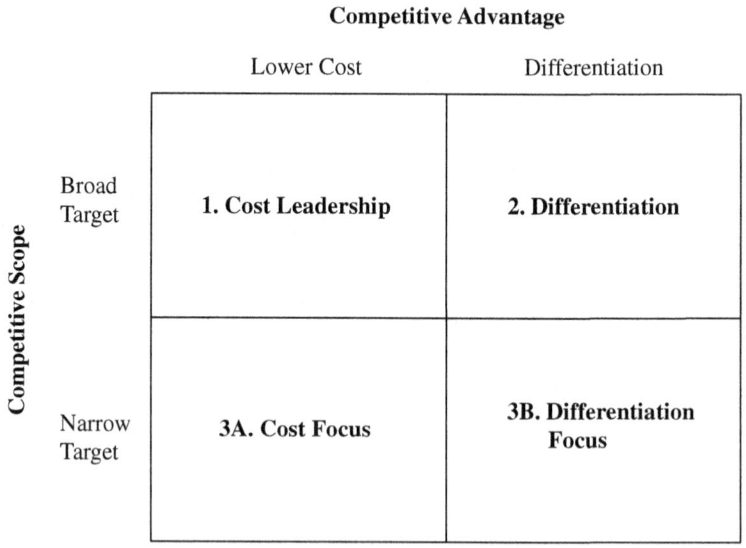

Fig. 9.   Four generic strategies.

Source: Porter (1985, p. 12).

COMPETITIVE ADVANTAGE

		Low Cost	Differentiation
COMPETITIVE TARGET	Broad Target	**Cost Leadership**	**Differentiation**
	Narrow Target	**Cost Focus** **Differentiation Focus**	
	Three Strategic Positionings	**Variety-based Positioning** **Needs-based Positioning** **Access-based Positioning**	

Fig. 10.   Seven generic strategies.
Source: Moon *et al.* (2014).

Later, in 1996, Porter presented a further augmented version of his framework by adding the concepts of variety-based, needs-based, and access-based positioning.[2] Although Porter never actually created a framework that incorporates these new concepts, they can all be considered to be a subset of the focus strategy. Figure 10 shows how they can be organized.

The above frameworks have been highly influential in transforming strategic management from simply informed conversation to rigorous academic discipline. However, they are not without flaws and three general points must be stressed[3]:

- *Failure to Distinguish Scope of Product vs. Customer Group* — While Porter distinguished strategies according to competitive scope, the nature of the scope is rather elusive. Porter later introduced the concept of needs-based, variety-based, and access-based strategies, but they overlap to a significant degree and do not

---

[2] See Chapter 4 for more detailed analysis.
[3] For further discussion, see Moon *et al.* (2014).

provide us with a clear-cut picture as to what exactly the firm's focus should be.

- *Stuck in the Middle* — There are actually many firms that choose to pursue several strategies simultaneously and still succeed. Porter's framework fails to account for the achievements of these firms.

- *Shifting Strategies* — Many firms frequently change their strategies according to business cycles and other variables. This goes against Porter's repeated assertion that strategies must be kept constant in order to create sustainable competitive advantage.

Figure 11 refines Porter's existing frameworks to provide a more comprehensive and realistic picture. The core difference is the introduction of a new dimension of competitive target (i.e., product or customer), which attempts to reconcile Porter's confusion when discussing the variety-, needs-, and access-based strategies. The competitive target for product is to provide a specific type of product or service for a broad scope of customers, while the competitive target for customer aims to serve a particular customer group with a wide

Customer Based Strategy

		Broad	Narrow
Product Based Strategy	Broad	**Broad Differentiation** ---------------------------- **Broad Cost Leadership**	**Customer-focused Differentiation** ---------------------------- **Customer-focused Cost Leadership**
	Narrow	**Product-focused Differentiation** ---------------------------- **Product-focused Cost Leadership**	**Narrow Differentiation** ---------------------------- **Narrow Cost Leadership**

Fig. 11. Eight comprehensive generic strategies.
Source: Moon *et al.* (2014).

range of products or services. Competitive target based on product or customer can be either broad or narrow for the competitive scope. These cases can be further subdivided based upon the competitive source, such as cost or differentiation. Therefore, by combining the three dimensions (competitive target, competitive scope, and competitive source), eight generic strategies are created to show a comprehensive and dynamic view. The following explains the key features of this model along with the four categories of Broad, Product-based, Customer-based, and Narrow strategies based on either cost or differentiation, using the case of the automobile industry as an example.

- *Broad Strategy* — Firms in this category attempt to provide a wide range of product or service varieties for a broad customer base, which can be achieved through differentiation or cost leadership. For example, Mercedes (high-end manufacturer) and Hyundai Motors (lower-end manufacturer) both attempt to provide a wide choice of automobiles for various customers, but the two firms have different strategic directions. Specifically, differentiation for Mercedes and cost leadership for Hyundai.

- *Product-based Strategy* — This refers to a strategy which attempts to meet the particular needs of a wide array of customers. This can also be based on either differentiation or cost leadership. While Land Rover and Jeep are both producers of off-road utility vehicles, the former chose to take the differentiation route by providing sophisticated features at significantly higher prices. On the contrary, Jeep chose to offer value prices for the quality of the product that it offers.

- *Customer-based Strategy* — Some firms attempt to provide a broad range of products or services to a narrow group of customers. Again, either a cost or differentiation approach can be taken as demonstrated by the following examples. Caterpillar, a leading construction and mining equipment manufacturer, offers tough and durable machines with superior performance. Furthermore, the level of customer service far exceeds that of its competitors in the same industry. Komatsu, another heavy machinery and mining equipment company, offers value products at a lower cost. Unlike Caterpillar, it has taken the cost leadership path to gaining competitive advantage within the customer-based strategy.

- *Narrow Strategy* — This strategy is applied to meet the particular needs of a particular group of customers. Companies such as AM General Corporation utilize a multi-scope strategy since it produces highly specialized military and special-purpose vehicles. The customer base is limited, the pricing is high, and the strategy is heavily focused on providing specific value. It is rather difficult to take a cost leadership approach because for a company to pursue this, it has to have a certain degree of scale and scope economies to attain cost advantage which is very hard to achieve in this kind of highly specialized industry.

At this stage then, what is stuck in the middle? Many companies have successfully pursued various strategies and survived. Stuck in the middle is in fact not a result of the wrong strategic choice, but rather a broadening of strategy. The real question is not whether companies can or cannot broaden their strategy, but rather whether they can broaden it without losing their competitive advantages. Hence, successful companies will expand without diluting their previous advantages.

Consider Toyota and Honda's entry into the US market. Although the success of numerous Japanese auto companies is generally accepted today, they were looked down upon in the early days of their entry into the US market during the 1980s. They were clearly not differentiators as foreign luxury brands such as BMW and Jaguar dominated this segment. Even in the lower-end segment, Hyundai was competing fiercely based on its cost leadership. However, why is it that 20 years later, four out of the seven best-selling sedans are those of Honda and Toyota that according to Porter have pursued a stuck-in-the-middle strategy?

The answer is quite simple; the majority of mid-sized car buyers in the US could not afford to buy an expensive BMW. At the same time, they were not willing to sacrifice their desire for quality and purchase a Sonata from Hyundai which at the time did not have a good reputation. In essence, these customers are both quality and cost conscious. By catering to these customers, Toyota and Honda were not being caught in the middle, but rather, they were utilizing a customer-focused strategy, which attempts to meet the particular needs of the middle-income buyers.

This new perspective can easily map out the evolutionary path of a firm. Consider two vastly different firms in the same industry, Hyundai and Mercedes. Hyundai started out in 1967 as a narrow cost strategy with a single product catering to one customer group in Korea (narrow cost). In 1976, it made tentative steps into the US and other countries based on cost-competitive automobiles (product-based cost leadership). In recent years, the firm has aggressively invested in overseas production bases and is becoming a broad cost leader in a wide array of automobiles (broad cost leadership). In this way, Hyundai was able to expand its product and customer base throughout the years without compromising its existing competitive advantage.

Mercedes Benz, on the contrary, started out by catering exclusively to higher-end customers. The medium-sized C-Class and larger E- and S-Classes were for more affluent customers (narrow differentiation). However, as time passed, it began introducing the smaller A-Class that caters to a broader range of customers (product-based differentiation). It is important to note that the introduction of the A-Class was not an attempt to be cost competitive, but was to pursue differentiation within a different target segment. It targeted the customers who wanted a higher-end car within that class of vehicles. If the purpose were to compete on price, most would look for a Honda or a Toyota rather than Mercedes. It is now increasingly offering a wider range of products in an array of classes to target such customers who look for luxury in different classes of automobiles (Broad differentiation).

The main concern for all firms is as follows: "How to sell what to whom?" The new model shows a more comprehensive framework to understand the answer to this question as it shows the dynamic and complex nature of firm strategies much better than the previous models.

Analysis

The above discussion aptly summarizes Porter's existing frameworks and further enhances their explanatory power. This is important given that his insight, while powerful, neglects the dynamic nature of global business and fails to account for many successful firms that shifted their strategies according to their needs. Furthermore, the ambiguity that frequently lingers over the relationship between Porter's new concepts of variety-, needs-, and access-based categories and his previous analytical frameworks is cleared up as well.

However, this study is limited to specific industries and the only in-depth case study example presented is the automobile industry. Considering the fact that industry structure has a profound effect on firm strategies, it remains to be seen whether this framework can explain the inner workings of other industries that are vastly different from the automobile industry. Nevertheless, the contribution of this work is that it succinctly ameliorates and further enhances Porter's previous approach. In addition, it provides a more effective context within which to analyze MNCs from developing countries as most of the so-called "Emerging Giants" are still in the intermediary stages which cannot be captured by Porter's framework.

Case Study 1: An Indian Blue Ocean[4]

HCL is a leading global technology firm with more than 150,000 employees across 49 countries and average annual revenue of US$9.9 billion as of June 2020. It is composed of three firms, HCL Technologies, HCL Infosystems, and HCL Healthcare. Having been founded in 1976, it is described as one of India's original IT garage start-ups. So, just how did a garage start-up develop into a global

---

[4]Some information of this case is abstracted from the Blue Ocean Strategy Official Website (www.blueoceanstrategy.com), The Hindu Business Line (Blue Ocean Strategy Helps HCL Tech Bag DSG Deal, January 20, 2006, & We Are Trying to Dominate the Multi-Service Space, July 2, 2006), https://www.dice.com/jobs/detail/Automation-Tester-HCL-America-Inc.-Cary-NC-22102/hcl001APP/6639629, and How HCL Tech balances its organic and inorganic strategy will determine its growth (Money Control, May 15, 2019).

conglomerate today? One of the ways to understand its growth is to consider the Blue Ocean approach.

In 2005, Mr. Vineet Nayar took over as CEO of the HCL group and on the same day a gift was left on his desk which was the book *Blue Ocean Strategy* by Kim and Mauborgne. Nayar claims that he decided to conceptualize the strategy and apply it directly to HCL. In essence, he wished to create uncontested market spaces within which his firm could grow and reap the benefits of an early-mover advantage.

Nayar realized that the application of the outsourcing business was becoming increasingly commoditized and under pricing pressures. Thus, HCL had to chase larger deals that would bring a significant transformation for the group. It made a concentrated effort to move up the value chain and go for multi-service deals with application and infrastructure components. Shortly after adopting its Blue Ocean Strategy, the firm made a number of successful joint ventures and partnerships with the likes of Boeing, AMD, NEC, and Celestica.

HCL's approach embodies a unique kind of disruptive innovation, which focuses on value centricity. This has deepened customer relationships, created new markets, and established strategic partnerships where there is collaboration, goal alignment, and substantive engagement. In this first stage, HCL had to create a strategy canvas (see Fig. 12), which is a diagnostic and action framework for

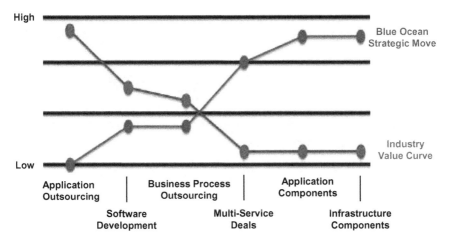

Fig. 12. HCL's strategy canvas.

building an effective Blue Ocean Strategy. It should include all of the current factors that the industry currently competes on and what customers receive from the existing competitive offerings on the market. Thus, its role is to first capture the current state of play in the known market space and then second to propel the firm to action by reorienting its focus from competitors to alternatives and from customers to non-customers of the industry.

As depicted in Fig. 12, HCL became acutely aware that the software development and business process outsourcing industries were intensely competitive, the margins were low, and offerings were commoditized. Therefore, HCL organized its priorities according to the Four Actions Framework explained in the first part of this chapter (see Fig. 3). The framework, by first eliminating and reducing, allowed for insight into how to reduce investments in highly competitive areas. Second, by raising and creating, HCL was able to lift buyer value and create new demand. This ultimately provided HCL with a move from an existing industry value curve to a Blue Ocean curve. The four actions in this framework are shown in Fig. 13.

In Fig. 13, key points include the elimination of the pure application outsourcing business and a reduction of the software and business process outsourcing segments, where competition was high. Alongside this, the raising of multi-service deals with the focus on upstream value chain activities was a high priority. By creating collaborative outsourcing, whereby client companies could select outsourcing criteria (application or infrastructure) and focusing on information management systems, HCL was able to enter into previously unexplored business segments and thus swim in its own Blue Ocean.

In order to sustain its growth in the future, HCL recently introduced its growth strategy of Mode 1-2-3 for Fiscal Year 2017 and beyond. Mode 1 strategy focuses on strengthening its core services, such as Application Services, Infrastructure Services, Engineering and R&D Services, and Business Process Outsourcing. Mode 2 aims to build future ready platforms through emerging technologies such as artificial intelligence, machine learning, and cloud platforms. Mode 3 is an ecosystem-driven strategy which is driven by strategic

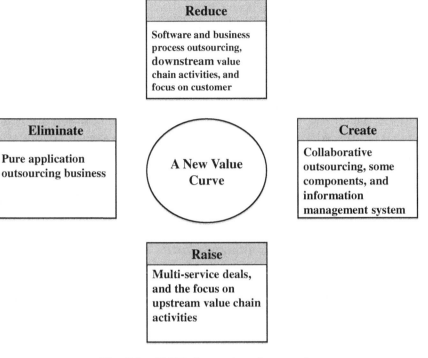

Fig. 13. HCL's four actions framework.

opportunities through Intellectual Property Partnership with tech companies such as IBM.

Over the years, HCL has been investing heavily in accruing firms that are consistent with its growth strategy for Modes 2 and 3. So far, the company has seen significant success as evident from the company's financial results. However, analysts have pointed out that while HCL's focus on emerging technologies is paying off with the growing expenditure on digital transformation, the company needs to further its organic business growth, expanding on its own capacity or core competence, as well. This is due to the fact that organic growth is important as it gives value proposition for clients.

Therefore, although HCL has been successful in its application of the Blue Ocean Strategy, it should be made clear that this approach should be considered an element of a whole strategy, not a single framework in itself. Thus, Blue Ocean should be accompanied with a Red Ocean Strategy for more sustainable growth.

Case Study 2: Toyota Stuck in the Middle?[5]

The Toyota Motor Corporation is a global company that is headquartered in Japan and was declared the world's second largest automaker in 2019 after Volkswagen in terms of global auto sales.[6] Toyota as a case study was covered in Chapter 2 with regard to Nonaka's knowledge creation within a firm. This time, we are going to look at Toyota again but from a different perspective. We have also previously discussed Porter's three generic strategies model in Chapter 1 and we will again revisit this model but from a slightly different perspective.

As mentioned before, although Porter's model is highly useful, there are two fundamental weaknesses within it: one is that it views the generics as being mutually exclusive and the other is that the model does not show how to shift strategies from one to another. It is argued that while Porter warns against being "stuck in the middle," some firms may actually benefit from competing in more than one generic strategy area. It is also argued that as a firm grows and develops, it may shift its strategy over time. We will thus highlight Toyota's simultaneous use of more than one generic strategy and then will look at how its generic strategy has changed over time, along its evolutionary path.

When the oil crisis broke out in 1973, American consumers began their shift to smaller cars which offered more fuel efficiency. However, US car manufacturers considered such vehicles as "entry-level" products that did not merit a high quality. Thus, the level of quality was

---

[5]Some information of this case is abstracted from the Toyota Website (www.toyota. co.jp/en), *The Economist* ("A Wobble on the Road to the Top," November 8, 2007), and https://notesmatic.com/2020/03/toyota-generic-and-intensive-growth-strategies/.

[6]Toyota's 2019 Global Vehicle Sales Trail Volkswagen's (US News, January 30, 2020), https://www.usnews.com/news/business/articles/2020-01-30/toyotas-2019-global-vehicle-sales-trail-volkswagens.

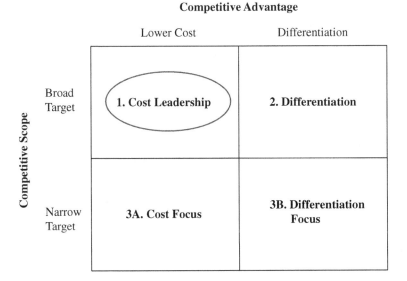

Fig. 14.   Toyota's strategy.

kept low in order to maintain price competitiveness even though US cars were not fuel efficient. However, Toyota entered the US market using a different approach based upon the experience it had with Japanese consumers who had a long-standing tradition of demanding small, fuel-efficient cars that were manufactured to high standards. As a result, Toyota began expanding beyond Japan and eventually into the US market. Using Porter's generic strategies model, we could place Toyota as initially having a cost leadership strategy, that is, a broad target market at lower cost while maintaining a certain level of quality. This strategy has been immensely successful for Toyota (see Fig. 14).

Until recently, Toyota has maintained this strategy and is still producing good-quality compact cars at reasonable prices. However, there has been further development in its strategy and that is the addition of the Lexus brand in 1989. Lexus is Toyota's luxury vehicle division and has become the highest selling luxury brand in the US. Currently, Toyota runs both the Toyota and Lexus brands simultaneously, thus expanding its strategy in two different directions. The Lexus brand could be seen as a form of differentiation focus, that is,

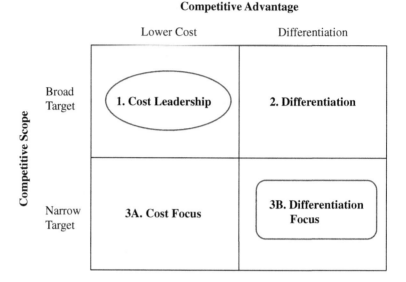

Fig. 15.   Evolution of Toyota's strategy.

a narrower target but a differentiated product. This generic strategy can be witnessed in Fig. 15. This proves that some firms, particularly larger firms, may be able to maintain more than one type of strategy at the same time without experiencing problems associated with being "stuck in the middle."

Regarding the second weakness discovered in Porter's model, the lack of dynamism, this model (Fig. 15) needs to be altered in order to make it more dynamic and thus easier to read. Toyota's strategic development will be shown using the new dynamic model. Cost focus is a common starting point for firms as they usually have an advantage in terms of cheap labor or natural resources, but lack vast amounts of technological know-how. Toyota, in a similar vein, launched its first prototype, the A1 passenger car, using the manufacturing process adopted by Ford Motors. This is shown in Fig. 16.

Toyota continued in much the same way for many years. That is to say, the company focused heavily on improving manufacturing procedures to increase profits and relay the benefits to its customers mostly in the Japanese domestic market. However, following the 1973 oil crisis, Toyota changed its approach and began to export

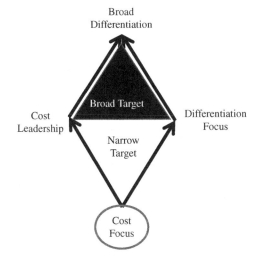

Fig. 16. Toyota's initial strategy.

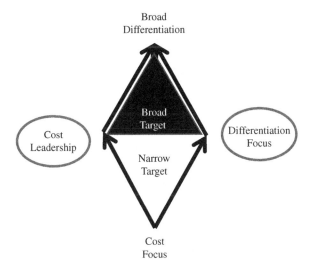

Fig. 17. Toyota's strategic evolution.

small, low-cost cars. The company maintained its cost focus but widened its target. Through this strategic maneuver, Toyota moved from a cost focus to a cost leadership position, which is represented in Fig. 17.

Lastly, as mentioned before, Toyota initiated its luxury division with the Lexus brand. In this way, it moved into the differentiation focus segment and continued to pursue it alongside its cost leadership strategy. This is a very common flow of events for a growing firm to follow, although it is usually only larger firms that are able to maintain more than one strategy at the same time. So, what is next for Toyota? According to our model the firm's final destination for its strategy is broad differentiation. This is where the firm seeks to be unique in the industry and at the same time serves as a broad competitive scope.

This can be well reflected by Toyota's intensive growth strategies through active market penetration and development, and product development. So far, the company sells in 190 countries, which shows a high level of market penetration. It has particularly achieved extensive penetration in foreign markets such as the US, China, India, Malaysia, and European markets.[7] At the same time, Toyota is committed to rapid production innovation to develop more fuel-efficient and safer vehicles for the market. In addition to improving passenger safety, the company is also investing in automated driving technology. By leveraging these strategies, Toyota could successfully increase its international customer base and market share in the automobile industry. It will be interesting to monitor Toyota's future developments with regard to this strategic position.

Case Study 3: A Makeup Strategy[8]

Porter's Generic Strategies framework is of immense value to the strategist, both in its original and extended forms. We have already

---

[7]Toyota's revenue distribution across the regions is as follows in 2019: North America (30%), Japan (25%), Asia (18%), Europe (11.5%), and Others (15.3%) (Visual Capitalist, 2020/8/18). https://www.visualcapitalist.com/visualized-how-much-revenue-automakers-generate-every-second/.

[8]Some information of this case is abstracted from Kanebo's Website (www.kanebo.com), Shiseido's Website (www.shiseido.co.jp/com), Jiangsu Longliqi's Website (www.longliqi.fuzing.com), Etude's Website (www.etude.co.kr), Amore Pacific's Website (www.amorepacific.co.kr), Isehan's Website (www.isehan.info), and Kose's Website (www.kose.co.jp).

Product Based Strategy	Customer Based Strategy: Broad	Customer Based Strategy: Narrow
Broad	**Kanebo** ----------------------------- **Jiangsu Longliqi**	**Shiseido** ----------------------------- **Etude**
Narrow	**Amore Pacific** ----------------------------- **Kose**	**Isehan** ----------------------------- **???**

Fig. 18. Asian cosmetic firms in the framework of eight generic strategies.

applied the three most basic generic strategies, four generic strategies, and the further extended seven generic strategies to previous case studies. However, we are going to take it a step further and apply the framework of eight generic strategies developed by Moon *et al.* (2014) to this case study.

This case study will analyze the Asian cosmetics industry utilizing the new eight generic strategies. Figure 18 illustrates the positioning of seven prominent Asian cosmetics brands within the eight generic strategies during the late 2000s, although it should be noted that some of these brands have evolved by moving to the alternative strategy over the last decade, a point which will be explained later.

Japan's Kanebo implemented a general differentiation strategy, as it not only offers a wide range of products to a broad base of customers but also goes the extra mile with salon services that both utilize and advertise its products simultaneously. For its part, China's Jiangsu Longliqi is placed as a general cost leader as it offers a wide variety of products to a large customer base and does so at a very low price.

Japan's Shiseido has a customer-based differentiation strategy. Although it has a broad product range, due to its high cost and exclusivity, it has a narrow customer range. Etude is a Korean cosmetics firm that also offers a broad product range but at a reasonable price. Its customer range is narrow as it is geared toward the cosmetic requirements among teenage girls.

Amore Pacific, another Korean cosmetics firm, has a much narrower range of products as it focuses only on skincare and makeup. It is pricey, but not overly so and thus is still accessible to a broad range of customers. Kose of Japan has a product cost leadership strategy. It has a narrow product range as it deals only with skincare yet a broad range of young customers with its Awake line and further targets its more mature customers with the Sekkisei line.

Japan's Isehan has a differentiated multi-scope strategy as it offers only one product, which is a special nanotechnology-based skincare product. Due to this exclusivity it also has an extremely narrow customer base. In this environment, there is no cosmetics firm that can match a cost leadership multi-scope strategy. Due to the problem of economies of scale, it is very difficult to have a narrow product range with a narrow customer base and do so at the cheapest price possible.

Applying this framework is a very useful method with which to base discussions around strategy. However, the placement of these firms within the framework is by no means static. Further suggestion of movement from strategy to strategy is possible depending on the firm's level of development. At the initial stage, a firm may base its approach in the narrow strategy and then at a later stage move to a product- or customer-based strategy. Ultimately, a broad strategy is the most desirable as the company becomes an all-round player rather than a niche one.

An example in this regard is Amore Pacific, which used to focus on skincare and makeup, but now offers a wide range of products to a diverse group of customers, thereby moving from product-based to a broad strategy. The company provides hair, body, and dental care products at a reasonable price. It also sells beverage, vitamins, and chewable pills, which contain ginseng, green tea, beans, and collagen as way to differentiate it from other products. Thus, the extension from three to eight generic strategies tackles the weaknesses found in Porter's previous work, and can be easily applied.

Discussion Questions

1. Do you agree or disagree that the Blue Ocean Strategy is an entirely new strategy proposition? Why?

2. Can you think of a product, similar to Yellow Tail wine, that has reformed the industry strategy canvas?

3. Do you agree that broad differentiation is the ultimate point for a developed firm? Why?

4. Does a firm have to choose only one strategy among protection-ist, competitive, and cooperative strategies? Can you think of a firm which uses more than one of these strategies simultaneously?

5. Why does Michael Porter condemn the concept of "stuck in the middle" so vehemently? Do you agree with him?

6. Besides the automobile and cosmetics industries, which other industries can we apply the eight generic strategies to?

CHAPTER 6

Measuring and Forecasting

Chapter Guideline

In the previous chapter, we saw how different scholars utilized Porter's model and then further enhanced its explanatory power. However, another crucial aspect of business is measuring and forecasting the strategic success or failure of a business operation. Well-known methods include various performance indices, financial statements, and investor reports. Since there is extensive literature available regarding conventional indices, this chapter will introduce methods and frameworks for forecasting and measuring that are beyond the conventional scope of analysis.

Summary of Previous Models

Various discussions on strategy are useful since they provide a short-cut to understanding complex business realities. Through Porter, we were able to gain an understanding on the fundamentals of strategic management. Furthermore, scholars such as Nonaka and Prahalad presented important insights into specific aspects of strategic management. Finally, the previous chapter illustrated a modified version which reconciled and further enhanced the explanatory power of Porter's models. However, businesses need to measure their success or failure in order to set realistic goals. Alongside this, effective forecasting is also required to make plans for the future, which will be the focus of this chapter.

6.1 Measuring the Intangible

Many great thinkers throughout history have repeatedly emphasized the importance of assessing oneself objectively. In this respect, the eminent Chinese military strategist Sun Tzu famously proclaimed that "if you know yourself and your enemy, you will not be in danger in one hundred battles (知彼知己 百戰不殆)." Such timeless wisdom is still valid in the world of business and therefore numerous methods for objectively tracking a firm's performance have been developed throughout history. Typical examples of business assessment tools include return on investment (ROI), return on assets (ROA), and cash flow which most business majors are bound to encounter somewhere along their academic and professional careers. However, as important as these measures are, they are limited to measuring "hard performance" that is strictly related to the tangible aspect of managing a firm. As we learned from Nonaka in Chapter 2, harnessing the intangible has become just as important as managing the tangible.

The Balanced Scorecard is a popular example of such a managerial tool designed to measure the intangible. Kaplan and Norton (1992) first introduced the Balanced Scorecard framework, which is a strategic tool to both operationalize and measure strategies of the organization or organizational units, such as strategic business units (Hansen and Schaltegger, 2016). Since the introduction of the Balanced Scorecard, many organizations from different sectors have applied this framework for various motivations (Malbasic and Marimon, 2019). *Harvard Business Review* has even identified the Balanced Scorecard as one of the most significant management ideas over the past 75 years (Gumbus and Lussier, 2006).

Academically, it has also had a profound impact on strategic management and has led to various spin-offs and criticisms. Some have extended or clarified the link between Balanced Scorecard and strategic management (Ahn, 2001; Brewer, 2002; Butler *et al.*, 1997; Hansen and Schaltegger, 2016; Kalender and Vayvay, 2016), while others have questioned the validity of the Balanced Scorecard concept itself due to lack of a solid theoretical foundation (Mooraj *et al.*, 1999; Nørreklit, 2000; Perkins *et al.*, 2014). Good or bad, what is evident is the massive stir created from the Balanced Scorecard concept. Therefore, comprehending the Balanced Scorecard is the first key step to gaining a balanced view on firm performance measures.

As the name suggests, the Balanced Scorecard is a managerial tool which provides managers a method to strike a balance between the tangible and intangible aspects of measuring and keeping track of firm performance. While financial measures are well developed and can give very important insights into the condition of firm operations, they are not sufficient. The Balanced Scorecard is a management performance and assessment framework, which tries to complement the existing financial statement to give a more comprehensive view on the efficacy of firm activity.

As Fig. 1 illustrates, the Balanced Scorecard comprises four major components of which three are non-financial perspectives: (a) customers, (b) internal business processes, and (c) learning and growth.

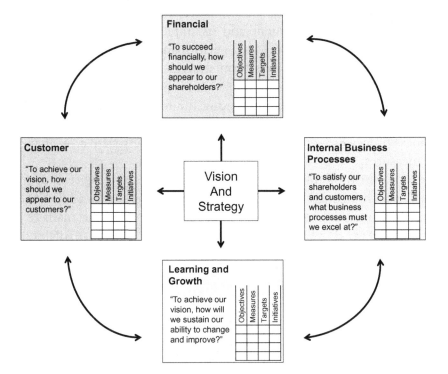

Fig. 1. Translating vision and strategy: Four perspectives.
Source: Kaplan and Norton (2007a).

- Financial perspective aims to measure the revenue growth, investment return, and cost reduction by using various financial indicators.

- Customer perspective consists of measures from the customer perspective, such as market share, customer satisfaction, loyalty, and acquisition of new market.

- Internal business process evaluates various processes (e.g., operational and innovative processes along the value chain) for creating and sustaining competitive advantages.

- Learning and growth perspective focuses on internal skills and capabilities such as employee skills, training, and education to keep changing and innovate.

These three non-financial perspectives are highly important for managers because financial measures alone cannot fill the void between strategy development and its implementation. Therefore, the Balanced Scorecard provides a performance management framework which connects the long-term strategic objectives with everyday and short-term actions. Kaplan and Norton (1996) further outlined the causal relationship among the four perspectives, "measures of organizational learning and growth → measures of internal business processes → measures of the customer perspective → financial measures."

In addition, Kaplan and Norton present four concrete processes which managers can follow to implement the additional three non-financial perspectives into the firm's strategic management (see Fig. 2). Each of these components will be explained hereafter.

Translating the Vision

The starting point of the explanation is the top section of Fig. 2. Translating the vision is simply aligning everyday actions among

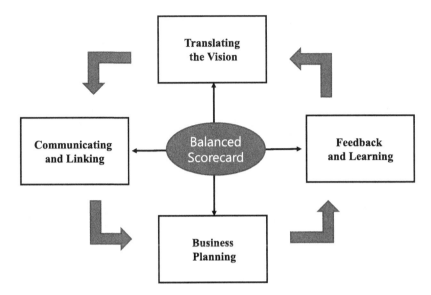

Fig. 2. Managing strategy: Four processes.
Source: Kaplan and Norton (2007a).

individual employees with the company's mission statement or strategic vision. Consider, for example, the mission statement "to provide superior service to targeted customers." While this may seem like a very clear goal, the understanding of the terms *superior service* and *targeted customer* may differ widely among employees. The "translating the vision" portion of Fig. 2, in essence, is a parameter which clearly defines the firm's vision so that employees can ensure that their everyday activities are aligned with the firm's overall strategic goal or vision.

Communicating and Linking

The next step is communicating and linking, which is a critical process since the translated vision must be disseminated down the organizational hierarchy. The Balanced Scorecard provides a clear way to follow and understand the firm's vision since it signals to all the employees what the firm is trying to achieve as a whole. Three specific steps can be taken to successfully achieve this feat (see Fig. 2):

- *Communicating and Educating* — Unlike the traditional top-down method of strategy execution, this requires the upper-level managers to disseminate the strategic vision all the way down to the lowest ranks of the firm. Furthermore, reverse communication from bottom to top must take place for any other input or enhancement that could be made to the strategy. For this process, the scorecard can provide everyone involved in the process a method to quantify and effectively communicate the strategic vision to each other.

- *Setting Goals* — The next step is transforming this vision into concrete sequences (objectives and measures) which everyone can follow. The personal scorecard (see Fig. 3) is the embodiment of this idea. With this scorecard in every employee's pocket, all firm constituents can constantly measure and check whether his or her actions are in line with the firm's overall strategic vision.

- *Linking Rewards to Performance Measures* — Incentives are powerful tools which drive people toward great achievements. Naturally, it is crucial to establish a connection between Balanced Scorecard measures and compensation. Employees should be rewarded when they successfully implement the strategic vision in the Balanced Scorecard. Of course, Kaplan and Norton note that this carries a certain level of risk since if the company does not have the proper measures included, it could lead to inefficiency. The best approach is still rather unclear, but it will become more evident as more companies adopt the Balanced Scorecard approach.

Business Planning

In order to coordinate the activities of individual departments and divisions, firms have to expend a massive amount of time and resources. Furthermore, because each part of the firm makes decisions

The Personal Scorecard

Corporate Objectives.

- Double our corporate value in seven years.
- Increase our earnings by an average of 20% per year.
- Achieve an internal rate of return 2% above the cost of capital.

Corporate Targets	Scorecard Measures	Business Unit Targets

Financial

Operating

Fig. 3. Personal scorecard.

Source: Kaplan and Norton (2007a).

on a different time table, managers also have to deal with time lags that could occur among different departments. The Balanced Scorecard can help alleviate this problem to a significant degree because it can integrate the different units within the firm under one strategic vision without separate coordination. As Fig. 1 demonstrates, the Balanced Scorecard gives a comprehensive guideline to link all important parts of a firm into one strategic direction.

After the strategic direction is clarified, the companies must also select the most important variables and incorporate them into the Balanced Scorecard. This affords an important support that all business units can mobilize to direct the firm's resources in the appropriate direction. The next process of business planning requires setting specific short-term targets for the Balanced Scorecard measures. Tangible goals are always very important because scorecard users can regularly check whether they are in line with the overall strategic vision and make changes if necessary. The final stage is to define the long-term objectives, for which managers must set tangible milestones for individuals to follow.

Feedback and Learning

The final point of the entire loop (see Fig. 2) is the "Feedback and Learning" process. The above three processes are crucial in actuating the strategic vision of a company, but the process in its totality needs to be reexamined to correct mistakes and further enhance the entire loop. Corporate reviews have existed in the past, but they have been usually focused on one aspect of the entire business and rarely assessed the efficacy of the strategic vision as a whole. With the Balanced Scorecard, the firm can now conduct thorough research and make the necessary changes.

Analysis

Kaplan and Norton's Balanced Scorecard has been immensely popular in the world of business and has been adopted by consulting firms worldwide. Prior to the Balanced Scorecard, most firms relied heavily on tangible indicators (mostly financial) to assess the position and condition of a firm. While these are important tools, it is no longer sufficient today as firm operations have become much more complex and multidimensional. Firms that are performing well may still be heading toward disaster if the profit is based upon activities that are not really in line with the firm's overall strategic vision. This is precisely why Kaplan and Norton's emphasis on measuring and integrating non-financial and intangible firm assets into the corporate strategy is a highly important aspect of strategy formulation in the business environment which requires constant innovation.

There are several criticisms, however, with the Balanced Scorecard. First and the most prevalent, is the subjective nature of the judgment criteria. When one looks at the specifics of the Balanced Scorecard, one can easily see that these are not based upon a systematic framework. Rather, it is an amalgamation of subjective indicators which the strategic planners of a company assess as being valid toward the overall corporate-level strategy. While the strategic vision itself inherently contains subjective elements, there is another difficulty in trying to objectively quantify a firm's intangible assets. This is associated with the next problem which is that if the Balanced Scorecard is used recklessly, it could end up being a list of positive metrics without accounting for the various trade-offs that arise when pursuing all the "positive" goals. Third, considering the huge amount of literature on the Balanced Scorecard, there has been scarce empirical research to support that an implementation of Balanced Scorecards leads to the improvement in firm performance (Paranjape *et al.*, 2006; Perkins *et al.*, 2014). Instead, a majority of studies have only been demonstrated in the anecdotal work of Kaplan and Norton (Perkins *et al.*, 2014). This thus raises further questions on the causality linkages within the scorecard (Nørreklit, 2000). Perkins *et al.* (2014) suggest that the overarching criticism of the Balanced Scorecards should be attributed to its lack of solid theoretical underpinnings. Despite these criticisms, Kaplan and Norton have presented us with a fresh new way to look at how to assess a firm's performance more comprehensively.

In order to put the Balanced Scorecard in a broader perspective, it is important to incorporate it into a more systematically designed framework. The diamond model (Porter, 1990) for competitive advantage offers an analytical framework which systematically organizes the determinants of competitiveness into four categories: (a) factor conditions, (b) demand conditions, (c) firm strategy, structure, and rivalry, and (d) related and supporting sectors. Although it was originally designed to analyze national competitiveness, the model has been widely used for industry- and firm-level analysis.[1] Figure 4 represents the Balanced Scorecard in terms of Porter's diamond model.

The Balanced Scorecard can be viewed as a detailed framework for a subset of the diamond model. For example, the customer perspective is a method to measure the demand condition that a firm faces, while learning and growth can be seen as an advanced factor condition, as illustrated in Fig. 4. Thus, what we can see from this analysis is that Kaplan and Norton's contribution is to advance our understanding of a sub-variable for each corner of the diamond.

It is always very important to keep the new knowledge that we gain into a single perspective so that we can have an all-encompassing and integrated view. Porter's diamond framework is one of those

---

[1] For evolution of the diamond model, see Rugman and D'Cruz (1993), Moon *et al.* (1998), Cho (1994), Cho and Moon (2000, 2013a, 2013b), Cho *et al.* (2008), and Cho *et al.* (2016).

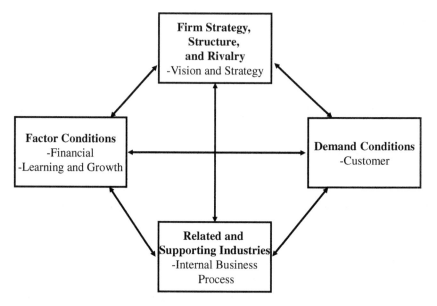

Fig. 4.   Porter's diamond model and the balanced scorecard.

powerful analytical frameworks that enable us to do so, and it is very important that we do not forget the big picture even when we are talking about specific sub-variables.

Later, in *The Strategy-focused Organization*, Kaplan and Norton (2007b) introduce a new tool, Strategy Maps, and a new approach that makes strategy a continuous process owned not just by top management but by everyone. As a result, they describe how the nature of the Balanced Scorecard has changed from a valuation tool to a comprehensive "Value-Based Management" tool. Several innovations and additional dimensions are included in the updated model, and for those who are interested, it is worth tracking the evolution of this influential framework.

6.2 Measuring Globalization

If the above section demonstrated the importance of measuring the intangible, now we turn our eyes to a wider scope and look at how to measure the hottest buzzword of our times: globalization. The word itself is used all the time, but the lack of precise definitions or measurements of the term is quite surprising. This may well be because of the highly complex, dynamic, and transformative nature of the term as well as its wide scope of impact. However, some bold scholars and professionals have forged ahead to create tangible measures for this unclear term and the A.T. Kearney/Foreign Policy Globalization Index is a good example of such a brave effort.

A.T. Kearney/Foreign Policy Globalization Index was one of the first globalization indices, and served as a prototype for many later indices (Gygli *et al.*, 2019). The Globalization Index was launched in 2001 and was revised every year until 2007 during which time it has presented a detailed analysis of globalization. While measuring globalization in and of itself is a difficult task, A.T. Kearney and Foreign Policy created a comprehensive index that analyzes the "globalness" of a nation by combining four major criteria: (a) economic integration, (b) personal contact, (c) technological connectivity, and (d) political engagement.

The index attempts to illustrate a balanced view of globalization, which is often myopically defined or measured because of the abstractness of the concept itself. By categorizing four major dimensions (see Dimensions of Table 1) and then subdividing each variable into several important sub-variables (see Items of Table 1), A.T. Kearney and Foreign Policy attempts to measure globalization in an objective manner.

After presenting the index, A.T. Kearney and Foreign Policy then provides an in-depth analysis of some of the most interesting trends of 2006.

- *Waiting for the Heavyweights* — The first trend is the rise of BRIC (Brazil, Russia, India, and China) countries, which is an exciting phenomenon with various implications for managers and there is immense potential with the untapped market segments of these countries. If these countries turn their eyes to rural development, the global market will expand to an unprecedented level. These

Table 1. Globalization index 2006.

2006 GI Rankings	Country	Change from 2005	Dimension: Economic	Dimension: Personal	Dimension: Technological	Dimension: Political	Economic Integration: Trade	Economic Integration: FDI	Personal Contact: Telephone	Personal Contact: Travel	Personal Contact: Remittances and Personal Transfers	Technological Connectivity: Internet Users	Technological Connectivity: Internet Hosts	Technological Connectivity: Secure Severs	Political Engagement: International Organizations	Political Engagement: U.N. Peacekeeping	Political Engagement: Treaties	Political Engagement: Government Transfers	2005 GI Rankings
1	Singapore	0	1	3	12	29	1	1	1	4	49	10	12	13	33	10	42	47	1
2	Switzerland	1	9	1	7	23	17	7	2	6	2	17	15	5	33	9	42	10	3
3	United States	1	58	40	1	41	62	36	18	33	52	6	1	1	1	25	58	38	4
4	Ireland	-2	4	2	14	7	4	5	3	3	9	26	20	8	11	1	31	23	2
5	Denmark	2	8	8	5	6	20	6	6	16	16	12	3	7	11	13	6	8	7
6	Canada	0	23	7	2	10	30	12	4	20	57	7	14	2	2	14	6	32	6
7	Netherlands	-2	21	11	6	5	11	52	8	11	40	9	2	11	5	17	6	6	5
8	Australia	4	18	36	3	27	55	3	14	32	50	3	5	4	33	18	31	37	12
9	Austria	-1	15	4	13	2	15	18	10	2	29	19	7	14	11	3	6	7	8
10	Sweden	0	19	12	9	9	21	16	11	9	39	1	9	9	25	8	6	15	10

Source: A.T. Kearney and Foreign Policy (2006).

new consumers will bring a new dimension to globalization and economic integration.

- *Rich Man's World* — Another interesting development identified is that many countries in the developing world have utilized globalization to their advantage and have achieved remarkable material wealth. They are now joining this elite tier within global capitalism. This phenomenon has significant economic as well as political implications as these new riches have the muscle to alter their countries in various ways.

- *The Toxic Few* — A.T. Kearney and Foreign Policy is keen to stress that globalization generates negative as well as positive effects. One of the most pronounced negative consequences of globalization is environmental degradation. This report presents a graph which shows the high positive correlation between emissions and globalization.

- *Cash on the Side* — Further consideration is given to the informal economy, which is the level of business activities that should be taxed by the government but are not. The less globalized a nation is, the larger its informal economy is, according to the report.

- *Latin America's Soft Left Turn* — Another focus is on Latin America that has been a hot bed of leftist ideology for a long time. From Fidel Castro to Hugo Chavez, many Latin American leaders speak for the validity of their socialist agendas and appeal to the mass public. However, an in-depth analysis of Latin America's globalization index shows a slightly different picture as nations in this region have made significant strides in the ranking. Despite the leftist façade, Latin America is increasingly becoming an integral part of the global free market system.

- *Buying into Dubai* — The final trend is the United Arab Emirate's recent aggressive move toward globalization that has made international headlines. Dubai is ambitiously aiming to become a new global financial powerhouse in a similar breadth to London and New York. As a result, policies have been highly business friendly and many immigrants from various corners of the world are moving into Dubai for new opportunities. The influx of human and financial resources promises an exciting future for this ambitious city.

The subsequent annual reports have used the same methodology as can be seen from the 2007 version depicted in Fig. 5. The top-ranking country is Singapore, followed by Hong Kong and the Netherlands. Surprisingly, the US ranks 7th, while all countries ahead of the US are noted for their small geographic size. Equally remarkable is the inclusion of Jordan and Estonia in the top 10.

Analysis

In recent years, globalization has generated more discussion and focus than any other term. Yet, despite the ubiquity of this term, there has not been a notable level of success in providing an accurate measure of this phenomenon until the A.T. Kearney and Foreign Policy Globalization Index emerged. The usefulness of this approach is immense as it not only gives a concrete standard of measurement but also provides a comprehensive overview of the meaning of this concept. While many people talk about globalization, they usually see one or two aspects of this phenomenon. By identifying the major variables and sub-variables, this index provides us with a more scientific and quantitative approach to globalization.

However, this index is not without problems as several aspects can be called into question. First, the major classifications are economic, personal, technological, and political (see Fig. 5). Unfortunately, these classifications are rather ambiguous and it is doubtful whether these categories can be seen as equal in terms of the level of scope. For example, the economic category seems to be more encompassing than personal or technological. Intuitively, one can assume that the weight of one sub-variable in the economic category may possibly outweigh the effect of personal or technology. A possible enhancement could be made by using economic, political, and social as the major categories. The second is the possibility of missing variables.

Political Engagement Including foreign aid, treaties, organizations, and peacekeeping	**Technological Connectivity** Including number of Internet users, hosts, and secure servers
Personal Contact Including telephone calls, travel, and remittances	**Economic Integration** Including international trade and foreign direct investment

Top 20 Rankings
1. Singapore, 2. Hong Kong SAR, 3. The Netherlands, 4. Switzerland,
5. Ireland, 6. Denmark, 7. United States, 8. Canada, 9. Jordan,
10. Estonia, 11. Sweden, 12. Britain, 13. Australia, 14. Austria,
15. Belgium, 16. New Zealand, 17. Norway, 18. Finland,
19. Czech Republic, 20. Slovenia

Fig. 5. Globalization index 2007.
Source: A.T. Kearney and Foreign Policy (2007).

Although the four variables are relevant in explaining globalization, other important areas such as migration are missing. In this respect, KOF Globalization Index, which was introduced by Dreher (2006) and is still in publication, seems to have complemented the limitations of A.T. Kearney/Foreign Policy Globalization Index by measuring globalization along the three dimensions of economic, social, and political aspects. KOF Globalization Index also includes criteria such as migration and culture under the dimension of social globalization.

In order to gain a more balanced view of the level of globalization of each country, I compare and contrast its results with other indices from various focuses. Specifically, I look at the rankings provided by the World Investment Report (UNCTAD, 2012), and three national competitiveness reports — the World Competitiveness Yearbook (Institute for Management Development, 2020), the Global Competitiveness Report (World Economic Forum, 2019), and the IPS National Competitiveness Research (Institute for Policy and Strategy on National Competitiveness, 2020). By comparing their rankings and data compilation, we should be able to gauge whether the Globalization Index is a reliable and competent source.

World Investment Report (*UNCTAD, 2012*)

The World Investment Report analyzes inward Foreign Direct Investment (FDI) performance and its potential, and ranks countries by their attractiveness in terms of investment environment. In measuring FDI Potential Index, the United Nations Conference on Trade and Development (UNCTAD) includes four key economic determinants (see Table 2) that capture the attractiveness of the market (market-seeking FDI), the availability of low-cost labor and skills (efficiency-seeking FDI), the presence of natural resources (resource-seeking FDI), and the presence of FDI-enabling infrastructure (UNCTAD, 2012). This FDI Potential Index was first proposed in 2002 and was published until 2012.

Table 2. Variables FDI potential index.

Market attractiveness	• Size of the market (GDP (purchasing power parity)) • Spending power (per capita GDP (purchasing power parity)) • Growth potential of the market (real GDP growth rate)
Availability of low-cost labour and skills	• Unit labour cost (hourly compensation and labour productivity) • Size of manufacturing workforce (existing skill base)
Presence of natural resources	• Exploitation of resources (value of fuels and ores exports) • Agricultural potential (availability of arable land)

Enabling infrastructure	• Transport infrastructure
	  – (road density: km of road per 100 km² of land area)
	  – (percentage of paved roads in total)
	  – (rail lines total route-km)
	  – (liner shipping connectivity index)
	• Energy infrastructure
	  – (electric power consumption)
	• Telecom infrastructure
	  – (telephone lines/100 inhabitants)
	  – (mobile cellular subscriptions/100 Inhabitants)
	  – (fixed broadband Internet subscribers/100 inhabitants)

Source: UNCTAD (2012).

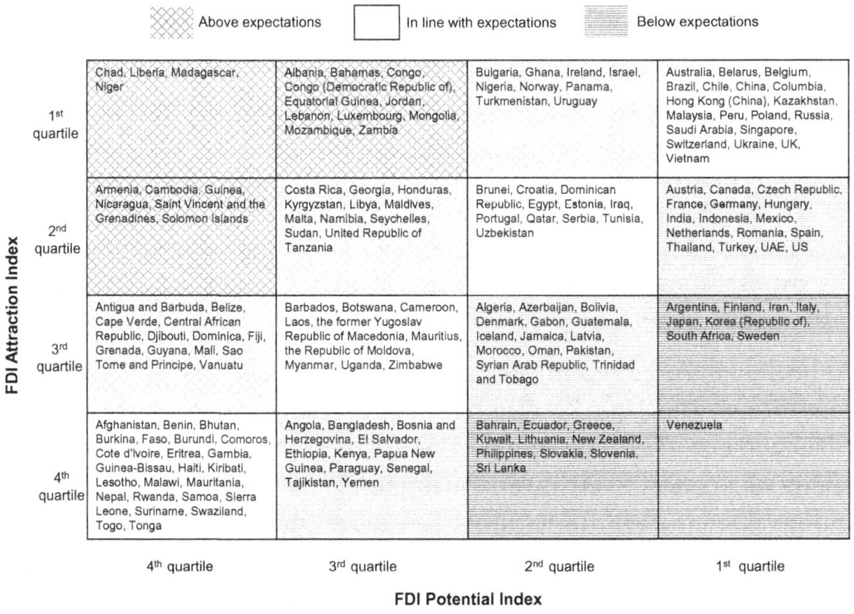

Fig. 6. FDI attraction index vs FDI potential index matrix (2011).
Source: UNCTAD (2012).

By comparing the performance in attracting FDI and FDI Potential Index, UNCTAD generates two distinctive country groups — significantly above or below expectations (see Fig. 6). According to UNCTAD (2012), the "above-potential" economies include resource-rich countries, small economies where single large investments can make a big impact on the performance, and countries in a "catch-up phase" which embarked on a course to improve investment climates like Albania. On the contrary, the "below-potential" group includes countries that traditionally have not been dependent on FDI for capital formation such as Japan and the Republic of Korea, countries that traditionally received low-level amounts of FDI such as Italy, or countries that are closed to FDI or maintain policies that are unattractive to foreign investors.

It is interesting to note that ten countries ranked in the group of "above or in line with expectations" also appear in the top 20 of the

Globalization Index 2007, including Jordan and Estonia; but, ten of the top 20 appear in the below-potential band of countries. This includes the US and the UK, which means they are regarded as poorly performing by the World Investment Report of UNCTAD, yet regarded more highly by the Globalization Index of A.T. Kearney and Foreign Policy. Therefore, there is a substantial gap in rankings between these two studies.

Three National Competitiveness Reports

Although all three reports assess the competitiveness of nations, their focus on evaluation is different. The International Institute for Management Development (IMD) defines competitiveness as "the ability of a nation to create and maintain an environment that sustains more value creation for its firms and more prosperity for its people" (IMD, 2010, p. 479). World Economic Forum (WEF) describes competitiveness as "the set of institutions, policies, and factors that determine the level of productivity of a country" (WEF, 2010, p. 4). On the contrary, the report by the Institute for Industrial Policy Studies (IPS) defines competitiveness as the relative position among rival countries (IPS, 2011, p. 68).

Table 3 shows the comparison among KOF Globalization Rankings and the three national competitiveness rankings for the top 20 countries. Given that the AT Kearny/Foreign Policy Globalization Index ceased publication in 2007, the KOF Globalization Index is selected instead for comparison. Although the number and specific countries of the top 20 are different across the four rankings, for all the three national competitiveness reports more than 50% of the top 20 countries appeared in the KOF top 20. It should also be noted that smaller economies such as Hong Kong SAR, Singapore, and Switzerland are dispersed throughout the ranking, whereas countries such as Estonia and Slovakia have shown a relatively high degree of globalization but did not rank in the Competitiveness Report Top 20.

While this of course only skims the surface of the many differences that exist among the wide range of reports available, it does highlight

Table 3.   KOF globalization ranking and three national competitiveness rankings.

Rank	KOF (2018)	IMD (2020)	WEF (2019)	IPS (2020)
1	Switzerland	Singapore	Singapore	Canada
2	Netherlands	Denmark	USA	Denmark
3	Belgium	Switzerland	Hong Kong SAR	Singapore
4	Sweden	Netherlands	Netherlands	Switzerland
5	United Kingdom	Hong Kong SAR	Switzerland	Sweden
6	Austria	Sweden	Japan	USA
7	Germany	Norway	Germany	Netherlands
8	Denmark	Canada	Sweden	New Zealand
9	Finland	UAE	United Kingdom	Hong Kong SAR
10	France	USA	Denmark	Australia
11	Norway	Taiwan	Finland	Finland
12	Spain	Ireland	Taiwan	UAE
13	Czech Republic	Finland	Korea, Rep.	Belgium
14	Hungary	Qatar	Canada	Israel
15	Portugal	Luxembourg	France	Germany
16	Canada	Austria	Australia	China
17	Ireland	Germany	Norway	Austria
18	Estonia	Australia	Luxembourg	Taiwan
19	Slovak Republic	United Kingdom	New Zealand	Kuwait
20	Singapore	China	Israel	United Kingdom

the need to be aware of the risk in taking these reports at face value. In order to understand the reports' ranking, we first need to understand how the data are collected, how the data are analyzed, and most importantly, for what purpose the data are compiled. For example, the IPS report specifically divides countries according to "country groups" in order to present a more accurate picture. In other words, comparing Hong Kong SAR with the US is rather meaningless because of the immense difference in size and structure between these two economies. Rather, Hong Kong SAR should be compared with other economies such as Switzerland and Singapore, while the US should be compared with Japan and other larger economies. Other institutes have their own different approaches.

It is also important to note that the specific variables for each report differ greatly. Extensive analysis will not be made here since it is beyond the scope of this chapter to provide an exhaustive analysis on this topic. However, the point that needs to be made for serious business scholars is that they must be wary of the fact that these indices are prone to mistakes and biases. Quoting them without a thorough understanding of the underlying mechanisms and constituent variables may lead to substantial problems.

6.3 Measuring the Future

The study of postulating probable futures or futurology is an interesting field, particularly in uncertain times such as the Coronavirus global pandemic or the revolutionary development of technologies such as artificial intelligence. Many prominent scholars (without actually calling themselves futurists) have provided us with a way of understanding the future. However, not many have actually attempted to provide a concrete guideline to measuring the future.

This concept of measuring the future has been promoted by Saffo (2007), a famous technology forecaster, who discusses concrete methods to effectively forecast the future. Unlike the popular myth of a person in robes chanting mystical incantations, futurists and forecasters use highly scientific and objective methods to analyze upcoming trends. Forecasting looks at how hidden currents in the present signal possible changes in direction for companies, societies, or the world at large. The difference between a prediction and a forecast is that the latter is based on firm logic and thorough analysis of the available current data. Having defined what forecasting is, Saffo proceeds to present clear steps toward making an effective forecast.

Define a Cone of Uncertainty

The cone of uncertainty is the process of visualizing the possibilities of various events that stem out from a moment or event. Various elements must be included in this cone such as the relationships among variables and the probability of realizing each event. However, the most important process is to define the "breadth" (of the cone), which is a measure of the overall uncertainty. One may visualize this process as akin to drawing a net to capture all the elements of uncertainty as part of the process to make an effective forecast. This is a very difficult yet important task as it provides the basic platform for future forecasting. The key to accomplishing this feat is to assign the proper weight to each probable event. Designating the probability of each possible outcome defines the breadth of the cone and thus the scope of analysis.

However, this task is inherently difficult due to the natural tendency for people to avoid uncertainty. Most prefer a yes or no approach to future events rather than acknowledging the fact that every event, no matter how certain or uncertain, has a certain degree of possibility to materialize. Consider the Y2K computer scare which engulfed the entire world right before the turn of the millennium. One group completely dismissed the event as improbable, while others went out to stockpile supplies in order to prepare for Armageddon. Although, in this case, the former group was correct, the reality was that it was only averted after the tireless work of many programmers who created systems to avoid the possibility of a Y2K catastrophe. As such, the probability was certainly there, although human effort and other circumstances mitigated digital Armageddon.

Look for the S-Curve

Contrary to intuition, most changes do not come incrementally. Rather, according to Saffo, change comes in an S-curve pattern, which starts off relatively quietly and then a drastic change occurs through some catalyst event. Consider Moore's Law predicting that circuit density on silicon wafers will double every 18 months. This forecast, made in 1965, has turned out to be largely true. The explosion point (or where the curve of the S starts to form) is the so-called digital revolution, which completely changed the industrial landscape in many fields including IT and electronics (see Fig. 7).

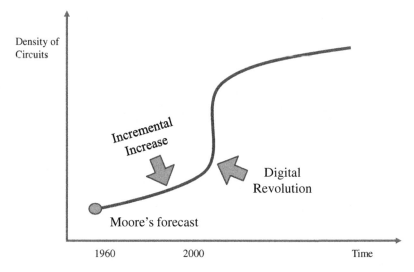

Fig. 7. Visual representation of Moore's forecast.
Source: Drawn based on Saffo (2007).

As one can see from Fig. 7, the key to effective forecasting is to identify the S-curve before it explodes upward as well as forecast where the inflection points are going to be. Recently, Ernst & Young (2020) suggested that the COVID-19 pandemic has thrust the global economy into a new S-curve (see Fig. 8). Prior to this, the global economy had been on what they term the "post-war S-curve," a process driven by globalization and information technology. However, almost overnight, the COVID-19 pandemic has pushed the world into a new renaissance as part of the "better world S-curve," where many people have been forced to adopt their lives toward remote working, virtual learning, and online shopping. Hence, in the new S-curve, whoever wants to get ahead of the trend must figure out when and how the trend will stabilize and plateau.

This curve shows why so many forecasters often make mistakes when analyzing future trends. Although many have the right idea, they miscalculate the speed at which the new trend will arrive. The Internet, for example, has been around since the 1980s and many

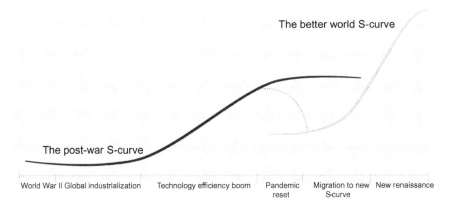

Fig. 8. COVID-19 and the migration to a new S-Curve.
Source: Ernst & Young (2020).

predicted that it would spread faster than it actually has, yet it still took a decade to reach the public and spread rapidly. By contrast, many people expected the current digital revolution to take a longer time, but the external disruption caused by the COVID-19 pandemic has instantly transformed every human domain, from consumer behavior to the nature of work (Ernst & Young, 2020). Baig *et al.* (2020) also suggested that we have jumped five years forward in consumer and business digital adoption in a matter of around eight weeks.

Even more important is the fact that we cannot eliminate the possibility of a trend reversing. Massive external shocks such as government regulations might eliminate the progress of the trend altogether. For example, advances in stem cell research in the US have taken a significant setback since President George W. Bush banned federal funding for the related technology during his administration.

Embrace the Things That Don't Fit

As clarified in Fig. 7, an effective forecaster must predict the inflection point before it actually hits. But, how does one get to achieve such a feat? One suggestion by Saffo is to pay attention to things that do not quite fit the current picture. Since humans have a natural tendency to avoid uncertainties, the general public tends to reject these out-of-place signals as an anomaly or an outlier, thus ignoring them. Consider the smart vacuuming robot designed by iRobot known as the Roomba. Although quite a few have been sold in the market, people still do not believe that the age of robots has truly arrived. The Roomba seems like a small anomaly or at best an enhanced version of the traditional vacuum cleaner. However, when one considers the strides made in robotics through various companies such as the Defense Advanced Research Project Agency's (DARPA) Grand Challenge, the Roomba is a clear indication that the robotics future is not a distant one.

Hold Strong Opinions Weakly

It can be easy for one to forecast that a certain event will unfold by using one piece of strong evidence as proof that it will materialize in the near future. However, this can often lead to erroneous conclusions because the real world is far more complicated and intertwined than to be simply explained by one or two major variables. Rather, Saffo suggests that it is more important to look at various pieces of interlocking information. Many people have difficulty in following this prescription because once one formulates a strong hypothesis and finds a couple of convincing pieces of evidence, all other signals are blocked out as negligible. In order to avoid this pitfall, an analyst must constantly be critical of his or her own forecast by collecting weak evidence that could potentially derail his or her hypothesis. This way, a forecast will truly be complete and effective as all variables will have been considered and exhausted.

Look Back Twice as Far as You Look Forward

Another common mistake that people make is to look for lessons from the not too distant past. History may be a good indicator for what is to come in the future, but an effective forecaster must ensure they are looking back far enough, instead of focusing on recent history. Therefore, when one looks back, it is vital to always look back at least twice as far as one looks forward. And, look back further if there is still uncertainty about forecasting the future. For example, by learning the historical experiences of dealing with past pandemics such as the Black Death during fourteenth century and the Great Plague of London in the seventeenth century, we can be more efficient when handling the Coronavirus global pandemic.

Know When Not to Make a Forecast

Many people get swept away with drastic changes and overestimate the impact that a new trend will have. The advent of the Internet has brought many into the dot com bubble and erroneous predictions about a "new economy" in which the rules of economic success will fundamentally change. However, after the dust has settled, it became apparent that most of the traditional economic logic was left intact and that the Internet, although an efficient and useful tool, was simply a conduit and not a game changer. This may also be applied to the recent development of technologies such as artificial intelligence and digital transformation. This shows that in order to make effective forecasts, it is important not to overstate the impact of drastic changes that happen and make an informed and critical forecast about what will happen once the dust settles and reality sinks in.

Analysis

As Kuhn (1962) once wrote, a scientific revolution is based on the accumulation of numerous anomalies which defy the pre-established scientific theory and widely accepted paradigm. These anomalies, according to Kuhn, are generally ignored or considered as outliers by most people. However, they have various levels of significance to the real innovators of the time and are the basis for forecasting the impending "paradigm shift." In other words, revolutionary paradigm shifts inherently cannot come in a linear format. Rather, when several phenomena, which cannot be explained by the previous paradigm, accumulate and stretch out, a paradigm shifts into a new dimension. The underlying logic behind Saffo's article is largely similar to that of Kuhn's 1962 book. Of course, Saffo has refined and significantly enhanced the explanatory power of the logic through various cases and further explanations. Still, the core message does not deviate significantly from that of Thomas Kuhn.

Saffo's article is illuminating in that it offers the readers a comprehensive look at how to understand the nature of revolutionary change. It is interesting to note that his analysis of the dot com bubble is similar to that of Porter's 2001 article, "Strategy and the Internet." Porter, at the time, concluded that the Internet has been overhyped and that when this excitement subsides and the dust settles, the economic forces of the past will come to play a more significant role again. While everyone was touting the "new economy," Porter's analysis turned out to be largely correct as the dot com bubble burst and people finally began to realize that the new economy was not that different from the old one. Such logic can additionally be applied to the post-pandemic era. Instead of considering an entirely new economic system, we should further examine how the existing strategies and wisdoms can help firms and people survive and thrive in the current "new normal."

Case Study 1: MUFG Bank[2]

MUFG Bank is an international private-sector entity headquartered in Japan. It was formally known as the Bank of Tokyo-Mitsubishi UFJ, which was created through a merger between the Bank of

---

[2] Some information of this case is abstracted from "Alignment" Kaplan and Norton, 2006, Harvard Business Press, The Palladium Consulting Group (www.thepaladiumgroup.com), The Bank of Tokyo-Mitsubishi UFJ Website (www.bk.mufg.jp), https://www.financemagnates.com/cryptocurrency/coins/japans-biggest-bank-launches-proprietary-cryptocurrency-this-year/, and https://www.bloomberg.com/profile/company/8315:JP.

Tokyo-Mitsubishi (BTM) and UFJ bank in January 2006. It was renamed MUFG Bank Ltd. on April 1, 2018 and is now the largest bank in Japan as well as the world's fourth largest bank by asset size. Its operations include deposits, loans, securities investment, financing, fund management, and other banking services.

The MUFG Bank's successful recovery from non-performing loan losses that plagued Japanese banking in the 1990s became a model to follow for many other Japanese banks. In fact, the year prior to the merger with UFJ, BTM repaid the Japanese government more than half of the US$7 billion the bank owed for its bailout during the banking crisis. In June 2005, it was the first of the four Japanese megabanks to complete payment of its public debt. Today, MUFG Bank focuses on building up its retail operations within Japan and is expanding corporate banking into emerging economies such as Southeast Asia. In particular, due to the emerging wave of digital technology, new business models are appearing in the financial sector, which are occurring rapidly in developing economies worldwide. How has it managed to attain this kind of success in such a short period of time and how does it intend to continue doing so? In 2001, MUFG Bank adopted the Balanced Scorecard method (hereby referred to as BSC) as a direct result of the intense pace of globalization and the need to articulate corporate strategy across diverse cultures.

Its long-term strategic goal is to become the world's premier financial group. However, this is largely dependent on the following factors: (a) gaining recognition as a globally active top Japanese brand, (b) sustaining growth in shareholder value, (c) enhancing operation quality and risk management, and (d) developing innovative products and services for its ever-expanding customer base. Although the bank once focused solely on the financial aspects of its business, it has since recognized the importance of these factors in order to become a top-tier financial services organization.

Initially, the bank could not see that it had a problem and was at first reluctant to implement the BSC method. However, when the various business units compiled their strategy maps, it became obvious that there existed little or no clear unifying concept of strategy among the corporate ranks. Thus, the strategy maps were compiled,

Table 4.   Strategy subdivisions.

Type	Definition	Example
Common	Bank-wide objectives, mandated throughout the organization on every scorecard	Enhance cost efficiency (financial perspective objective)
Shared	Interdivisional objectives shared between two or more units that were expected to cooperate to achieve the result	Streamline credit approval process (internal perspective operational efficiency objective)
Unique	Intra-divisional objectives describing an activity expected to be fulfilled independently by that group	Maintain knowledge of your customer files (internal risk management)

Source: Kaplan and Norton (2006).

compared, and analyzed which ultimately led to a new strategy map being created. Here, strategies were subdivided into those that were common to the whole group, those shared by more than one unit, and those unique to a particular unit (see Table 4).

In this way, the organization was able to formulate an overall strategy while maintaining each business unit's autonomy. The organization also realized that it had to move from a bottom-up to a top-down structure within each business group in order to disseminate aims, goals, and strategies more easily, but retain a horizontal alignment between the business units themselves. Thus, despite its initial reluctance, the MUFG Bank was able to achieve significant synergies among its business units by utilizing the BSC.

Case Study 2: Business Strategy of the Government[3]

South Korea's Ministry of Security and Public Administration (hereby referred to as MOSPA) was established in 1998 when the country's Ministry of Government Administration and the Ministry

---

[3]Some information of this case is abstracted from the MOPAS website (www.mopas.go.kr), The Balanced Scorecard Institute (www.balancedscorecard.org), and The Palladium Consulting Group (www.thepalladiumgroup.com).

of Home Affairs were combined. It is responsible for various tasks including government innovation, government organization management, e-government, and decentralization. However, when the two ministries were combined in 1998, they discovered that they themselves were lacking organizational focus. It was an uncoordinated, disruptive, and unorganized period of time and in order to bring the two ministries together and focus their efforts, the BSC was introduced.

At first, the organization lacked a strategic center, and thus, after completing its strategy maps, the organization realized that its top priority was to provide the best public service to its customers: the Korean people, central government agencies, and local governments. Thus, it shifted its focus to a more balanced indicator comprising customers, internal business processes, and a learning and growth viewpoint (see Fig. 9). This shift allowed the organization to more

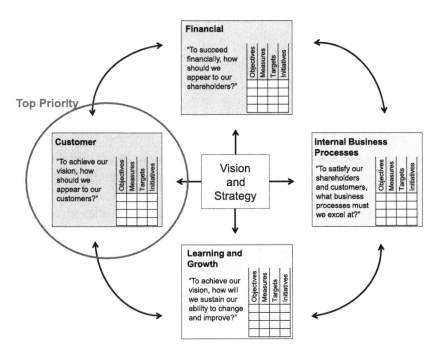

Fig. 9.   The balanced scorecard for MOSPA.

Source: Kaplan and Norton (2007a).

easily achieve its priority of satisfying its "customers." Essentially, the Ministry determined that it needed to adopt various innovation-oriented methods used in the private sector in order to become more competitive.

Besides its already considerable financial accomplishments achieved through the merger of ministries, the newly formed MOSPA implemented a variety of changes and improvements in the areas of internal business processes, learning and growth, and customers. The following are examples of some of the multitude of changes that were made in the organization:

- *Internal Business Processes* — A horizontal distribution of administrative functions of power between local authorities and a top-down structure were implemented.

- *Learning and Growth* — Continuous training for all government employees was implemented. In addition, regular workshops were held to which private and public sector guest speakers were invited.

- *Customer* — Information services and transparency regarding policy developments were improved, while the opportunity for customer feedback regarding new policies were improved.

As a direct result, Minister Myung-Jae Park at that time stated, "We are witnessing remarkable progress in meeting the strategic objectives of the ministry." Thus far, the outcome has resulted in the MOSPA being inducted into the Palladium Consulting Group's 2007 Hall of Fame with regard to its effective use of the BSC. This achievement has afforded the Ministry the right to a consultation session with Dr. Robert Kaplan himself in order to solidify its future goals and the further implementation of the BSC.

Thus, with the previous two case studies, we have seen how effectively the BSC can be applied in both the public and private sectors. It is important though to recall the analysis part of section one, which would suggest that further development could be more effective using the diamond model rather than the BSC approach.

Case Study 3: New Zealand's Robotics Industry[4]

As mentioned previously, forecasting is not a case of looking into a crystal ball, palm reading, or cartomancy. There is a distinct difference between predicting and forecasting. Specifically, forecasting is based on sound logic and a thorough analysis of available data. In order to make an effective forecast, one must define a cone of uncertainty; look for the S-curve; embrace things that do not fit; hold strong opinions weakly; look back twice as far as you look forward; and know when not to make a forecast. Using these six basic rules, almost any firm can attempt to forecast its future.

Robotics firms are the enterprises of the future and have already made the seemingly impossible possible. So, what is next for these robotics firms if we have already developed robots with manufacturing, cleaning, dancing, and talking capabilities?

Given its remoteness from much of the world, New Zealand has been undertaking efforts to increase its connections to the global economy beyond tourism and agriculture. New Zealand's robotics research is one way through which the country strives to become an important player in the tech sector. The country is renowned for specializing in unmanned aerial vehicles (UAV) and autonomous underwater vehicles (AUV) technology (see Fig. 10). Wizard Robotics, for example, was one of the first companies to introduce civil robotics to New Zealand, and it covers all areas of autonomous aviation and marine vehicles and provides autonomous solutions to agriculture, forestry, mining, gas, and oil companies. While its work is undoubtedly vital, as the development of the robots can help human life, we must ask, what is next?

In order to best gauge what is next for New Zealand's robotic firms, we must first define a cone of uncertainty. The cone of uncertainty in Fig. 11 shows, on the left, the areas of robotics development such as Sony's development of a fully mobile dancing robot; Sanyo's

---

[4]Some information of this case is abstracted from Wizard Robotics website (www.wizardrobotics.com), https://www.roboticsbusinessreview.com/health-medical/new-zealand-robotics-rd-seen-path-global-trade/.

Fig. 10. Unmanned aerial vehicle (left) and autonomous underwater vehicle (right).

Source: Images extracted from websites www.safmc.net and www.links999.net.

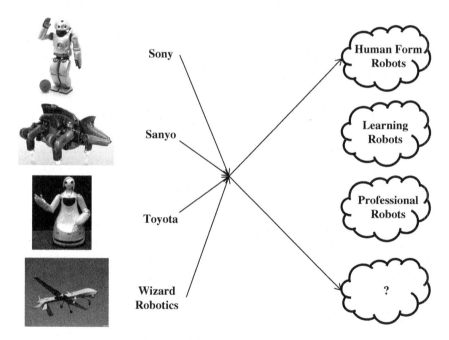

Fig. 11. The cone of uncertainty.

development of a home guard robot; Toyota's development of service robots such as guides; and Wizard Robotics' development of UAV and AUVs. These are all beginning to reach a convergence point which is represented by the center of the diagram, such as full mobility, speech ability, and little requirement for human control. Now, the cone of uncertainty opens up into the future on the right side. This represents the possible areas for further development with some suggestions that New Zealand's robotics may or may not wish to consider.

Second, New Zealand's robotics should look to the S-curve in order to understand the trends which are going to take place within the robotics industry. Despite its rapid development, the industry is seen as quite novel and unusual, but not exactly a very concrete and promising engine for future growth. However, with further technological advances, it is likely that robots will become an increasingly large part of our lives and thus more necessary. When society reaches this stage (the lower curve of the "S"), there will be a massive and sudden increase in demand. Wizard Robotics would do well to stay a step ahead of this trend.

In order to stay a step ahead of this trend, we must embrace the things that do not fit. Currently, with the COVID-19 pandemic, the global economy has accelerated the adoption of artificial intelligence (AI) technology, and thus the wide use of robots will be an imminent reality. If we embrace this uncertainty, we will be more prepared when it occurs.

In addition, Saffo advises to hold strong opinions weakly. New Zealand's robotics should not be overly confident that AI robots will be a surefire possibility. In fact, they should keep in mind the possibility that it could be wrong. To make sure, they should collect evidence that counters its future hypothesis, to be prepared for the worst but continue to hope for the best. Rule 5 states that effective forecasting requires looking back twice as far as looking forward. Thus, New Zealand's robotics should look back to not only the developments made in the robotics industry five years ago but also the general trends which developed over the past ten, twenty, and thirty years. A detailed analysis starting from the birth of robotics technology in the 1950s would be a good starting point. From there, contrasting the rise of the Japanese robotics industry with the fall of the US robotics industry in the 70s and 80s would further enhance the understanding of the crucial elements for success.[5] As Saffo noted, history does not repeat itself, but it does rhyme. Contrasting the success and failure of the two cases would be very useful in devising companies' future plans.

Discussion Questions

1. Would you add a variable to the Balanced Scorecard? If so, which variable and why?

2. The analysis suggests that the diamond model is a more comprehensive model than the Balanced Scorecard. Do you agree? Which do you prefer? Discuss.

3. How would you improve A.T. Kearney and Foreign Policy's globalization index?

4. Among the indexes presented for measuring globalization, FDI, or national competitiveness, which do you think is the best? Discuss.

5. Do you believe forecasting is a viable source for firms to base their strategy on?

6. Saffo provides six rules for effective forecasting. Do you believe some of them are redundant or can you add a seventh rule?

---

[5] See Porter (1990), pp. 224–238 for historical analysis on robotics industry.

CHAPTER 7

Global Perspectives on Strategy

Chapter Guideline

Now that we have looked extensively at the world of business strategy, it is time to add a more global perspective to our academic endeavor. This chapter will discuss some articles which have had crucial impacts on the field of global business strategy. These articles will lay the foundation for gaining a comprehensive overview of the meaning of global business strategy from various perspectives.

Summary of Previous Models

We began this book with Porter's analytical frameworks to establish a basic understanding of business strategy and then proceeded to look at some alternative views by authors such as Nonaka as well as Prahalad and Ramaswamy. Afterward, we looked at works by authors such as Moon, and Kim and Mauborgne who attempted to further extend Porter's framework. Lastly, we looked at various ways to measure and forecast business opportunities. Based on a thorough understanding of business strategy, we now turn to the connotations of global business strategy and will look at several milestones. Although their theoretical frameworks were introduced in the 1980s, they give us foundations for understanding the recent wave of global competition, such as the battle for technological hegemony between the US and China.

7.1 Global Competitive Strategy

Throughout the 1970s, many Western companies faced a formidable challenge from their Japanese counterparts who were armed with low-cost labor and efficient production methods. Many scholars have analyzed this phenomenon and pointed out the various determinants behind Japan's success, such as Rehder (1979) who looked at Japanese management practices. He believed that its remarkable efficiency was due to the country's cultural heritage and that Western companies must adopt certain aspects of Japanese organizational know-how to counter this threat. Others, such as Drucker (1981), point to more comprehensive cultural reasons which he dubs Japanese habits, or rules, of competitive success including the following: (a) taking competitiveness seriously, (b) considering national interest ahead of personal interest, (c) making external relationships important, and (d) and not seeking final victory over opponents with whom one still has to live. As valid as these comments have been, they focused on cultural characteristics derived from a belief in Japan's uniqueness. While this may provide a certain degree of explanation, it does not present a clear prescription.

Hamel and Prahalad (1985) take on a more descriptive approach and analyze why Western companies failed to meet the Japanese challenge from a strategic management perspective. According to the authors, the main problem with past countermeasures adopted by Western companies is that they were solely focused on expanding economies of scale. While this is important, there are many other variables which decide the winners and losers of global competition. In this respect, the frantic outsourcing among Western companies of their production activity to low-cost countries (at that time) such as Taiwan and Korea was not an effective countermeasure from a global strategic perspective. The authors proceeded to illustrate the missing variables through a series of examples.

Thrust & Parry

The term "thrust and parry" refers to the new type of competition that unfolded between multinational companies during the 1980s.

For example, the French tire maker Michelin attacked the American market by utilizing the profits it had generated in Europe to drive out Goodyear. In response, Goodyear struck back in Europe in order to drive Michelin out of America. These two giant tire makers in essence attacked each other by cross-subsidizing their operations across the Atlantic. The lesson to note here is that the key to winning this competition is not in expanding economies of scale. Rather, the flow of cash into each other's home market was where the true game lay. The Japanese understood this nature of global strategy and utilized it to their best advantage in their assault on Western multinationals.

At this point, the authors emphasize that it is important to distinguish between global competition and global business. Global competition, as seen from the Michelin vs. Goodyear case, requires cross-subsidization in order to gain global brand and distribution positions. This shows that global competition is determined by the strategic intent of competitors, while global business, on the contrary, requires a global market as the domestic market is too small to achieve the minimum volume needed for cost efficiency. Therefore, global business remains the more traditional realm, based on economies of scale and efficient (low-cost) production.

Identifying the Target

The battle between companies through cross-subsidization is aptly described in the section above. However, on a larger scale, the global war for business is focused on brand dominance. Relying simply on scale economies and reducing production costs will not bring victory in this intense war for global brand recognition. In order to provide a shortcut toward understanding the complex global competitive landscape, Hamel and Prahalad present the following framework (see Table 1).

The three major categories in this framework are building a global presence, defending a domestic position, and overcoming national fragmentation. In the context of the 1980s, the Japanese competitors were in the process of building a global presence, while American companies such as RCA, GE, and Zenith were desperately defending their domestic dominance. At the same time, the Europeans were

Table 1.   A global competitive framework.

	Build Global Presence (Japanese)	Defend Domestic Dominance (American)	Overcome National Fragmentation (European)
1965	Access Volume		
		Response lag	Response lag
1970	Redefine cost-volume relationship		
		Match costs	
1975	Cross-subsidize to win the world		Reduce costs at national subsidiary
		Amortize world scale investment	
1980	Contiguous segment expansion		Rationalize manufacturing
		Gain retaliatory capability	
1985			Shift focus of strategic responsibility

Source: Hamel and Prahalad (1985).

overcoming national fragmentation. By following the corresponding segment in Table 1, one can see what kind of tactic each competitor (from left to right (1) Japanese, (2) American, and (3) European) followed, in chronological order. Further explanation about these three categories will follow in the coming sections.

Loose Bricks in America

"Loose Bricks" refer to market segments which were largely ignored by Western MNCs that Japanese competitors exploited in order to make their initial landing in European and American markets. For example, in the 1960s, the Japanese gained a competitive advantage in the small-sized portable television segment (see the first column of Table 1). This was mainly due to the fact that Japanese local demand conditions overwhelmingly favored smaller-sized televisions due to the limited space in Japanese homes. The European and American manufactures were caught off guard and soon paid for their mistakes as the Japanese incrementally built their brand name through exploiting this loose brick and ultimately began to dominate the entire market with more diverse product types.

Zenith and RCA were caught off guard and desperately sought to defend their home markets through outsourcing and cutting production costs (see the second column of Table 1). However, the more they tried to pursue such actions, the more ground they lost as the Japanese were cross-subsidizing their operations in the US market through the abundant revenue they were generating in the Japanese domestic market. The failure of these American multinationals to understand the true nature of global competition led to these half-hearted and ineffective countermeasures, which ultimately gave way to their Japanese competitors in the American television market.

Loose Bricks in Europe

The story was a little different in Europe, but the result was the same. Although Japanese companies, just as they did in the American market, entered the European market, they faced restrictions. In such an environment, they sought to overcome this problem by establishing production bases in Europe. This allowed these Japanese companies to sell products other than small-sized portable TVs in the European market. They also found partners and distributors within the European markets that helped them establish a strong brand presence in Europe. The end result is that these Japanese companies were able to exploit a loose brick in both markets and eventually expand their product lines, along with their brand names.

Regaining Cost Competitiveness (European Companies)

In the European case, the problem is far more severe because of the fragmented nature of the region's television manufacturers. For example, Philips, after successfully building enough scale economies and aggressively reducing production costs, still faces the problem of a fragmented management structure. As shown in the third column of Table 1, the European manufacturers must overcome national fragmentation in order to compete effectively in the global market. Hamel and Prahalad suggest three concrete steps that these firms can take in order to counter the Japanese competitive threat: First, analyze the precise danger of national fragmentation. Second, create a system in which managers can track global competition and devise effective countermeasures. Third, educate executives on the need for cohesion and organizational reform.

New Concepts

Based upon the above discussion, it is clear that three new concepts emerge. The first is the concept of worldwide cost competitiveness, which refers to the minimum share of the global market required to gain economies of scale. Next, as explained through the discussion on cross-subsidization, is retaliation, which refers to the minimum market share the company needs in a particular country to be able to influence the behavior of key global competitors. The last is home country vulnerability that relates to the risk harbored by concentrating on the domestic market without branching out internationally.

New Strategic Thought

In conclusion, firms cannot survive global competition unless they look at it from a wider scope. Without an effective incorporation of the three new concepts explained above, firms will lose further ground and ultimately perish. In fact, few firms have made a distinction between short-run tactics and long-run strategic intentions of global competitors. As seen from the failure of how Western firms responded to the entrance of Japanese firms, defensive-minded competitors are doomed to lose if they have no appreciation of strategic intent.

Analysis

Prahalad and Hamel provide us with piercing insight into the reasons why many Western companies were taken over by Japanese competition in the 1970s and 1980s. They were able to rise from the ranks of low-cost manufacturers to world-class multinationals because of their aggressive and comprehensive approach in knocking down the walls protecting the Western market. In this way, these Japanese firms have been at the cutting edge of global competition in most manufacturing segments until the early 2000s.

It is important to note though that the Japanese are now in the position of being caught up or surpassed by Korean, Chinese, and other manufacturers from developing economies. The competitive landscape has changed significantly since the time Prahalad and Hamel's article was written, and these new competitors are competing in a fashion that is even more dynamic and complex than that described in their article. As this book progresses into the later chapters, we will discuss more on how global competition has changed from Hamel and Prahalad's description. However, as is true for any intellectual development, it is important to know more about the specific details. Still, this article provides us with a very firm foundation for understanding the nature of modern global competition.

Hamel and Prahalad's strategic intent in particular still provides useful implications toward understanding the success of Korean and Chinese firms. The long-term strategic intents have made it possible for these companies to tolerate the short-term financial losses across some sectors in order to develop future advantages. For example, Samsung Electronics has cross-subsidized the new business sector of semiconductors for almost ten years despite continuous losses, using the money earned from the cash cow sector of sugars and textiles. Moreover, although the project of "Made in China 2025" has been mainly initiated and subsidized by the Chinese government, it is also the long-term goal for creating future competitiveness by aiming to shift from low-end to high-end manufacturing.

Another important work by Hamel and Prahalad (1994), entitled *Competing for the Future*, deals with the concept of future competition and how to prepare a firm to stay ahead. While the analysis is much more complex and in-depth, the core message is the same: managers must seek constant innovation, broaden their scope, and accept and integrate unfamiliar methods into their management practices. The answer to winning global competition, as well illustrated by the two authors, is to always hold a much longer orientation, and wider vision and scope than your competitors. However, Hamel (2009) argued that in a turbulent world, as prediction is difficult and long-range planning is of limited value, generating diverse options and creating conditions in which new strategies can emerge and evolve are critical to rapidly adapting to the changing environment.

7.2 Global Cooperative Strategy

A famous Korean proverb notes that "Even lifting a piece of paper becomes easier with two people working together." The idea here is that cooperation rather than competition may be more desirable in many situations. In the world of business, this age-old lesson is expressed in terms like strategic alliances, which facilitate the coordination of relationships between firms and partners. Such interdependencies affect the ability of firms to compete and/or create economic wealth (Eng, 2007).

While strategic alliances across borders are quite common nowadays, they were not as evident during the 1960s and 1970s. The change came with the 1980s when increased economic deregulation led to the increased flow of global capital and thus promoted more diversified entry modes. As Dunning (1995) noted, a series of new developments during the 1980s and 1990s have transformed the activities of economic agents. The world has moved toward embracing a new trajectory of market capitalism which is characterized by alliance, relational, and collective actions. What is implied here, as represented in the term "Alliance Capitalism" (contrasted with "Hierarchical Capitalism" of the past), is that firms are moving toward a more eclectic mode of wealth creation that combines both competition and cooperation.

One of the first scholars to present a comprehensive view on this phenomenon of increased strategic alliances is Kenichi Ohmae (1989). While Hamel and Prahalad provide us with a framework for understanding modern global competition, Kenichi Ohmae presents a comprehensive view on the importance of strategic alliances or global cooperation. The starting point of Ohmae's discussion is explaining the three main reasons why strategic alliances have become increasingly important in global business strategy.

Californization of Need

Globalization has led to an interesting phenomenon which Ohmae (1989) calls "Californization of Need." This term refers to how consumer preferences and needs have increasingly converged due to increased information dissemination and a global lifestyle. For example, everyone essentially wishes to live and shop in California. For example, Koreans, Japanese, Turkish, and French alike all have a Big Mac for lunch, have Starbucks coffee afterward, while wearing Levi's Blue Jeans and carrying an Apple smartphone in a Gucci bag. But, why does this phenomenon mandate strategic alliance?

The answer is that firms must cater to a wider audience than they did in the past, which indicates that the scale of production must be substantially increased compared to the past. Therefore, firms must incur a high level of fixed cost in order to possess the capability to cater to a wider audience. The problem is that many firms do not have the capacity to do so nor is it desirable to do so even if a firm possesses immense capital. Rather than trying to cater to this significantly wider customer base by incurring the fixed cost alone, it makes much more sense to forge alliances to distribute the necessary cost.

Dispersion of Technology

Dispersion of technology refers to the technological aspects that have fundamentally shifted the global competition from a variable cost game to a fixed one. Technological complexity embedded in products has evolved drastically over the years, which means a single product now requires so many other cutting-edge technologies that one firm cannot possibly have the expertise to become global leader in all categories. Combine this with the fact that all these firms wish to sell to as many customers as possible, then we can see why every cutting-edge technology simply disperses so much faster than it used to.

Consider the evolution of cameras. In the past, cameras were analog devices that required very simple parts and components such as camera lens, gears, shutters, and a sturdy plastic body. A single firm could undertake the production of all the necessary components without compromising its competitive advantage. This has all changed with the digital revolution; now, the camera has evolved drastically. It is today near impossible for one firm to be proficient in all aspects of production without incurring tremendous fixed costs. For example, a digital camera today needs cutting-edge software, technology, and solutions such as Charge Coupled Device (CCD) sensors, flash disk memory, and Complementary Metal Oxide Semiconductor (CMOS) memories. Furthermore, even if these software technologies could somehow be produced in-house, it would make little sense to keep it in-house when these separate technologies could be sold to various other firms for increased revenue. The only solution in this case is to seek allies that are specialized in each of the necessary components and establish a long-term partnership with them.

The Importance of Fixed Costs

The need to cater to global consumers with similar needs and the wide dispersion of technology mean that firms must now play the fixed cost game in order to succeed. Take building a brand name, for example. In the past, firms could go about it alone since the brand name had to be recognized by a much smaller group of consumers. Now, with global competition, unless the brand name is recognized by a wider audience, a firm does not even get a chance to sell its product. Achieving global exposure and recognition is a herculean task which requires immense fixed costs. Rather than incurring all the fixed costs, it is much wiser to seek alliances to amortize the risk associated with making such a significant investment.

Consider the example of an American firm that has developed a new pharmaceutical product to be marketed all over the world. In the past, firms did not have a global consumer base to cater to, so it simply used its own sales force for domestic distribution. However, if the firm wants to distribute the new product in Japan, should it incur a massive fixed cost and establish its own sales force in Japan or should it seek an alliance? The answer Ohmae gives is the latter.

Dangers of Equity and the Logic of Entente

The question that we must ask at this point is why so many firms prefer to go it alone rather than establish alliances. The answer is equity control. When a firm invests in a joint venture or acquires another firm, the chief concern is return on investment (ROI) and the dividends that are generated with it. Based on this concern, firms want total control or at least dominance in the form of equity share in order to maximize ROI and the dividends. This is why most firms want a 51% equity share in an alliance as this provides majority of the control. However, Ohmae criticizes such a control-obsessed approach for two reasons.

The first is that this hierarchical mentality will inevitably lead to conflict between the partners. The parent company with 51% equity share will frequently question the competence of the other side when ROIs do not increase rapidly or substantially. Although ROIs simply cannot increase very quickly, most equity shareholders are very willing to pull the plug unless the investment pays chart-topping returns. The second problem is that even when this arrangement generates a good ROI, the parent firm will start to think of what will happen if it had 100% control instead of 51%. Looking at the cash flow and revenue generated, the parent firm overlooks the massive fixed costs that it did not have to install due to the alliance and only focuses on the potential benefit of 100% ownership.

Ohmae insists that this kind of destructive relationship rarely, if ever, leads to success. Instead, two things must change. First, firms must view alliances as a marriage rather than a parent to subsidiary relationship. Second, firms must realize that the primary focus should not be on ROI but on Return on Sales (ROS). Unlike an ROI-orientated approach which demands that the subsidiary *work for* the parent, ROS orientation means that both partners will focus on the sales of the operation for mutual benefit and *work together*. Thus, the new logic of entente or strategic alliance requires a fundamental shift in perception from a parent–child relationship to a parent–parent relationship based on mutual respect and cooperation.

Analysis

Ohmae brings in a fresh new perspective to global business strategy by shifting the focus from competition to alliance. If Hamel and Prahalad presented us with a fresh new perspective in understanding the nature of global competition, Ohmae adds another dimension by focusing on global alliances. The key message from Ohmae is that in the new global business landscape, firms cannot survive without a sound strategic alliance, which allows them to amortize the massive fixed costs needed to compete effectively. It is interesting to note that while these authors all observed the same symptoms, they prescribe polar opposite solutions.

As useful as the above two articles are, they both need to be incorporated into a larger framework. While all these authors are leading business intellectuals, it is important not to be overwhelmed by their brilliance and keep a larger framework in mind when reading their articles. Figure 1 shows how these two articles stand in the context of a comprehensive global strategy (refer to Chapter 5 for further details about the model).

This illustration shows that although both articles have presented the readers with illuminating insights, they are still only describing part of the broader picture. Hamel and Prahalad have succeeded in highlighting the true nature of global competition, but have missed the fact that alliances can significantly ease the process of competing in the new global arena. This though does not mean that Ohmae's antithesis is entirely valid either.

First of all, Ohmae's discussion of fixed costs and the need for alliance is highly relevant in the more complex, global industries. Backer and Rinaudo (2019) suggested that the more complex the business environment becomes, the more such relationships make sense, particularly in the current era when open innovation strategy is

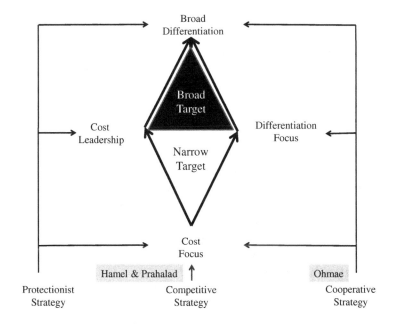

Fig. 1. Hamel and Prahalad, and Ohmae in the comprehensive global strategy.
Source: Moon (1993).

widely adopted for both, leading latecomer firms to develop ideas or solutions. In the dynamic and technology-based industries, innovations are rarely developed and commercialized within a single firm, even for the major players (Chesbrough, 2003; Chesbrough and Appleyard, 2007). According to the open innovation paradigm, the research and development systems among firms are open with permeable boundaries (Chesbrough *et al.*, 2006). Under the open innovation system, firms can either sell their technologies to the external market (outbound openness) or use the external sources for further innovation inside the firm (inbound openness) (Dahlander and Gann, 2010).

The problem with Ohmae's logic though is pronounced when seen from the wider context of the global economy. Strategic alliances are useful for firms to amortize the immense fixed costs and hence operate more smoothly in the global business context. This benefits the consumers as it brings more consumption options at a lower cost and disperses technology rapidly. However, when this picture is taken too far, we can imagine a scenario in which mega-alliances and acquisitions can create immense barriers to the entry of newcomers. This has the potential to kill the competitive spirit that is vital for a healthy business environment, while established firms will not want to share their core competencies with each other (Porter, 1990). The outcome of such a trend is that it will lead to more ineffective strategic alliances (Liou *et al.*, 2011). In short, although Ohmae's article has added a very important new dimension to global business strategy, we should not regard it as a replacement to competition. Rather, it is simply another weapon that can be kept in the firm's arsenal of a wide array of strategic weapons that can be deployed.

7.3 Comprehensive Synthesis?

Cooperation or competition? What is the answer to global strategy? The obvious answer is "both," but this logical response does not do much in terms of providing a practical prescription. Fortunately, we have Sumantra Ghoshal to explore a synthesizing framework of the two extremes.

Ghoshal (1987) outlines the need to provide managers with an organizing framework which synthesizes various perspectives. As the concept of global strategy gained increasing prominence during the 1980s, related literature flourished, yet no one synthesized all approaches into a single framework (see Table 2).

The easiest way to follow this synthesis is to look at the far-left column first in Table 2. It outlines the strategic objectives that all firms must achieve in order to have a successful global strategy. Simply put, a global firm looks to achieve efficiency, manage risk, and learn to innovate through its global strategy. However, an important point to remember is that each of these goals has trade-offs and conflicting ends in the actual implementation process.

The next part to look at is the sources of how to achieve these different objectives. National differences, scale economies, and scope economies are the base upon which firms can find the means to achieve these important strategic objectives. Combining these two

Table 2. Global strategy: An organizing framework.

	Sources of Competitive Advantage		
Strategic objectives	National differences	Scale economies	Scope economies
Achieving efficiency in current operations	Benefiting from differences in factor costs — wages and cost of capital	Expanding and exploiting potential scale economies in each activity	Sharing of investments and costs across products, markets and businesses
Managing risks	Managing different kinds of risks arising from market or policy-induced changes in comparative advantages of different countries	Balancing scale with strategic and operational flexibility	Portfolio diversification of risks and creation of options and side-bets
Innovation, learning and adaptation	Learning from societal differences in organizational and managerial processes and systems	Benefiting from experience — cost reduction and innovation	Shared learning across organizational components in different products, markets or businesses

Source: Ghoshal (1987).

broad categories in a three-by-three matrix, Ghoshal presents a comprehensive framework that synthesizes all preexisting works. Below is a detailed analysis of each objective.

Strategic Objectives

- *Achieving Efficiency* — With a global strategy, this seeks to visualize the cost advantages of global integration vis-à-vis the benefits of responding to national differences. In other words, different industries and companies gain or lose competitive advantages depending on the level of integration (which is to standardize the firm's value chain regardless of the market) or differentiation (which is to tailor the firm's value chain depending on the market). For example, the consumer electronics industry would benefit from high integration and low differentiation, while the packaged foods industry, which depends highly on local consumer tastes, will benefit more from differentiation rather than integration. This classification can even map the difference in companies within the industry. For example, in the automobile industry, Toyota is closer to integration, while Ford or Fiat is more toward differentiation. The level of analysis can go down to individual tasks executed by the firm (see Fig. 2).

- *Managing Risks* — There are four types of risks that firms face in conducting their operations. The first are macroeconomic risks, which are basically exogenous variables beyond the firm's control. The second are policy risks, which are government policies that affect the conduct of firms. The third are competitive risks, which are strategic responses by competitors that may undermine the firm's position. The last are resource risks, which occur under a condition where the firm may not have the necessary resources to implement its global strategy. The key to a successful global strategy then is to analyze all of these risks when making strategic choices.

- *Innovation, Learning, and Adaptation* — These are the three methods with which a firm may enhance its capabilities by

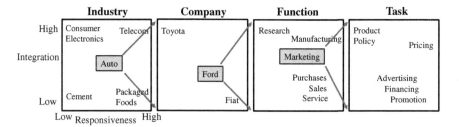

Fig. 2.   The integration-responsiveness framework.
Source: Ghoshal (1987).

operating in multiple environments. Through exposure to diversity, the firm can internalize what it has learned and enhance its competitive advantage. This is quite different from previous theories, such as Dunning 1995, which believe that a firm goes abroad in order to exploit the market imperfections based on its pre-established advantages in a new market, but similar to the imbalance theory (Moon and Roehl, 2001; Moon, 2007), which explains that firms often go abroad to search for advantages.

Sources of Competitive Advantage

- *National Differences* — Different nations have a range of factor endowments, which can lead to inter-country differences in factor costs. A firm can therefore gain cost advantages by configuring its value chain so that each activity is located in the country that has the least cost for the factor that the activity uses most intensively. This is the concept of comparative advantage-based competitive advantage (Kogut, 1985). However, it should be noted that while comparative advantages among countries can provide competitive advantages for firms, the realization of such benefits is not automatic but depends on complex organizational factors and processes. In essence, the difference between the traditional trade theory and Ghoshal's view is in the number of variables. The traditional view focuses on factors such as labor and capital, while Ghoshal includes more variables, such as quality, quantity, and configuration of its material, human, and institutional resources.

- *Scale Economies* — Just like the first source, scale economies are well studied and there is rich literature available on this subject. This goes back to the basic economic principle on how increased economies of scales lead to reduced production costs and ultimately enhanced competitiveness. However, again, this is still a limited and static view point toward scale economies. A more dynamic view can be adopted by adding the concept of a "learning effect." Firms with larger scales can accumulate more experience and thus lead to even more cost cuts. Still, we must note that scale economies may harbor negative effects. A larger scale also means an increase in the potential for a response lag. This may prove especially detrimental in a global business environment which is becoming increasingly complex and unpredictable and thus it is very important to balance scale and flexibility.

- *Scope Economies* — The last and least well understood is the concept of scope economies. While economies of scale refer to a decrease in the average total cost by expanding the production of a single product, economies of scope refer to a similar benefit reaped from expanding the production of multiple products. For example, there are scope economies if the cost of the joint production of two or more products is less than the cost of producing them separately. Scope economies focus on the synergistic effects created when a firm diversifies its products and markets. A more detailed explanation can be seen in Table 3.

The logic of scope economies arises from a diversified firm's capability to share costs across the activities of the value chain that its competitors cannot imitate if they do not possess similar capabilities

Table 3.   Scope economies in product and market diversification.

	Sources of Scope Economies	
	Product Diversification	**Market Diversification**
Shared physical assets	Factory automation with flexibility to produce multiple products (Ford)	Global brand name (Coca Cola)
Shared external relations	Using common distribution channel for multiple products (Matsushita)	Serving multi-national customers worldwide (Citibank)
Shared learning	Sharing R&D in computer and communications businesses (NEC)	Pooling knowledge developed in different markets (Procter and Gamble)

Source: Ghoshal (1987).

of diversification. Such sharing can take place across segments, products, or markets (Porter, 1985). For example, in the soft drink industry, bottling and distribution are local in scope, while the designing of efficient bottling plants is integrated. Coca-Cola has externalized those functions that are purely local in scope. Similarly, IBM has externalized its PC business by setting up an almost stand-alone organization. Yet another example is Proctor and Gamble which may incur costs by developing a separate product for a specific market. However, this effort leads to knowledge creation that creates a synergistic effect for other products as well.

Prescriptions in Perspective

As emphasized before, the usefulness of this model lies in its synthesis. This helps managers formulate a comprehensive global strategy that takes into consideration all the important variables. Another notable contribution of this model is that it highlights the existence of trade-offs between different strategies. When individual strategy prescriptions are analyzed separately, they all seem valid and useful. However, in reality, by choosing one strategy, one must forgo the opportunity to pursue another path. Consider, for example, the decision to choose from different sources of competitive advantages. If a firm wishes to exploit factor costs in different locations, it must sacrifice some opportunities to enhance scale efficiency and thus forgo various synergistic effects. In sum, this framework shows that managers must make the appropriate strategic choices and be aware of the different trade-offs according to the objective and the surrounding context that they face.

Analysis

Ghoshal summarizes and synthesizes the existing discussions into one coherent framework. As we have seen in Hamel and Prahalad and in Ohmae, a unilateral focus on one aspect of global strategy leaves behind many gaps that are not accounted for. If a firm decides to pursue Hamel and Prahalad's prescription and aggressively pursue cross-subsidization and attack the competitor's home market, it may miss the opportunity to forge strategic alliances, an opportunity that can significantly reduce the firm's operating cost. However, if a firm decides to unilaterally pursue Ohmae's prescription, then a firm may face the problem of lacking a competitive edge by compromising its own advantage in an obsession to forge strategic alliances. Instead, Ghoshal aptly points out the existence of a variety of strategic options and, more importantly, the trade-offs that inevitably accompany each choice that a manager makes.

Despite the creative and well-structured framework of Ghoshal, some sources of competitive advantages derived from the global strategy may be restricted under some specific situations. For example, trade conflicts like that between the US and China will make it difficult for MNCs to exploit the national differences from each other through strategic alliances. Firms then should adopt a more sophisticated strategic design to avoid or pursue alternative channels that are less affected by restrictions from the external environmental. In addition, firms from less developed countries will even find it difficult to go abroad and compete against established global firms from advanced countries due to their liability of origin (Bartlett and Ghoshal 2000). Hence, there will be differences in choosing appropriate strategic options between first movers from developed countries and latecomers from developing countries.

Case Study 1: Arçelik is No Turkey[1]

Arçelik, founded in 1955, is a household appliances manufacturer based in Turkey. The company is controlled by Koc Holding, one of Turkey's largest and most prestigious groups, and is the market leader

---

[1] Parts of this case study are extracted from Arçelik's Official Webpage (https://www.arcelikglobal.com/en/), https://www.dailysabah.com/business/turkish-home-appliance-manufacturer-arcelik-continues-production-in-russia/news, https://www.nytimes.com/2020/08/27/business/turkey-currency-crisis.html.

in Turkey's appliance sector with its Arçelik and Beko brands. It is also the third largest household appliances company in Europe in terms of sales. The company engages in the production and marketing of durable goods, components, consumer electronics, and after-sale services. Its products include white goods, consumer electronics, small home appliances, and kitchen accessories. Arçelik now operates in more than 100 countries, through its 23 production facilities in 9 countries.[2] It offers products under its own 12 brands in the household appliances sector, including the two European brands Beko and Grundig, the well-known German manufacturer that it had acquired after Grundig went bankrupt in the early 2000s. Internationally though, Arçelik is probably best known for its Beko brand.

Arçelik was once, not long ago, just a small domestic firm in Turkey, a country not known for its competitive edge in the white goods sector. It is thus difficult to imagine how such a firm has gone from strength to strength when the odds were seemingly stacked against it. This case study will highlight all of the points mentioned by the scholars above: Hamel and Prahalad, Ohmae, and Ghoshal; thus, it will provide us with an excellent example of a firm that has gained global recognition through truly global strategic endeavors.

Hamel and Prahalad on Arçelik

Koc is by far the largest and most important MNC of Turkish origin and is viewed as a dominant force in the Turkish economy and a rising giant in various sectors. What is more remarkable is the pace and aggressiveness at which Koc Holding has globalized its business in recent years, in particular its subsidiary, Arçelik. From the perspective of Hamel and Prahalad, we will first look at how Arçelik has (a) built a global presence, (b) defended its domestic position, and (c) attacked the loose bricks in Europe.

---

[2] Turkey, China, Romania, Russia, South Africa, Thailand, Pakistan, India, and Bangladesh.

Arçelik was originally focused on producing metal furniture, which was a high-demand product in Turkey at that time. However, as the country began to experience an industrial boom, the firm saw bricks come loose in the consumer appliance market and it quickly moved its operations into home appliances. By 1960, Arçelik had become a major Turkish manufacturer of washing machines and refrigerators. Had it not seized the opportunity of the loose bricks in the consumer appliance market at that time, Arçelik would probably still only be producing metal furniture in Turkey.

Arçelik licensed most of its technology from GE and Bosch Siemens and was permitted to utilize the technology only for the domestic market. However, as of the early 2000s, the majority of these licensing agreements expired and Arçelik began to devise ambitious plans to burst into the global market. It has taken a highly diversified path to building a global presence, through acquisitions of foreign firms subsidized by its domestic profits and by establishing international distribution channels that are consistent with the global competition model of Hamel and Prahalad (see Table 4).

Arçelik made the majority of its acquisitions, including several prestigious Western multinationals such as Grundig and Blomberg, as a way to acquire advanced technology and build distribution channels overseas. More importantly though, these efforts sought to improve the disadvantageous brand image associated with being from a developing country. As a direct result of its acquisitions, it has gone from strength to strength in Europe and is now beginning to enter the Asian market as the European markets reach a saturation point. For example, recently, Arçelik acquired the production and sales companies operating in Pakistan under the Dawlance brand in 2016. In 2019, it also acquired majority stake (57%) in Singer Bangladesh for US$75 million as part of an approach toward creating a strong presence along the historical Silk Road.

Many firms that expand this quickly and aggressively may be in danger of national fragmentation, so it is essential that national subsidiaries continue to interact with the organization. Arçelik is obviously aware of this danger and has implemented rigorous employee training and education programs across the board in order

Table 4. Arçelik's acquisitions, strategic alliances and joint ventures in 2000s.

Firm	Year	Country	Entry mode*	Purpose
LG	2000	Korea	J.V.	Technology
Beko	2001	Austria	A	Branding/Distribution
Blomberg	2002	Germany	A	Technology/Branding/Distribution
Bregenz	2002	Germany	A	Branding/Distribution
Leisure	2002	United Kingdom	A	Distribution
Favel	2002	UK and Ireland	A	Distribution
Arctic	2002	Romania	A	Branding/Distribution
Alba	2004	UK	JV	Technology/Production
Grundig	2004	Germany	A	Technology/Distribution
Alba	2007	UK	A	Branding/Distribution
Changzhou Casa-Shinco	2007	China	A	Distribution/Production
Fisher & Paykel	2007	New Zealand	SA	Distribution

Note: *Entry modes: acquisition (A), strategic alliance (SA), joint venture (JV).
Source: Information sourced from www.arcelik.com/tr.

to make all employees aware of the connectivity that exists between the brands. They are not to be treated as separate entities but as complementary arms to a center entity.

Ohmae on Arçelik

As highlighted before, Ohmae emphasized the concept of the "Californization of need" to describe the general convergence of global consumer tastes. This integration has led to a wider base of global consumers, which increases the importance of scales of production. Therefore, Ohmae recommends strategic alliances as one course of action to relieve the burden of achieving increased scales of production. He additionally points out that as products have become more technologically advanced, it has become increasingly difficult, if not impossible, for one firm to provide all of the essential components that are required to manufacture a product. There may also be heavy fixed costs associated with branding. While branding is essential for the success of any firm, firms often wish to avoid the associated costs. Arçelik has successfully managed to avoid all of the above pitfalls mentioned by Ohmae.

By pursuing a highly aggressive path of strategic alliances and acquisitions, Arçelik has been able to spread its costs and simultaneously increase its scale of production. This aggressive internationalization acted as an enabling switch for this previously domestic original equipment manufacturer (OEM) company to advance into an original brand manufacturer (OBM) with solid technology and brand reputation.

Furthermore, strategic alliances have enabled Arçelik to distribute the high costs of technology development and acquisition. Had Arçelik attempted to internalize all these activities, the costs and time required would have made it an insurmountable task. Instead, the firm pursued partnerships with Korean multinational LG to develop air conditioners and with the British firm Alba for distribution and finance operations. Arçelik's moves have been quite successful as the company has been able to establish itself as the third largest supplier of white goods in the European market without having to incur significant fixed costs.

Lastly, Arçelik has been successful in avoiding fixed costs associated with branding. As a Turkish firm, it has advantages in some Eastern European markets such as Azerbaijan, Romania, and Uzbekistan and does not have to work as hard at branding as it does in other markets. In markets such as Germany, the UK, or the US, its brand may be looked down upon simply because of its country of origin (COO). As a Turkish firm, Arçelik faced significant COO disadvantages, which could raise issues regarding the level of the quality of the good. Rather than attempting to build up its Turkish brand, Arçelik was able to circumvent this negative COO problem by purchasing recognizable, trustworthy, and highly valued brands from more developed countries. Grundig is an excellent example of this strategy, as it has a 95% recognition rate in Germany. Yet, few even know that this former German white goods giant is now a subsidiary of a Turkish firm. For Arçelik, acquisitions, joint ventures, and strategic alliances are a quiet affair, thus allowing it to leverage the branding that is already in place.

Ghoshal on Arçelik

Ghoshal integrated a number of theories and thoughts on global business strategy into one cohesive framework. There are three aspects to his framework: (a) achieving efficiency, (b) managing risks, and (c) fostering innovation and learning.

Again, Arçelik has managed to be successful on all of these fronts. In order to achieve efficiency, and thereby, competitive advantage, a firm must know when to standardize and when to tailor the firm's value chain. While there are clear-cut cost advantages to full integration and standardization, this is not always possible to realize. In particular, the global white goods sector is characterized by a myriad of consumer preferences due to distinct national preferences for cooking style, residential structure or size of the home, and the climate. Arçelik has been able to encompass both extreme pyramids through diversified branding. In less developed markets, where standardization is possible, Arçelik has chosen to purchase locally popular, economical, and technologically simple brands. However, in more advanced markets, a certain level of differentiation is required as consumers are more sophisticated and require a higher quality of goods.

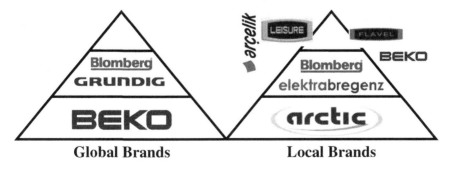

Fig. 3. Arçelik's brand portfolio.

Thus, Arçelik has endeavored to acquire globally popular, more expensive, and technologically advanced brands (see Fig. 3).

The company has also been successful in managing risks despite Turkey's chronic economic volatility. With a strong background and experience in risk management in Turkey, Arçelik was able to easily understand and penetrate risky foreign markets such as Uzbekistan and Azerbaijan. Armed with this knowledge, it was fairly easy to penetrate other markets, seen as less traditionally risky, such as Germany and the UK. However, there are other types of dangers in these advanced markets such as competitive or resource risks. Had Arçelik entered those markets without being aware of the competitive risk, it would have had a difficult time competing against more established multinationals. Yet, by entering those markets under the guise of "one of us," Arçelik was able to overcome both competitive and resource risks that exist in more advanced nations. In addition, in responding to the COVID-19 pandemic, Arçelik took many early measures learning from its operations in China. Those experiences helped the company implement effective measures in all other facilities around the world and continue to meet the needs of its customers.

Lastly, by entering different markets around the world, including those in Europe and the Asia-Pacific, Arçelik learned how to continuously innovate. This is a key to the success of any global company and Arçelik has, in a very short period of time, learned from its experiences, thrived through internationalization, and effectively competed head-to-head with more established firms while enjoying a monopolistic position in its home country. For example, despite the potential risks from Brexit, the company opened an R&D center in Cambridge in 2016, in order to take advantage of a British tradition for scientific innovation, particularly to conduct the research applicable to smart appliances.

Discussion Questions

1. The "thrust and parry" concept came out in the 1980s. Do you think that this can still be applied to today's world or did

the nature of competition evolve significantly? What are some examples?

2. Can the concept of "loose bricks" be likened to the "blue ocean" idea? Discuss the similarities and differences.

3. The "Californization of need" seems similar to the notion of standardization. How is it different from the standardization argument?

4. If firms were to arrange strategic alliances on a 50/50 basis, would they continue to function and achieve their objectives more easily or with more difficulty?

5. What could be the potential benefits and challenges for firms to make alliances in the same or different industries?

6. Can firms really ever effectively manage risk? If so, how can they effectively manage the four risks mentioned by Ghoshal?

7. Which of the three approaches — Hamel and Prahalad, Ohmae, and Ghoshal — do you find most effective in explaining the case of Arçelik and why?

8. How should firms effectively balance the relationship between competitive and cooperative strategies in the current fast-changing and uncertain era of pandemics and high technologies such as artificial intelligence and digital transformation?

CHAPTER 8

Developing and Extending Analytical Models

Chapter Guideline

The concept of global business strategy is quite difficult to grasp because of its complex and multidimensional nature. Even in the overabundance of business literature written on global business strategy, there is still little consensus and much room for further development. In this chapter, we will look at the works of scholars who have attempted to provide main analytical frameworks in order to help scholars, managers, and students gain a better understanding of global business strategy.

Summary of Previous Models

After studying various business models, we have elevated our analysis to the global level by looking at prominent scholars who have attempted to assess global business strategy from various perspectives. As illuminating as their works have been, we could see that there are still many loopholes and missing variables that have not been accounted for. Even Ghoshal's synthesis was not clear enough and does not provide a systematic framework to analyze the degree of globalization.

8.1 Coordination–Configuration Model

We now come back to Porter once again in order to gain an overar ching perspective on global competition and strategy. The starting point for Porter's analysis is the fact that previous literature has only given a partial view of how global business strategy should be conceived (Porter, 1986). The purpose of his work is to explore international competition under the context of competitive strategy. In this regard, the key question that needs to be answered is how a firm's activity in one country affects or is affected by what is going on in other countries.

Patterns of International Competition

Two important concepts, "multi-domestic" and "global," are introduced by Porter for modeling global strategy. These terms set the two opposing continuums that describe the pattern of international competition depending on the industry. A multi-domestic industry, as the name suggests, is an industry in which competition in one country is independent from competition in other countries. The competitive advantage of a firm, therefore, is specific to the country because an advantage in one nation largely does not transfer into another. An appropriate example would be the packaged foods industry, which is characterized by a myriad of consumer tastes and preferences. Global industries, on the contrary, are the polar opposite of multi-domestic industries since competitive advantage in one nation has a significant impact on the other. The commercial aircraft industry is a good example where economies of scale and product standardization are the key ingredients for success. The distinction between these two types of industries has profound implications. Understanding the determinants of industry structure is then the most important idea.

Causes of Globalization

Then, what makes an industry global? An industry becomes global when there is competitive advantage to be derived from integrating

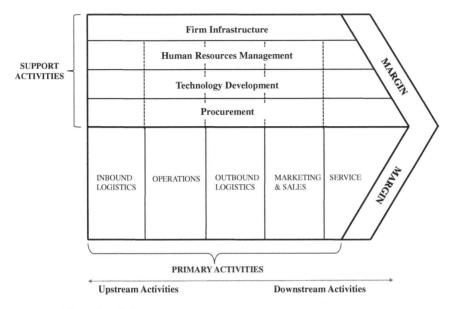

Fig. 1. The value chain.
Source: Porter (1986, p. 24).

activities across many different countries. In order to specify what integrating activities means, the value chain is introduced (see Fig. 1).

The important point here is the distinction between upstream and downstream activities. Competitive advantage in downstream activities is largely derived from performing country-specific activities, while upstream and support activities are generally those that can be derived from one or more source countries. The heart of global strategy is to perform these activities in a global context to maximize the firm's competitive advantage. But, how does a firm achieve this feat? What kinds of tools are available? Here, an important basis for a framework emerges which Porter calls *configuration* and *coordination*. Configuration refers to the location in the world where each activity in the value chain is performed, while coordination refers to how similar activities performed in different countries are coordinated with each other. Table 1 illustrates several examples that can help the reader grasp this Coordination–Configuration (C–C) concept.

Table 1. Configuration and coordination issues by category of activity.

Value activity	Configuration issue	Coordination issue
Operations	Location of production facilities for components and end products	Allocation of production tasks among dispersed facilities Networking of international plants Transfer of process technology and production know-how among plants
Marketing and Sales	Product line selection Country selection Location of preparation of advertising materials	Commonality of brand name worldwide Coordination of sales to multinational accounts Similarity of channels and product positioning worldwide Coordination of pricing in different countries
Service	Location of the service organization	Similarity of service standards and procedures worldwide
Technology Development	Number and location of R&D centers	Allocation of research tasks among dispersed R&D centers Interchange among R&D centers Development of products responsive to market needs in many countries Sequences of product introductions around the world
Procurement	Location of the purchasing function	Location and management of suppliers in different countries Transfer of knowledge about input markets Coordination of purchases of common items

Source: Porter (1986, p. 26).

As we can see from Table 1, various parts of the global value chain can be configured and coordinated in order to enhance the competitive advantage of a firm. With this understanding, Porter defines global strategy as one in which a firm acquires competitive advantage through configuration and/or coordination among dispersed activities. This concept can be summarized into a simple yet powerful analytical framework as illustrated in Fig. 2.

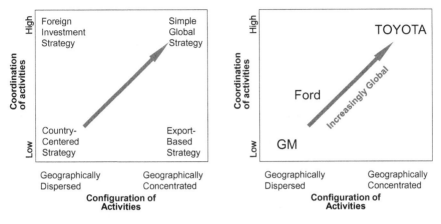

Fig. 2.   The dimensions of international strategy (left) and the auto industry (right).
Source: Porter (1986, pp. 27–28).

As depicted on the right-hand side of Fig. 2, Toyota has concentrated all of its production facilities into one location while coordinating other activities that must be performed within close proximity to their consumers. GM, on the contrary, chose the complete opposite route and decided to take a country-centered strategy with separate brand names and production facilities for each market in which the company wishes to operate. As the arrows indicate, all automobile firms are moving more toward what Porter sees as the final stage (the upper right corner) in order to maximize the benefits derived from internationally coordinating and geographically concentrating different activities in the value chain.

Thus, the question arises, when should firms concentrate their activities globally and/or coordinate dispersed activities? A firm should concentrate its activities when there are economies of scale, a proprietary learning curve, a comparative advantage of one or a few locations for performing the activity, and advantages of co-locating linked activities such as R&D and production. In other words, when locating linked or similar activities in one spot generates synergies, the advantages of concentration outweigh those of dispersion. On the contrary, dispersion of activities is more favorable when customer needs are different according to the location and/or communications and transportation conditions. Coordinating these geographically dispersed activities may lead to numerous advantages such as increased knowledge base, local responsiveness, and the ability to exploit favorable local conditions (such as the exchange rate and tax incentives).

Configuration/Coordination and the Pattern of International Competition

The activities from which a firm can derive competitive advantage depend on the industry and countries. For example, as mentioned before, commercial aircraft industries are characterized by immense competitive advantage derived from concentrating R&D and production activities. Furthermore, firms in the film industry are more likely to derive competitive advantage from coordinating their various activities in countries with similar languages and cultures. The important message here is that the specifics of how to coordinate/configure the various activities within its value chain depends on the structure of the industry which the firm operates in.

The Process of Industry Globalization

Industries move from being multi-domestic to global for several reasons. Exogenous variables such as general technological advancement, buyer needs, government policy, or country infrastructure exert major influences. For example, when a buyer needs to become homogenized for electronic products, having global outreach and economies of scale provides crucial advantages to firms that possess such capabilities. As these influences strengthen, an industry becomes global because of the immense benefits that can be reaped from going global. For example, thanks to globalization, within ten years, the iPhone has already been well established as one of the most successful consumer products of all time in terms of the global unit sales since its launch year. Since 2007, when the first iPhone was introduced to the market, Apple had achieved almost 1.2 billion units of sales by 2017 (*Wall Street Journal*, 2017).

Global Platform

The term global platform is another way of describing how individual countries should no longer be regarded as standalone entities. Rather, individual countries should be regarded as components of the whole picture. This distinction is important because it is a significant deviation from the traditional concept of comparative advantage which views a nation's factor endowment as the ultimate source of advantage. While the traditional view of factor endowment is still valid, it needs to be defined broadly and incorporated into the term "global platform." This platform not only includes these traditional elements but also demands sophistication, technical personnel, infrastructure, and local operating environment (such as competition and rivalry). The importance of traditional determinants such as low-cost labor and abundant resources is decreasing, while more complex drivers, such as those listed in the previous sentence, are becoming far more significant. Therefore, in deciding whether to operate in a country or not, the traditional perception of a nation's factor endowment is insufficient and must incorporate a more rigorous and comprehensive view which sees individual countries as part of a larger entity.

Strategic Implications of Globalization

In light of the above analysis, it is evident that when an industry goes global, firms must rethink the way they formulate strategy. Traditionally, the focus has been on how to adapt to the conditions of certain locations and optimize a firm's operations accordingly. However, from the above analysis, we can see that the issue has an additional dimension, which concerns how to link and coordinate activities performed in individual countries in order to derive the maximum advantage from a global industry. Figure 3 depicts the strategic choices that firms can make in a global industry.

The following provides a more specific explanation for each category.

Geographic Scope

	Global Strategy	Country Centered Strategy
Many Segments	**Global Cost Leadership or Differentiation**	**Protected Markets**
Few Segments	**Global Segmentation**	**National Responsiveness**

Segment Scope (left axis label)

Fig. 3. Strategic alternatives in a global industry.
Source: Porter (1986, p. 46).

- *Global Cost Leadership or Differentiation* — A firm's strategic choices are defined either by cost leadership or differentiation. These choices are realized through coordination and/or configuration of its activities by selling a wide array of products to consumers in many countries.

- *Global Segmentation* — This is a strategy in which a firm caters to a specific segment in many countries. A good example is luxury cars, such as Mercedes, which is a homogenized segment in various countries.

- *Protected Markets* — Firms can shelter themselves from global competition by finding markets that are protected by the national government. Because the market is protected, a firm can produce a wide array of goods regardless of competition.

- *National Responsiveness* — Firms can choose to cater to a particular nation's needs even though the industry itself is global. Unconventional needs among customers, for instance, can create a feasible condition for this kind of approach.

The four strategic choices elaborated above reflect obvious trade-offs. However, each is often not mutually exclusive from one another as many firms pursue one or more strategies simultaneously. This point will be further elaborated as the chapter progresses.

Analysis

As always, Porter presents us with a sweeping picture of a highly complex phenomenon.

In essence, this analysis is based on his fundamental grasp of competition: advantages are derived from low cost or differentiation and industry is the most important unit of analysis. Because each industry has different structural compositions, some become global, while others remain multi-domestic. From this theoretical foundation, Porter asserts that a firm should employ a global strategy when the benefits derived from coordinating and configuring its value chain activities over a wide array of countries are substantial. The costs and benefits of a global strategy mostly depend on the industry structure and the level of advantage that can be derived from a different mix of global coordination and configuration. Porter went on to analyze the various implications this foundation has for firm activities in the global business strategic context.

Porter's contribution is significant in two ways: First, he fused his value chain framework with globalization in order to provide an analysis from the functional level. This is significant because, realistically, firms have differing degrees of globalization depending on each value activity it performs. Second, Porter's analysis provides us with important insights as to why an industry globalizes and how a firm's function can be dispersed in various countries to maximize the benefits of globalization. However, theoretically even this seemingly flawless analysis actually contains some problems as will be seen in the following sections.

On the contrary, empirically, Porter's view of "global strategy" is not fully supported in practice (Verbeke, 2013). The seminal work of Rugman and Verbeke (2004) challenged the concept of global strategy for MNCs by demonstrating empirically that the majority of the

Fortune Global 500 firms operated regionally, not globally. Their 2004 study has triggered a subsequent stream of research on the *regional* nature of firm internationalization (Verbeke and Asmussen, 2016; Kim *et al.*, 2020). Over the last fifteen years, there has been a growing consensus among scholars that most MNCs pursue regional rather than global strategies (Banalieva and Dhanaraj, 2013; Rosa *et al.*, 2020).

Porter emphasized the potential benefits of a global strategy, whereas international business scholars have stressed the challenges and costs of pursuing such an approach. In addition, the seemingly uncontrollable external factors also influence firms' strategic options for their global businesses. For example, the rise of anti-globalization sentiment since late 2010s and the recent COVID-19 pandemic have further had a significant impact upon the geographic orientation of MNCs (Rosa *et al.*, 2020). These external factors increase the hidden vulnerabilities in the global supply chains, which propel firms to reconfigure their global activities in a more resilient and flexible manner. For example, various firms have tended to establish a number of regional factories rather than focus on extreme specialization in a single country.

8.2 3D Global Model

Moon (1994) critically reviews Porter's approach and presents his own enhanced framework. The starting point of Moon's criticism is the issue of configuration in Porter's approach (see Fig. 3). According to Porter's model, a purely global strategy requires geographical concentration and a high level of coordination. In terms of configuration, a more geographically concentrated configuration implies a more global strategy and geographic dispersion leads to a weak global strategy.

This logic is highly problematic if we apply it to the service industry. Consider two airline companies, American Airlines and Eastern Airways. As an international company, American Airlines has 635 aircrafts and serves 161 destinations for which it has to coordinate various activities in geographically diverse areas. Eastern Airways, on

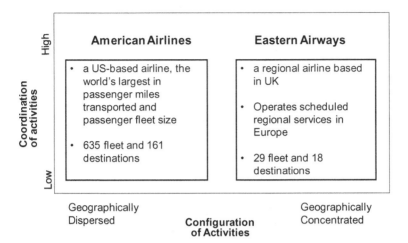

Fig. 4. American Air and Eastern Air according to Porter's framework.

the contrary, is a regional airline based in the UK with 29 aircrafts and serves only 18 destinations. As such, it has a high level of coordination along very limited geographic locations. In terms of Porter's framework, these two firms can be depicted as in Fig. 4.

Clearly, there is something wrong with Fig. 4 as American is depicted as less global when compared to Eastern. Figure 4 would look more appropriate if "Geographically Concentrated" and "Geographically Dispersed" are switched. This begs the following question: "Why did Porter make such a mistake?" The first reason is Porter's overemphasis on economies of scales. As he argued, global industries have increased scale benefits, mostly due to homogenization of demand, which means that concentrating production activity in one location is more advantageous. Yet, with technological innovation and flexible manufacturing processes, firms can now benefit more from coordinating their dispersed production activities.

The second reason is that Porter's approach is too specific as it focuses on the experiences of Japanese automakers during the 1970s. After their success with the so-called "purely global strategy," these companies are now moving toward dispersing their activities over many different countries. Therefore, one can see that Porter's framework may be useful for analyzing a specific global strategy at a specific time, but does not truly capture the evolving nature of global industries.

A New Framework of Global Strategy

Given the issues mentioned before regarding Porter's approach, Moon proposes a new framework that separates the upstream and downstream activities. There are two different paths toward a purely global strategy and this can be divided into production-seeking global strategy and market-seeking global strategy (see Fig. 5).

Note that the horizontal axes have been replaced with "number of countries" and the vertical axes with "production coordination" and "marketing coordination." By separating the marketing side and production side, this framework gives a more precise picture for understanding the exact path of globalization for these different firms. Furthermore, by choosing the number of countries, instead of configuration, we can now more specifically measure the degree of dispersion for a global firm.

Here, one can see that the two automakers, GM and Toyota, have taken on very different paths in terms of global strategy.

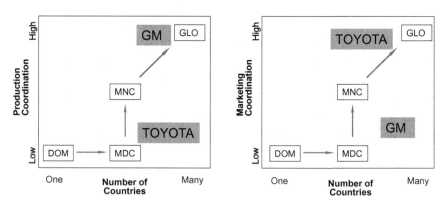

Fig. 5.   Production-seeking strategy vs. Market-seeking strategy.
Source: Moon (1994).

Instead of a singular framework in which GM is deemed less global than Toyota, one can see that they have simply taken different routes toward the same end. While GM dispersed its production activities in many countries, Toyota concentrated its production activities in relatively few locations. In terms of marketing, Toyota coordinates activities in many countries, while GM, although it has markets in many countries, maintains a relatively lower level of coordination. In essence, global strategy does not have to take one singular path. Toyota decided to focus more on penetrating global markets, while GM's strategy was more focused on using global resources efficiently.

Three-Dimensional Framework and Patterns of International Expansion

When we put all the above information together, a new 3D framework for understanding global strategy can be drawn (see Fig. 6).

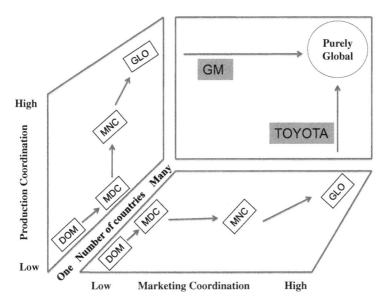

Fig. 6. Global expansion paths.
Source: Moon (1994).

With Fig. 6, we can now map the global expansionary path and the final destination. While the two auto giants took different expansionary paths, GM focused more on production coordination, while Toyota took on marketing coordination. Despite this, the final destination should be the same as a purely global strategy, which consists of both high production coordination and high marketing coordination. Thus, in order for GM to become a more global firm, it must increase its marketing coordination, while Toyota needs to expand its production coordination. The essential message here is that neither firm is more global than the other. The two firms are just *differently global* as they are each focused on different aspects in their journey to reach the final stage.

A general implication for global strategy can be derived from this framework. All firms start out as purely domestic (DOM) competitors and then move on to become multi-domestic (MDC) players which can be achieved by increasing either production or marketing in several countries. After a firm establishes itself in several countries, it will then seek to move on to become a multinational corporation (MNC) by coordinating the activities it performs in various countries. When this coordination becomes heightened and expansion reaches into many more countries, it then becomes a global corporation (GLO). However, at this stage, there is still an imbalance between the two activities depending on the strategy focus. In order to correct this imbalance and become purely global (purely GLO), the firm must now seek higher coordination and international expansion in the activity that it previously neglected. GM needs a higher level of marketing coordination, while Toyota needs more production coordination to attain a purely global strategy.

This framework is significant in that it provides a concrete and quantifiable framework to track a firm's globalization path. Furthermore, this analysis gives conceptual clarity to the often overused and convoluted distinction among global, multinational, and multi-domestic firms. One can now easily understand the degree and specific direction that firms take in order to take advantage of globalization.

Analysis

The previous section provides an enhanced analytical framework for understanding the complex and often misunderstood concept of globalization. While many indices of globalization and transnationality have been available, they have always been biased in one way or another (Nielsen and Nielsen, 2013; Qian *et al.*, 2008, Marshall *et al.*, 2020). Hence, the new 3D framework presented here provides an opportunity to analyze globalization in an easy yet comprehensive manner.

At the same time, this 3D framework can be extended. An important point that readers should recognize is the fact that the number of countries is used as an indicator in this case. While this is clearly an enhancement from Porter's framework, a technical problem still remains. For example, if firm A has two production facilities located in China and two located in the US, while firm B has one production facility each in Belgium, Finland, the Netherlands, and Sweden, firm B can be considered to be more global than firm A. However, when one considers the physical distance, the story becomes quite different as China and the US are quite far away while those four European countries are very much clustered around each other. This could potentially be an area of further study to adjust the 3D framework according to physical distance.

8.3 DDC Model

Moon and Kim (2008) further advance the previous model introduced by Moon (1994) and provide a rigorous quantitative methodology that can be readily applied to analyze the degree of globalization of multiple firms in an industry.

The two authors start off by criticizing the various existing frameworks. First, the integration and responsiveness framework by Prahalad and Doz is flawed (at least in its original format) because it fails to provide a comprehensive framework which encompasses both production and marketing. Next, Porter's configuration and coordination suffers from a similar bias since it is only suitable to analyze the manufacturing industry. When the service industry is examined through this lens, the framework clearly loses its explanatory power (Refer to Fig. 4).

As this analysis shows, there are several problems with the prior frameworks as they are either flawed or biased toward one side (see Table 2). Therefore, what is needed is a comprehensive framework that encompasses production, marketing, and the number of countries in which both these activities are coordinated. With such a theoretical foundation, one can determine a more precise degree and path of a firm's globalization.

Functional Division

Porter (1986) is the first scholar to bring the globalization analysis down to the functional level through the value chain, which is the right place to start. However, he failed to consider that different firms configure and coordinate their activities in a wide variety of patterns. Unlike Porter's thoughts, there are various paths available in terms of dispersing a firm's value chain activities. Therefore, in order to map the complex and diverse nature of a firm's globalization path, a different framework is needed which focuses on the functional division of the value chain, not the firm itself.

Different Paths of Functional Activities in Global Expansion

Then, how do we map the globalization strategy of a variety of firms that take different paths from each other? Furthermore, if firms disperse their value activities differently from each other, how can we map this in a comprehensive framework? The key to the answer is to first clarify the terms, multi-domestic and global. While many scholars have discussed these two concepts, most have been biased toward one or the other and thus failed to take a balanced view.

What clearly emerges from synthesizing the various viewpoints is a functional division. Firms having a core competence in the production functions tend to take a more *global strategy*, while firms

Table 2. Comprehensive comparison of existing models and a new model.

	Configuration–coordination model	Integration-responsiveness model	Extended model		DDC model
	Porter (1986)	Prahalad and Doz (1987)	Harzing (2000)	Moon (1994)	
Diversification					
P	Configuration	•	•	Number of countries	Production diversification
M	•	Responsiveness	Responsiveness	Number of countries	Marketing diversification
D¹	•	•	•	•	o
Coordination					
P	•	Integration	Interdependence	Production coordination	Production coordination
M	Coordination	•	•	Marketing coordination	Marketing coordination
D²	•	•	•	o	o
Functional division	•	•	•	•	o

Note: P, production; M, marketing; D¹, division of the production number of countries and the marketing number of countries; D², division of the production coordination and the marketing coordination; •, missing; o, included.

Source: Moon and Kim (2008).

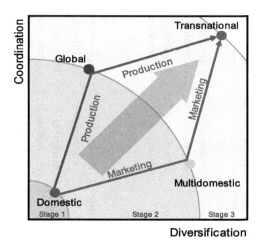

Fig. 7.   DDC model.
Source: Moon and Kim (2008).

having advantages in marketing activities would take a more *multi-domestic strategy*. Now that the functional divisions and terminologies are clarified, we can proceed to look at the Dynamic Diversification Coordination (DDC) model, which shows the firm's globalization path according to the functional division (Fig. 7).

What we can see from this model is a two-way path to becoming a transnational corporation: global and multi-domestic. Firms with a production focus will take the global path, while firms orientated toward a marketing focus will take the multi-domestic path. Both activities require coordination and diversification, but production will lean more toward coordination, while marketing will lean more toward diversification, at least in the first two stages. However, in the final stage, both production and marketing will be widely diversified and highly coordinated to take full advantage of a global strategy.

Empirical Analysis

While this section will not provide a full presentation of the empirical analysis based on the DDC model, it is still important to note the two hypotheses proven.

- *Hypothesis 1a* — There is a division of functions in the process of global expansion.

- *Hypothesis 1b* — Firms take a global strategy for the production function, while they implement a multi-domestic strategy for the marketing function.

By verifying the above two hypotheses, one can gain a better understanding of a firm's globalization path. This approach has contributed to the existing literature in two major ways. First, it shifted the unit of analysis down to the functional level and therefore added analytical rigor to the field. Next, the DDC framework showed a more specific methodology to quantify and map the globalization path of various firms. Instead of fixing the analysis on one side or the other, this new framework can account for the wide array of firms that exist within the same global industry.[1]

Analysis

What we have seen is a clear progression and improvement from model to model, with each improving and correcting the previous one's flaws and imperfections. So, have we reached the ultimate power of explanation with the most updated model? Those are questions that can only be answered with the repeated application of the model to a variety of firms and industries. While the concepts of production and marketing do indeed cover most, if not all, of a firm's functions, the successful application of the model to a multitude of industry types has yet to be conducted. While all the above analytical models generally classified the primary value chain activities into two categories of production and marketing type, the supporting activities, technology development in particular, may have different patterns of internationalization. Therefore, the development and improvement of Porter's original work remains largely theoretical.

---

[1] For more discussion and empirical tests, see Moon and Kim (2008).

In addition, should we infer that all firms have the goal or dream to reach the transnational stage? If firms are to halt their progress on the DDC model, should we assume that they have failed? Can they then be deemed as unsuccessful ventures? It is possible to say that the uncertainty from the anti-globalization mood may have affected the pattern of firms' internationalization. For example, the cover story published by *The Economist* (January 24, 2019) entitled "The steam has gone out of globalisation" stressed that "slowbalisation will lead to deeper links within regional blocs. Supply chains in North America, Europe and Asia are sourcing more from closer to home."

Such a changing pattern shows implicitly that firms may seek to halt their path toward a higher degree of globalization due to the changing global environment. Hence, although the DDC model is a useful tool for the analysis of a firm's progression, it should be used with mild caution when analyzing the different positions among firms in different industries.

Case Study 1: Hyundai Motors[2]

The Hyundai Motor Company is a division of the Hyundai-Kia Automotive Group and is South Korea's largest, and the world's fifth largest, automaker in terms of units sold per year.[3] Despite its vast size, it has not always played a significant role on the global stage in terms of automobile development and manufacturing. During its humble beginnings, the firm was forced to rely on licensed technology (mostly from Japan) and was largely considered internationally as a peripheral, low-cost manufacturer. However, over time, the company has built up its strength and has recently become the world's fifth largest automaker. We can apply the models explained in this chapter to analyze the long-term evolution of the firm's development

---

[2]Some information of this case is abstracted from the Hyundai Motors official website (www.hyundai-motor.com), Kim and Moon (2006), and Moon (2016, 2018).

[3]https://www.forbes.com/sites/donaldkirk/2020/04/03/hyundai-motor-group-faces-turbulent-times-as-coronavirus-drags-down-sales/#69117ef45ae5.

path. In this respect, we will begin with Porter's "configuration and coordination" model; next, we utilize Moon's extension of Porter's model, and then finish with the DDC model.

Before we formally analyze Hyundai Motor Company's global strategy, we need to explain a little background information on its history. The firm was established in 1967, and in 1968 it produced two models for the South Korean market, the Cortina and the Granada using the Ford brand. In 1975, the firm produced its first Hyundai self-branded car for the Korean market which was known as the Pony. At this point, the firm produced and sold its automobiles only in the domestic market, but hired foreign expertise to improve the quality and design of its cars (Italian firms for design; Japanese engineers for the engines; and British experts for R&D).

In 1976, Hyundai began to export its cars to Ecuador and the Benelux countries, and in 1986 the firm finally entered the US market. Following this endeavor, it then opened a short-lived production plant in Canada and set up a design center in the US in 1990. Despite the initial failure in expanding production overseas, Hyundai opened another production plant in India in 1996 and then went on to establish production plants in the US as well as R&D centers in Germany and the US. Following these initial successes, Hyundai Motor Company has spread its operations out across the world for production, R&D, and sales (see Table 3).

Let us analyze the firm's growth paths and patterns. We will begin with Porter's configuration and coordination model which is shown in Fig. 8 in a basic fashion. Using this framework, we can map Hyundai's development over the course of its history (see Fig. 9).

According to Porter's C-C model, Hyundai would have its starting point in the bottom right-hand corner as the firm began as a purely domestic automaker. Therefore, its configuration of activities was concentrated and coordination of its activities was quite low. However, over time, although Hyundai remained geographically concentrated in only South Korea, it began to widen its corporate outreach through exports and thus began to coordinate a wider array of activities worldwide.

Fast forward to recent years and we can see a sprawling global conglomerate with a strong outreach and brand name. Hyundai

Table 3.   Hyundai motors' assets worldwide.

Region	Significant assets	Country
America	Manufacturing plants	US, Brazil
	R&D centers	US
	Sales offices/Regional headquarters/branch offices	US, Canada, Mexico, Brazil, Colombia
Europe	Manufacturing plants	Russia, Czech Republic, Turkey
	R&D centers	Deutschland
	Sales offices/Regional headquarters/branch offices	Netherlands, Norway, Deutschland, Russia, Spain, UK, Italy, Czech Republic, Turkey, Poland, France
Asia and Pacific	Manufacturing plants	Korea, India, China
	R&D centers	Korea, India, Japan, China
	Sales offices/Regional headquarters/branch offices	India, Japan, China, Australia, Malaysia, Indonesia, Cambodia

Source: https://www.hyundaimotorgroup.com/About-Us/Group-Performance.hub.

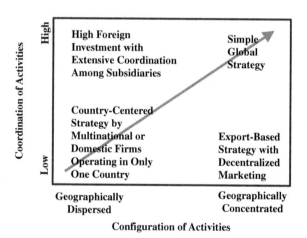

Fig. 8.   Configuration and coordination model.
Source: Porter (1986, p. 28).

Motors has a geographically dispersed configuration of activities comprised of regional headquarters, regional offices, production plants, and R&D facilities in different countries across a number of regions.

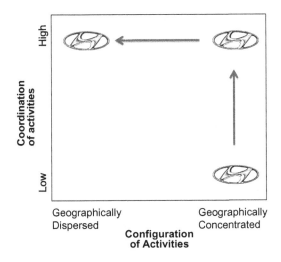

Fig. 9. Hyundai motor's historical development.

The firm also has a high level of coordination among its activities with a large number of subsidiaries scattered across the globe, which maintain a high level of interaction with the central headquarters in Korea. Thus, according to Porter and as represented in Fig. 9, Hyundai managed to obtain global positioning (as indicated by the top right-hand corner) in the middle of its development phase and has since moved away from that position to the status of a less globalized firm (as indicated by the top left-hand corner). In order to clarify this position, let us now look at Moon's extension to Porter's model.

As highlighted previously, Moon argues that Porter made a fundamental error in labeling his axes in the configuration and coordination model, which can be confirmed by the progression of Hyundai Motors. Although it has been traditionally argued that Hyundai has focused more on a production-seeking global strategy, using Moon's altered framework, it can be argued that the firm has in fact focused more on a market-seeking global strategy. This can be confirmed when looking at the number of production facilities Hyundai holds compared to the number and dispersion of regional HQs, regional offices, and overseas subsidiaries. Figures 10 and 11 are graphical illustrations of both Hyundai's production-seeking global strategy and its market-seeking global strategy, respectively.

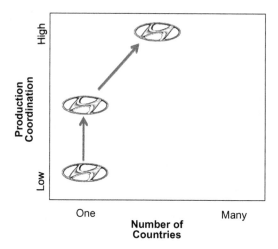

Fig. 10.   Hyundai motor's production-seeking global strategy.

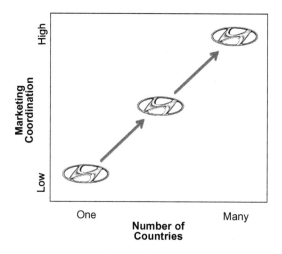

Fig. 11.   Hyundai motor's market-seeking global strategy.

When we compare Fig. 11 with Fig. 6, we can see that in terms of a production-seeking global strategy, Hyundai has not yet reached the global stage and can be more accurately described as a multinational with a potential to become a global firm. However, in terms of a market-seeking global strategy, Hyundai is indeed a global firm and has followed a path of shifting from a domestic firm to a multinational

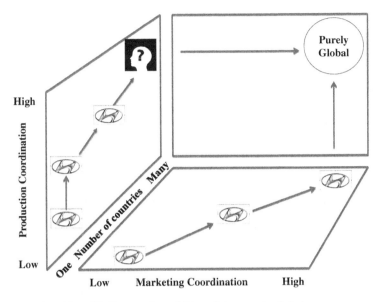

Fig. 12. 3D Perspective of Hyundai motor's global strategy.

firm to the penultimate global firm status. This can be depicted more succinctly from the 3D perspective as shown in Fig. 12. Thus, using this extension of Porter's model, we can see that in terms of production, Hyundai has yet to move into a global position while it has achieved a global status from a marketing perspective. Once the firm moves into a global stance in production, Hyundai will then have to deal with how to amalgamate the production and marketing aspects of its operation in order to transform it into a purely global firm.

Moon and Kim (2008) further extended the 3D model to the DDC type as explained in Section 8.3. An empirical analysis through the DDC model provides us with a more accurate analysis of Hyundai's global strategy. Table 4 shows that the DDC model is the most effective model in fully utilizing the variables of production, marketing, diversification and coordination, compared with other models which utilize the variables only partially. Finally, Fig. 13 illustrates the empirical data for the DDC model to show the relative position of the major automakers.[4]

---

[4]For full empirical result, see *Ibid.*

Table 4.   Variables for measuring global expansion.

	C-C model (Porter, 1986)	I-R model (Prahalad and Doz, 1987)	WIR (UNCTAD, 1995, 2002)		Extended model		
			TNI	NSI	Moon (1994)	Harzing (2000)	Contractor et al. (2003)
Production	•	Integration	FATA FETE	•	Production coordination	Interdependence	FETE
Marketing	Coordination	•	FSTS	•	Marketing coordination	•	FSTS
Diversification	Configuration	Responsiveness	•	Number of countries	Number of countries	Responsiveness	FOTO
Coordination	o	o	•	•	o	•	•

Notes: FATA, foreign assets as a percentage of total assets; FSTS, foreign sales as a percentage of total sales; FETE, number of foreign employees to total number of employees; FOTO, number of foreign offices to total number of offices; TNI, Transnationality Index; NSI, Network Spread Index; WIR, World Investment Report; •, missing; o, included.
Source: Extracted from Kim and Moon (2006).

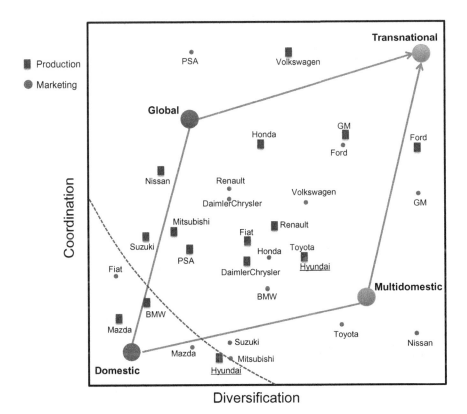

Fig. 13. Integrated scatter diagram.
Source: Extracted from Kim and Moon (2006).

The results show that Hyundai Motors does indeed, as suspected, have a lower level of transnationality from a production aspect than from a marketing aspect. Thus, we can conclude that the firm does need to shift its focus toward a more global level of production. Once Hyundai reaches such a level of marketing and production functions together, its focus will be the integration of the two in order to achieve a purely global or transnational business strategy.

Following Toyota's mass recalls in 2010, Hyundai has begun to place more effort into quality control, while at the same time it has been reluctant to expand its production capacity, although most of its global plants have already reached full capacity. The *Financial Times* (2013) commented that Hyundai seems to be too cautious to further expand globally. Because of such constrained production situation, some regions (e.g., the UK) were even unable to receive a sufficient amount of vehicles, which in turn affected Hyundai's global sales performance. As a result, the *Wall Street Journal* (2015) reported that Hyundai showed a fifth consecutive decline in its net quarterly profits since 2014. The above episode shows that the careful and precise evaluation on both internal capability and external environment is very important for the sustainable growth in firms' global expansion.

Discussion Questions

1. In his CC model, Porter classified the top right-hand corner as being a global strategy. How would you classify the other three corners using Porter's definitions in Fig. 2?

2. Porter made an error in classifying the axes in his CC model. What other weaknesses did you note? What are then the strengths of the model? Discuss.

3. Moon divides Porter's model into two sections: production and marketing. Is this the only way to divide the firm's strategies? Can you think of a third path that a firm might follow?

4. Do you agree with Moon that production and marketing strategies must be coordinated before being able to become a truly global firm? If not, why?

5. To what extent do all firms want or need to be transnational?

6. In line with the DDC model, what specific suggestions can you provide for Hyundai Motors? Discuss.

7. Do you think regionalization can be considered as being less globalized? If not, can you give a counterexample?

CHAPTER 9

The Grand Debate Over Standardization Strategy

Chapter Guideline

We now turn to the debate between "standardization" and "differentiation." Globalization would seem to have two paradoxical effects as firms increasingly standardize to meet homogenous tastes while also differentiating to meet the individual needs of consumers in different locations. So, what is the answer? The simple answer would be to say "it depends," but this response, although logical, does not provide us with a useful insight. Furthermore, this kind of simplification leaves us little room to explore the pros and cons of this exciting debate. This chapter will look at some prominent scholars who have sought to provide us with answers on this topic.

Summary of Previous Models

So far, we have examined the various concepts of business strategy and what it means to elevate these concepts to a global level. In the previous chapter, we looked at a few analytical frameworks that help comprehensively assess the degree of internationalization among firms. Now, we turn our eyes to the nature of the phenomenon itself and try to answer the classic question of "whether to standardize or differentiate when doing businesses abroad." With this chapter, we will gain a firm understanding of this polemic debate and use it as a platform to add another piece to the puzzle.

9.1 The Grand Thesis: *The World is Flat*

Thomas Friedman's *The World is Flat* (2005) became an instant best-seller and earned critical acclaim as well as sharp criticism. The core message of the book is that globalization has leveled the competitive playing field between developed and developing economies. He attributes this trend mainly to various technological advances in computer and information technology, which grant anyone with a laptop and internet connection access to technology and information. In 2007, he published *The World Is Flat 3.0* by adding new materials to keep up with the evolving digital age. He described the transformed global landscape as "Globalization 3.0" in which individuals from the periphery (emerging economies) are now a *tour de force* in the globalization story. Friedman metaphorically described this leveled playing field as a "flat world." Despite being heralded as a revolutionary concept, Friedman was not the first one to come up with this term. A flat world was prophesied by the eminent business and economics scholar Theodore Levitt in his article of "The Globalization of Markets" published in 1983. Levitt has written numerous articles that have changed the manner of people's thinking about important matters, and this article is the most noteworthy (Tedlow and Abdelal, 2004).

Living in the Republic of Technology

The starting point of Levitt's article is the dissemination of technology that has led to the inclusion of previously untapped areas of the global economic system. Through the spread of new technology, the world is integrating into singularity and this has led to the emergence of a homogenous market base at an unprecedented scale. Thus, his subtitle "Republic of Technology" aptly represents this global trend in which the world surges toward singularity since technology is the main driving force.

In order to articulate his point further, Levitt distinguishes the two terms: global corporation and multinational corporation. A multinational corporation operates in many different countries but differentiates its strategies according to the market in which it operates, while a global corporation has a multinational outreach but provides all markets with a standardized product. Levitt's conclusion is that the world is increasingly gravitating toward being in favor of the global corporation.

Vindication of the Model T

One may counter Levitt and assert that national dissimilarities are indeed still very real and that many firms differentiate according to markets and reap great success. Levitt does not deny this and mentions that there are several strategies that individual firms can adopt in order to gain global commercial success. However, the aggregate trend is that the world is moving toward increased standardization and homogenized taste. Consider Ford's Model T, the first mass produced automobile. The Model T demonstrates that despite individual differences and preferences, ultimately, customer's needs boil down to high-quality goods at a low cost.

Expanding this logic to the global scale, we can see why so many Japanese automobile companies (with highly standardized products) were able to achieve massive success in the global market. Of course, Japanese automobile companies lost some market position because they did not differentiate according to local markets. Still, overall, the formula for success enjoyed by these Japanese companies comes down to two simple variables, low cost and high quality. Thus, a company that can take full advantage of this kind of approach is one that is an expert in one great truth (a global company) rather than one that knows about many different aspects (a multinational company). Levitt's famous analogy, the fox and the hedgehog, aptly portrays this relationship in which a fox, who knows a lot about many things, represents a multinational, while a hedgehog, who knows everything about one great thing, represents the global company.

The Remaining Differences and Accepting the Inevitable

According to Levitt, the remaining national differences are mainly a reflection of people's misguided beliefs. Multinationals erroneously assume that they must differentiate in order to succeed, while customers also believe that their tastes are fixed. But, when customers are presented with high-quality goods at a low cost, the national barrier and remaining differences can actually be nullified. The only problem is that both marketers and customers alike do not understand this fact. In this regard, the implication is that truly successful firms are those that can actually go beyond this mode of thought and boldly pursue standardization and move on to become global companies. Despite all the differences and seemingly insurmountable barriers, the overarching common denominator is that consumers desire low-cost and high-quality goods and standardization is the key to providing these timeless values.

The Earth is Flat

Now made even more famous by Thomas Friedman, the notion that the earth is flat succinctly portrays Levitt's message. Friedman (2020) said over the last 15 years, the world has been technologically shifting from a connected to an increasingly hyperconnected global economy. Hence, globalization has become faster, deeper, cheaper, and tighter than ever before. However, the world is still round and many national differences persist and will continue to exist in the future. Therefore, the key is to treat the world as flat and focus on creating a consumer base that can be preserved. Rather than assuming a static view of customer preference, truly successful companies will actually mold their customers into liking them. Furthermore, the current technological and institutional developments are becoming increasingly favorable to this trend. Developments such as rapid dissemination of IT technology, drastic improvements in transportation in terms of both technology and cost, reduced trade barriers through the World Trade Organization (WTO), and numerous Regional Trade Agreements (RTAs) all support the general gravitation toward a flatter world.

Analysis

It is quite interesting to look back at Levitt's (1983) article a few decades after it was written. The question really boils down to the following: "Is the world becoming more similar or different?" Differences are still prevalent and a large portion of the world's population is still left out of the global economic system. As we will see in the following sections, many scholars have criticized Levitt from various perspectives. In this sense, his prophecy may not have been entirely accurate. However, what is undeniable is the general trend, the direction that the forces of globalization are steering this world toward. Let us go back to Saffo's S-Curve that we discussed in Chapter 6 and illustrate Levitt's prophetic analysis in this analytical framework (see Fig. 1).

According to Saffo (2007), change comes in an S-curve pattern in which it starts slowly and incrementally and then suddenly explodes. Figure 1 maps a hypothetical globalization S-curve. The 1940s and 1950s saw the end of World War II and the establishment of the Breton Woods system. From the 1960s to the 1980s, the world slowly headed toward economic integration through multilateral frameworks such as the General Agreements on Tariff and Trade (GATT).

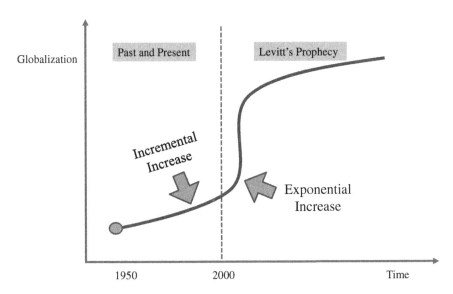

Fig. 1. Levitt's prophecy in Saffo's S-curve.

Later, the 1990s were marked by the sudden disintegration of the Soviet Union and former communist economies.

The 2000s were characterized by increased regional and bilateral trade agreements as well as the increasing influence of the World Trade Organization. Moreover, a larger number of developing countries have increased their participation in the global economy via global value chains (GVCs). For this, governments around the world have played a particularly important role as investors or promoters for global integration. *The Economist* (2019) suggested that the period of 1990–2010 was the golden age of globalization, commenting that "commerce soared as the cost of shifting goods in ships and planes fell, phone calls got cheaper, tariffs were cut and the financial system liberalized." Throughout this decade, it seemed that globally integrated firms were destined to become the future model (*Wall Street Journal*, 2020). In fact, globalization has sometimes been described as an irreversible process (Verbeke *et al.*, 2018). Since the late 2010s though, a variety of "de-globalization" forces, such as rising nationalism, trade wars, reshoring or nearshoring, and the COVID-19 pandemic, have gained some momentum around the world. So, what is the likely impact of these factors on globalization in the future?

As mentioned in Chapter 6, an effective forecaster must predict the inflection point before it actually hits, and Levitt's 1983 article can be understood as he forecast the inflection point in Fig. 1. Whether or not the world economic system will hit this inflection point between "incremental increase" and "exponential increase" is one of the most central questions in many academic disciplines, including international business.

Regardless of whether or not Levitt's prophecy materializes in the future, many scholars have been in line with Levitt's prophetic message that the world is heading toward a flatter and homogenized platform. Porter (1986) and Prahalad and Doz (1987), for example, characterized global industries as those having low responsiveness and high integration. For example, in a global industry, a firm's competitive position in one country is significantly affected by its position in other countries. Commercial aircrafts, semiconductors, automobiles, and smartphones are appropriate examples under this category.

Accordingly, a firm must integrate its activities on a worldwide basis to capture the linkages among countries that can then maximize scale benefits and cost advantages.

Morrison (1990) refined this logic and delved deeper into the specifics. He concluded that global industries are those that have intense levels of international competition, which leads to the marketing of standardized products worldwide. Therefore, industry competitors usually have a presence in all key international markets and promote high levels of international trade. Isenberg (2008), in his analysis of start-up companies, asserted that successful entrepreneurs must not be overwhelmed by the prevailing national differences. He urged that only those who boldly ride the wave of globalization through a global strategy can achieve a sustainable competitive advantage. As can be seen from this extensive list of follow-ups, many scholars do believe (of course to varying degrees) that the world is heading in the direction that Levitt envisioned in his 1983 article. More recently, Verbeke *et al.* (2018) suggested that the world needs more — not less — globalization, to achieve the net efficiency benefits of novel resource combination processes across multiple host environments for the long-term sustainable growth of firms.

9.2 Antithesis: The World is Spiky

Now, we will take a look at the antithesis to Levitt's hypothesis: the "differentiation" story. Douglas and Wind (1987) assert that global standardization is merely one of a number of strategies that may be successful in international markets. Rather than viewing globalization as a unilateral process in which standardization overrides all strategies, Douglas and Wind paint a much more complex and diverse picture where both standardization and differentiation become more pronounced due to globalization. As the two scholars are both marketing specialists, this article is heavily focused on that aspect among firms. The authors contend that increasing global integration has taken place and that a global perspective in a marketing strategy is highly crucial. Yet, this does not mean that a marketing strategy must follow a singular formula of standardization. In fact, global products and brands are appropriate for only certain market segments, while others need a more differentiated approach.

The Big Debate: Global Standardization vs. Differentiation

The biggest debate in international marketing strategy has been between implementing a uniform worldwide strategy and adapting to specific local market conditions. Proponents of standardization argue that implementing a uniform strategy creates international synergies, maximizing a firm's global competitive advantage. Others, however, have argued that a uniform global strategy could lead to the crucial mistake of neglecting some important market segments. Douglas and Wind conclude that uniform standardization is not only dangerous for a firm's competitive advantage but also impossible at times because of external barriers such as government regulations. In order to articulate this argument further, the three underlying assumptions of Levitt's global standardization philosophy are refuted one by one:

- *Homogenization of the World Wants* — As Ohmae (1989) aptly put it, "Californization of needs" integrates the global population into a single set of demands. To what extent is this true? Not so much, according to Douglas and Wind as they point out that there is a lack of empirical evidence to support this claim. Moreover, many companies actually adopt unique, tailored approaches to individual markets. The Coca-Cola Company is the epitome of a global company and actually markets many products that are customized to local tastes such as the sports drink Aquarius in Japan. Another reason why this assumption is flawed is because of the growing body of evidence which indicates significant differences within countries. In other words, what Levitt and other standardization proponents argue for homogenization of needs is in fact limited to a very specific population segment in multiple countries. In every country, there are certain pockets of global consumers, but a majority of them are out of this standardization story.

- *Universal Preference for Low Price at Acceptable Quality* — Can we view low price and high quality as a universal value which can override all other differentiators? Douglas and Wind disagree based on three counterarguments. First, low price positioning is a vulnerable strategy that is unsustainable in the long run. New technological innovations, for example, can quickly nullify such an advantage. Second, there is a severe lack of evidence to support the universal preference theory. Price-sensitive segments have existed universally, but there is no clear indication that it is on the rise due to increased globalization. Finally, standardized low-price products in one country can mean a high price in another one. For example, a US$10 pair of shoes would be considered as a good deal in the US, but the same standard-priced product would be regarded as very expensive in Ghana. Therefore, without differentiation, standardized low-price products can fail to tap into many global segments.

- *Economies of Scale of Production and Marketing* — Integration of firm activities can lead to significant economies of scale as firms can reduce the average production cost per unit. This logic, though, neglects three factors. First, flexible factory automation allows economies of scale to be achieved at much lower levels of output. Second, cost of production is not a major component of total cost, for example, marketing cost can become even more substantial than production cost. Last, marketing strategy should be based on various components such as brand names and advertising.

Requisite Conditions for Global Standardization

The point of Douglas and Wind is not that standardization is a completely invalid strategy, but that it can only be successful under certain exogenous conditions as outlined in the following list:

- *Existence of Global Market Segments* — Simply put, without a demand for standardized goods, the supply cannot be sustained. In industrial markets, where differentiation of goods is rather insignificant (e.g., cement), standardization would be a good choice. However, industries that are highly sensitive to local tastes (e.g., food) need to be differentiated. A global segment for consumption is a prerequisite for global standardization.

- *Synergies Associated with Global Standardization* — Standardizing a product leads to numerous synergistic benefits because action in one country can enhance the performance in another. For example, if a company develops a detergent suitable for the Japanese market, then it will probably boost the product's success in similar countries such as Korea. This kind of synergistic benefits must exist if the global standardization is to be a viable choice.

- *Availability of an International Communication and Distribution Infrastructure* — Without a convenient worldwide distribution system and communications network, standardization cannot succeed. Technological innovations in both of these areas have made global standardization a more feasible choice, but there are still significant barriers.

Operational Constraints to Effective Implementation of a Standardization Strategy

Achieving globalization is not difficult but does come at a cost. The following section outlines the external and internal constraints pointed out by Douglas and Wind.

- *External Constraints* — Four external constraints inhibit firms from pursuing a global strategy. First, government policies and trade restrictions (tariffs and quotas) severely limit a firm's ability to standardize globally. For example, high tariffs force firms to differentiate their pricing, which makes uniform pricing an impossible option. Second, marketing infrastructure, such as available media outlets, may differ from country to country. A standardized marketing approach, therefore, becomes undesirable. Third, differences in availability and cost of resources may force a firm to change its product design or component. For example, a global paper manufacturer must modify or replace its wood fiber content when producing in countries where timber is scarce. Last, competition structures are also different among countries. In certain countries, lower-end products are at the heart of competition, while in others higher-end ones are more important. In this respect, adopting a singular competitive strategy will ultimately lead to failure.

- *Internal Constraints* — There are two noticeable constraints for a global strategy. First, if a firm had no prior global operation whatsoever, it can adopt a standardized approach without much internal difficulties. However, for most firms, this is not the case as they already have preexisting global operations which need to be restructured to fit a standardized strategy. Dislocating the firm's previous global commitment such as joint ventures or partnerships requires significant costs, which could have a severe adverse effect on the firm. Second, local management motivation and attitudes could pose another problem as standardization requires centralized planning and diminishing the authority of previously autonomous entities within the firm. This has a very high potential for internal conflict that can lead to significant losses for a firm.

A Framework for Classifying Global Strategy Options

Douglas and Wind conclude that global standardization is only feasible when certain conditions (both internal and external) are met. Rather than viewing global standardization as the optimum strategic choice, Douglas and Wind emphasize that it is one out of many choices available. Therefore, rather than viewing the choice as either standardization or differentiation, the appropriate way to look at it is a mixture between the two extremes. Figure 2 illustrates the possible strategic mixes available for a company.

As Fig. 2 illustrates, no firm can actually pursue a purely differentiated or standardized strategy. Depending on the category, location, and industry, firms will take various mixes of the two elements to optimize their operation.

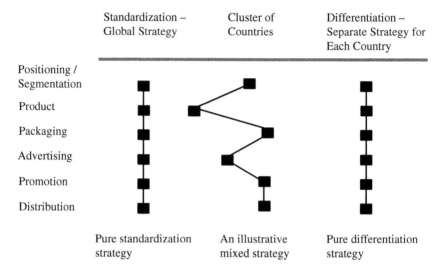

Fig. 2. The standardization–differentiation continuum.
Source: Douglas and Wind (1987).

The core message of Douglas and Wind is that standardization is not a silver bullet in the world of globalization, but a viable option only under very specific circumstances. Furthermore, in most cases, the optimal strategy requires an appropriate mixture of both extremes because national dissimilarities in many perspectives pervade in reality. Therefore, the firms are destined to run into major obstacles if they devise and implement their strategies without considering the vast discrepancy between the standardization theory and reality.

Analysis

Douglas and Wind convincingly counter Levitt's argument and many scholars have followed this antithesis from various angles and perspectives. Rugman and Verbeke (2004), for example, asserted that very few multinational enterprises have the ability to sell standardized products and services around the world, thereby refuting the type of globalization originally advocated by Levitt. After an empirical analysis of the largest 500 international firms in the world, the two authors confirmed that most firms are not "global,"[1] but are rather regional companies with the majority of their presence in the triad (Europe, Japan, and North America) region.

Similarly, Garvinn and Levesque (2008) urged that a multiunit enterprise, which is characterized by a geographically dispersed organization with a high level of autonomy, is the norm among the top 500 companies. Furthermore, Ghemawat and Hout (2008) insisted that a growing number of firms from emerging economies are building their global positions through a focused and vertical business. These firms spot opportunities to pull apart and reconfigure existing value chains in order to deploy capital more efficiently. An even stronger assertion came from Greenwald and Kahn (2005) as they argue that global consumer demand is still highly segregated since separate local environments are still characterized, in both obvious and subtle ways, by contrasting tastes, a number of government rules, various business practices, and different cultural norms. Thus, the authors proclaim that all strategies are essentially local.

It is true that in some cases differences have become even more pronounced and many firms are adopting ever more eclectic strategies. However, one must pause to think whether Douglas and Wind's article is truly an antithesis to Levitt. While the authors' intention may have been something close to it, in retrospect it seems that standardization and differentiation are actually different sides of the same coin. What this means is that rather than viewing standardization or differentiation as an end point, it would be more appropriate to view these two concepts as different paths to reach a certain final point. Recall and Kim's Dynamic Diversification Coordination model, which we discussed in the previous chapter (see Fig. 3).

Using Fig. 3, we can actually visualize Levitt's thesis being on the global path, while Douglas and Wind's thesis is on the multi-domestic path. The point is that the two apparently conflicting theories may

---

[1] Rugman and Verbeke (2004) defined "Global" as having sales of 20% or more in each of the three parts of the Triad, namely, North America (or NAFTA), the European Union, and Asia, but less than 50% in any one region of the Triad.

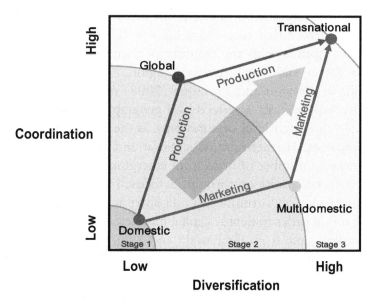

Fig. 3.   Moon and Kim's DDC model.

Source: Moon and Kim (2008).

simply just be describing different paths to the same final destination.

9.3 Another Antithesis: The World is Not Flat

Joining the criticism mentioned above, Professor Pankaj Ghemawat of Harvard Business School also disputes the idea that the future global economy will be fully globalized, integrated, and homogenized. Although the global economy has been increasingly integrated over the last few decades, it is still far from the theoretical extreme of total integration (Ghemawat, 2003). Ghemawat (2001, 2007) suggested that national markets may be distant along the four dimensions — cultural, administrative, geographic, and economic (CAGE). According to Ghemawat, Levitt's analysis does not help us understand the convergence in any of these distances.

- Cultural distance refers to the attributes of a society mainly by interactions among people, such as language, religion, ethnicity, values, and social norms.

- Administrative attributes include laws, policies, and institutions that are required or enforced by governments.

- Geographic distance involves the attributes of countries that affect cross-border economic activities mostly driven by natural phenomena, such as physical distance, time zones, and climate.

- Economic distance refers to differences that affect cross-border economic activities through dimensions such as the gap between the rich and poor, and other differences in costs and quality including natural, financial, human, and more advanced man-made resources (infrastructure, information, and knowledge).

Moreover, Ghemawat's (2007) noticeable article entitled "Why the World isn't Flat," presents an antithesis to Thomas Friedman's famous *The New York Times* article and subsequent book *The World Is Flat: A Brief History of the Twenty-first Century.* The core part of Ghemawat's argument is that globalization and standardization proponents are simply wrong and that they have overexaggerated the globalization myth. While many assume that the world is heading toward an integrated and connected world, the truth is that only a fraction of the global population is in this globalized world, while the overwhelming majority is still out of the loop.

The 10% Presumption

The fraction of those involved in the globalized world, according to Ghemawat, is only about 10% of the world's population. A large majority of the world is still not engaged in activities that fall under the category of "globalization." Representative globalization indicators such as immigration, investments, patents, and phone call revenues are all around the 10% mark. The only exception is trade, which is around 20%.

A Strong National Defense

The reason behind these surprisingly low numbers is the prevailing nationalist and protectionist sentiments which still define the world. Even Infosys, the crown jewel of the Indian IT industry and Friedman's favorite example, is not exempt from this paradigm. Yes, Infosys does serve many American clients halfway across the globe through a wired and connected world. However, this is not just because the boundaries are becoming nullified but also because a large part of Infosys investment is actually American capital. The national origin of the capital investment is one of the main reasons why Infosys caters to the US market. Expanding on this conjecture, Ghemawat further points out that most investments are intra-regional and largely domestic. The so-called "free flow of global capital" is an overblown myth which neglects the reality that even today an overwhelming majority of fixed capital is from domestic or regional sources.

Turning Back the Clock

Ghemawat does not deny that there has been some progress toward what globalization proponents call an integrated world. Yet, the proportion of this phenomenon has been severely overblown in most literature and this trend has the potential of being reversed. In times of economic crisis or large calamities, countries tend to turn to protectionist barriers. In other words, unlike globalization proponents who argue that worldwide integration is an inevitable and powerful force, Ghemawat points out that it is very fragile and has overwhelming potential to be dismantled.

More recently, Ghemawat (2018) suggested five predictions or SMART predictions that are likely to affect the long-term trend of globalization, which in turn requires firms to fundamentally change their global strategies:

- South by southeast: Despite some success stories in Latin America, Western Asia, emerging Europe, and Africa, the largest gains have been concentrated in East and South Asia. China and India alone account for more than 25% of global growth over the last decade.

- Modest trade growth: How fast trade actually grows relative to GDP is likely to depend on further progress in services trade. However, this requires us to do so with the regulatory environment as the principal barriers.

- Accelerated globalization along other dimensions: Other dimensions of globalization drive by people and particularly information flows have shown recent increase. Digitization has helped people connect more effectively across borders.

- Regionalization and multipolarity: It has become increasingly important to think of the global economy in terms of regional aggregation, as an individual country is less likely to be able to drive growth by itself. Hence, it is useful to investigate multipolarity at various levels of aggregation.

- Trading places? US–China rivalry: Despite the multipolar context, a key question remains on the relative strength of the two largest poles, the US and China. Although it still seems unlikely for China to take over the US, it is evident that there will be significant tensions between the two countries.

Analysis

Samuel Huntington, in his controversial book *The Clash of Civilizations and the Remaking of World Order* (1996) categorized the globalized elites as the "Davos Man." These figures, according to Huntington, are those few who believe in the pursuit of global mass consumption under the leadership of elite corporations, media moguls, and bankers. Furthermore, constituents of the Davos Man are the ones who follow the global standardization trend and are the core consumers and proponents of global standardization. Thus, this type of global culture is only a limited phenomenon shared by a small portion of the global population. Ghemawat's analysis is on a similar yet even more critical line as he even poses the possibility of this limited globalization to actually unwind. Therefore, what we accept as a given fact may not be so solid after all.

There are other possibilities in this regard. The so-called Davos Man may be powerful and wealthy enough to hold together the current level of global connectivity and perhaps even increase it. Through their influence and with governmental cooperation, it may be entirely possible to make globalization a truly international trend and, moreover, one that has a positive effect on all the lives it touches. Yet, Tedlow and Abdelal (2004) said politics is fundamentally unlike technology in terms of its influences on globalization. Derived from the study of history, it shows that governments chose openness before World War I, but they chose protectionism thereafter. Again, they have then chosen openness in the 1990s, but pursued nationalism in more recent years. At the same time, it should be noted that the technology involved such as the steam engine or atomic weaponry cannot be reversed once it has been invented (Tedlow and Abdelal, 2004). It may then be too idealistic to perceive the continuous engagement of government toward globalization. But, being somewhat idealistic may be what the world needs rather than focusing on the gloomier outlooks provided by Ghemawat and other such scholars. That is not to suggest that Gehmawat's theory should be entirely discounted, but we need to recall an old saying, "Always plan for the best, but prepare for the worst."

Case Study 1: Amore Goes to France[2]

When people think of South Korea's (Korea, hereinafter) economic strengths, they tend to consider shipbuilding, automobiles, steel, and information technology (IT) as the key sectors. However, there is one Korean company that has made significant strides in an industry that Western companies traditionally dominated: the cosmetics industry. Amore Pacific is Korea's leading high-end cosmetics brand which

---

[2]Some parts of this case study are extracted from the Amore Pacific Website (www.amorepacific.com), *The New York Times* (Not to Be Outdone — The New Urban Spa, August 11, 2005), the DHC Website (www.dhccare.com), https://retailinasia.com/in-markets/japan-korea/korea/south-korean-cosmetics-to-seduce-europe/, and http://www.koreatimes.co.kr/www/nation/2020/09/694_295463.html.

became immensely successful among the growing middle- to upper-class segment of Korean women. Amore Pacific's spectacular rise from being a humble, local niche player to a global cosmetic powerhouse is a success story and one that demonstrates the power of a carefully thought-out global standardization strategy.

The exponential rate of economic growth from the 1960s transformed the war-devastated Korea from one of the poorest nations in the world to a major global trading power. The Korean population's concern quickly gravitated from basic survival necessities to more advanced utilities such as aesthetic beauty. Amore developed its products using ingredients that have long been tried and tested by Korean women, who are considered to be very sophisticated consumers of cosmetic products. These ingredients are viewed as being completely natural and highly beneficial toward enhancing women's beauty; some notable products include green tea, Korean red ginseng, and bamboo. In terms of product range, Amore focused on using these three key ingredients in items such as anti-aging, cleansing, moisturizing as well as in the cosmetics lines. The results were very positive and Amore Pacific became a household name in Korea.

The firm's success did not stop in Korea. Amore's formula for success, high-quality cosmetic products with natural ingredients, had a strong appeal among other Asian consumers who had similar tastes. Amore's reputation began to spread in the region, and in particular it was popular in Japan, which is renowned for its sophisticated cosmetics industry. Before long, Amore Pacific products were competing with the likes of Shiseido and SK-II (a Proctor and Gamble brand) of Japan. Thus, products developed initially only for the Korean market could be applied in the exact same form throughout the Asian market, particularly Japan and then China. However, this may not seem unusual as it is common for regional markets to share similarities in tastes and therefore demands. The real test would come when launching Amore Pacific in Western markets such as Europe and the US.

Having achieved success in Asia, Amore Pacific has then sought to launch its products on the global stage. In this respect, Amore Pacific realized what other Asian cosmetics firms have not, that is, all women essentially pursue the same values when it comes to cosmetic products. They want effective anti-aging and cleansing properties using the most natural and effective ingredients. Thus, Amore Pacific was able to market its products, which were created in Korea for Koreans, to women in the US and even in Europe where the cosmetics market is known for being particularly sophisticated leading to difficulty in gaining a foothold. In fact, the company was even able to play up the "Asianness" of the products' ingredients in line with the trend that considered Asian products as rooted in ancient knowledge of natural ingredients. Elevating a previously local product to the regional and finally to the global level, Amore Pacific is now a formidable global force in the cosmetics industry.

When entering the European market, the head of Amore Pacific Europe stated that "the company's aim today is to widen its geographical presence beyond Asia" (Retailing Asia, 2018). He said the priority of Western brands is the effectiveness and quantity of active ingredients, which is different from Asian products that consider "the smell, the touch, and the pleasure that a cream brings" as all equally important. Despite the challenges, the company emphasized that there is a need for guidance for European consumers to make them willing to work Korean products into their routine. This thus implicitly shows that rather than taking consumers' preferences as a given, firms also have to persuade and transform the heterogenous markets into homogenous one.

There are some additional drivers internally and externally that can help Korean firms realize their goal. Internally, Korean cosmetics merge traditional Asian ingredients with ultra-high-tech components. Externally, the Korean Wave of pop culture has the potential to create enthusiasm among Europeans for Korean makeup products. Thus, in line with what Levitt has pointed out, as markets become more homogenized, the potential for massive growth, through the development of an appropriate standardized product, increases exponentially. Still, the case of Amore Pacific is a little counterintuitive. While Levitt focuses on low-cost and high-quality products being the most likely candidates for standardization, Amore Pacific's products cater to those interested in high cost and high quality. Therefore, Amore Pacific is not only a good example of product standardization but of the ability to homogenize a luxury product in the global arena.

In a similar vein, Japan has witnessed the rise of one of its skincare leaders, the Daigaku Honyaku Center (DHC), which was established in 1972. Similar to Amore Pacific, the company has built a strong reputation in Japan as a skincare company that utilizes natural benefits provided by a recognizable yet unsophisticated raw material. In contrast to Amore Pacific though, DHC started out using a key ingredient, which was more recognizable to the Western customers than to Asian ones — olives.

Intuitively, one could assume that Japanese consumers may have been reluctant to try olive-based products since it is not a familiar ingredient for Japanese consumers. Furthermore, Douglas and Wind would have us believe that access to Japanese consumers would be challenging given the discrepancy in taste between Japanese and Western consumers. Familiarity and security are two friends that are difficult to separate, and people across the globe tend to prefer products with ingredients which they are familiar with. However, due to a Japanese desire to emulate Western ideals, Japanese women were quick to try the product.

The product was a huge success and DHC quickly became a household name throughout Japan and later in Korea and China as well. DHC skincare products, although manufactured in Japan, have been able to seamlessly integrate themselves into Western cosmetics markets. In Europe, olives are considered to have amazing restorative powers and thus the product instantly appealed to consumers there and in the US. Furthermore, there has been a growing trend in the West related to the use of Asian products. Although olives are common in Europe, consumers there may feel that the Japanese aspect of the product merely adds to rather than detracts from its appeal (see Fig. 4).

The cases of Amore Pacific and DHC both represent a high level of standardization, although the starting points are significantly different. There seems to be a desire on both sides of the globe to

Standardization Point

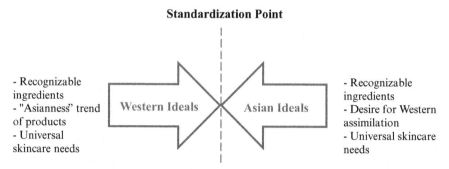

- Recognizable ingredients
- "Asianness" trend of products
- Universal skincare needs

Western Ideals   Asian Ideals

- Recognizable ingredients
- Desire for Western assimilation
- Universal skincare needs

Fig. 4.   Standardization point.

assimilate one another to a certain extent. Thus, standardization comes from a meeting point in the middle of the spectrum rather than from the extreme point on one side or another, as the term standardization seems to suggest as shown in Fig. 4. Perhaps then we can conclude that standardization is merely the desired meeting point among aspects of differentiation, which would certainly integrate both Levitt and Friedman's notion of "the world is flat" with Douglas and Wind's theory of "the world is spiky."

Case Study 2: Mythical Standards[3]

The "golden arches" are noted as the epitome of globalization, homogenization, and standardization. Of course, we are talking about McDonald's, the American fast food chain that has developed into a global empire. However, is McDonald's really that standardized? Can a product as personal as food be completely standardized? Douglas and Wind would answer to the contrary, while Levitt would be more than happy to use McDonald's as a representative case for his argument.

McDonald's was a local firm that focused on producing goods that catered strictly to an American taste. Still, the concept of the

---

[3]Some parts of this case study were extracted from McDonald's official website (www.mcdonalds.com), Wall Street Institute Materials (www.wsikorea.com), and https://www.businessinsider.com/mcdonalds-international-menu-items-2016-9# mcdonalds-indias-veg-pizza-mcpuff-1.

restaurant soon gained global appeal. The concept included hot, tasty, and inexpensive food that could be delivered to the consumer in rapid time. As successful as the concept was, the product itself was proving difficult to sell. McDonald's was hugely lucrative in America, but less so in Europe and least of all in Asia. The simple explanation for this is that different tastes exist in those regional and even individual markets.

Let us take a look at the Bulgogi Burger. This is an item that is specifically geared toward the Korean market and is not available in neighboring Japan or China. The Bulgogi Burger is not available in Japan, as the Japanese prefer their localized version of the Teriyaki Burger. In Italy, where people are picky about their cheese, the burger patty is draped in parmigiano reggiano, not just the regular run of the mill cheddar cheese slice. In Germany and Switzerland, both countries famous for beer, one can purchase a nice cold glass of local brew along with a McDonald's burger. In the Middle East, all the meat must be *halal* (Muslim dietary laws), while in Israel the products must be *kosher* (Jewish dietary laws).

The Bulgogi Burger, among others, represents the highest level of differentiation and shows that even a global and supposedly standardized firm, such as McDonald's, must cater to unique tastes on a country, regional, and even religious basis. The McDonald's story thus may confirm Douglas and Wind's hypothesis. Although it should be pointed out that despite its differentiation, the core products, such as the Big Mac, Double Cheese Burger, and McChicken Sandwich, are still massively popular all over the world. The local and regional versions constitute a smaller proportion of the menus, which McDonald's offers to its customers. Moreover, some menus developed to customize local customers, such as vegetarian items served by McDonald's India, turn out to be popular in many other of their outlets around the world. These cases thus confirm Levitt's argument for the customer's homogenous tastes among countries.

Another point that must be addressed is the difference in appropriate strategy based on functional-level division. While product standardization and differentiation remain separate concepts, it seems that marketing strategy, for the most part needs to be thought of in terms of differentiation. This can be seen in the examples provided below:

- Stevedores at an African port believed that a box with the international symbol for "fragile" (a silhouette of a broken wine glass) contained broken glass. Rather than wasting space by keeping the boxes, they threw them all into the sea!

- "Irish Mist" (an alcoholic drink), "Mist Stick" (a curling iron from Clairol), and "Silver Mist" (Rolls Royce car) all flopped in Germany as the word "Mist" means dung/manure in German.

- Managers at one American company were startled when they discovered that the brand name of the cooking oil they were marketing in a Latin American country translated into Spanish as "Jackass Oil."

- American Motors tried to market its new car, the Matador, based on the image of courage and strength. However, in Puerto Rico the name means "killer" and was not popular on its hazardous roads.

- An international golf ball manufacturing company packaged its items in packs of four for convenient purchase in Japan. Unfortunately, the pronunciation of the word "four" in Japanese sounds like the word "death" and items packaged in fours are thus unpopular.

- Walmart copied its operational system in the US when it entered the German market. One element of this system is to have a person at the door smiling and greeting people by saying "Welcome to Walmart." This works in the US, but is not so comfortable for Germans who associate such behavior with a close level of intimacy.

The above examples are funny, but they also raise a question on whether to standardize or not at the global level. Thus, as mentioned previously, a production and marketing strategy may require different paths and should not be simultaneously standardized.

Discussion Questions

1. Do you agree with Levitt's theorization of global versus multinational firms? Do global firms always have the advantage? Discuss.

2. Levitt used the analogy of a hedgehog and a fox. Can you think of firms that represent either the fox or the hedgehog?

3. Do you agree with Douglas and Wind's prerequisites for global standardization? Can you think of other prerequisites that may be required for globalization?

4. Are standardization and differentiation just two sides of the same coin? Can both lead the firm to the same outcome? Discuss.

5. Do you think McDonald's is pursuing more differentiation or more standardization? Discuss.

6. Do you think the global economy will be more standardized or differentiated in the post-COVID era? Discuss.

CHAPTER 10

All Together Now...

Chapter Guideline

Standardization or differentiation? Globalization or localization? These dichotomies seem to be inherently conflicting. The debate over standardization has left us with more questions than answers. What is the more appropriate strategy in an international setting? Can these apparently contradictory terms be reconciled to create a more comprehensive framework to understand the complex nature of global strategy? Yes, they can. The previous chapter highlighted the points of debate, and this chapter will provide some answers to the questions that linger in our minds.

Summary of Previous Models

We are now at the penultimate chapter of our long journey through the world of global business strategy. Based on a conceptual grasp of business strategy, we have delved deep into the issues pertaining to its elevation to the global level. The result was a series of analyses by scholars who express seemingly contradictory points, but are still convincing in their own right. Now, we will look at some scholars who have sought to fuse all the existing studies together to create a truly overarching view on the complex and multidimensional nature of global business strategy.

10.1 Global Strategy: The Context

"To globalize or not to globalize, that is the question." This modified version of Hamlet's soliloquy used to be the most important question in International Business during the 1970s and 1980s. Consequently, many studies have tried to shed light on this question, and many scholars have presented evidence that global strategy or increasing the degree of globalization leads to better firm performance (Vernon, 1971; Grant, 1987; Daniels and Bracker, 1989; Geringer *et al.*, 1989; Glaum and Oesterle, 2007; Sharma, 2011).

Globalization, of course, is not the panacea to solve all the problems that a firm faces. This is a very important point to note as globalization can just as easily detract from profitability as it can contribute toward it since going global requires incurring significant costs. For example, some studies argued that cross-border business carries risks and creates complexities which ultimately reduce the market performance among firms (Lu and Beamish, 2001). Moon (2016a, 2016b) suggests that despite the potential negative impact of globalization, its positive impact tends to be more prominent in the long term. Similarly, Efrat and Shoham (2012) call for a time series approach, as the impact of internationalization on firm performance normally evolves over time and may not be immediately evident. Other studies have suggested moderating factors should be incorporated for evaluation such as management structure, firm age, firm behavior, and market orientation (Cacciolatti and Lee, 2016; Carr *et al.*, 2010; Lin *et al.*, 2011). Therefore, the question of "whether to globalize or not" has now evolved into "how to globalize more effectively." In this sense, Yip's (1989) framework provides a succinct analysis of "whether and how to globalize" firm strategy. The key point of Yip's analysis is illustrated in Fig. 1, which he calls "Total Global Strategy."

Following Fig. 1, we can see that formulating a global strategy requires three concrete steps:

- *Developing Core Business Strategy* — Every competitive firm possesses some kind of core, firm-specific advantage. This concept is similar to what Porter described as "strategic fits" (see Chapter 4) and is a necessary condition for firms to go global.

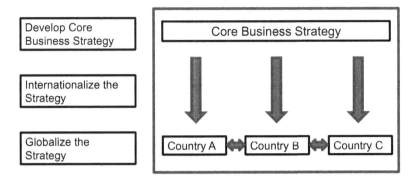

Fig. 1. Total global strategy.
Source: Yip (1989).

- *Internationalizing the Strategy* — This is when a firm elevates its firm-specific advantage to the global arena. It requires coordinating and configuring the firm's value chain activities according to the global setting.

- *Globalizing the Strategy* — The final stage is to generate synergies from linking dispersed activities. The numerous activities performed in various locations all combine to create a strong global strategic fit.

In this case, the exogenous (industry globalization drivers) and endogenous (an organization's ability to implement a global strategy and resources of business) variables all converge into setting global strategy levers. By considering these variables, we can assess the costs/benefits of implementing a global strategy.

What is Global Strategy?

Yip distinguishes multi-domestic strategy and pure global strategy, and explains their implications on five dimensions:

- *Market Participation* — In a multi-domestic strategy, countries are selected purely based on their market potential. However, in a global strategy, countries are selected on not only their market potential but also based on their impact on the overall strategy.

- *Product Offerings* — Products are tailored to match local tastes and needs in a multi-domestic strategy. On the contrary, a purely global strategy offers fully standardized products regardless of the market.

- *Location of Value-Added Activities* — All activities occur in each country in a multi-domestic strategy. But a global strategy requires a fully integrated and dispersed value activity which takes full advantage of differences among countries.

- *Marketing Approach* — In a multi-domestic strategy, just like product offering, marketing is completely customized for individual countries. At the same time, global marketing requires a uniform approach regardless of countries.

- *Competitive Moves* — A multi-domestic strategy does not have to consider the impact on competition in other countries, while global strategy managers must always keep in mind that a decision made in one location has an impact on another.

Benefits of Global Strategy

So, what are the advantages of global strategy? Yip provides the following answers:

- *Cost Reductions* — A company can increase the benefits from economies of scale by pooling production or other activities at a global scale. A second benefit comes from exploiting low factor costs in different countries, while a third one is exploiting flexibility such as operating in multiple locations depending on economic situations.

- *Improved Quality of Products and Programs* — Firms with global strategies can focus on a few standardized products and programs. This means that they can concentrate their resources to increase the quality of these selected few.

- *Enhanced Customer Preference* — Global availability, serviceability, and recognition can enhance customer preference. Global suppliers, such as fast food and credit card companies, can provide a multinational customer with a standard product around the world and gain international familiarity.

- *Increased Competitive Leverage* — A global strategy provides more opportunities for offense and defense. As Hamel and Prahalad (1985) described, a firm can gain a wider array of weapons in its strategic armory by globalizing its operations.

Drawbacks of Global Strategy

At the same time though, there are clear trade-offs in pursuing a global strategy:

- *Increased Coordination Costs* — A firm must incur substantial costs in terms of implementing appropriate mechanisms, at least in the initial phase of globalization.

- *Customer Preference Trade-off* — As Douglas and Wind (1987) pointed out, standardized products may not be able to satisfy all the tastes among customers and may lead to losses in certain markets.

- *Lower Responsiveness* — Since a global strategy requires homogenous marketing regardless of location, firms may be slow to react to changing local needs.

Finding the Balance

Considering these strengths and weaknesses with the global strategy, the most crucial decision that firms have to make is to what *degree* a firm should globalize. Of course, this decision must be based on careful consideration of various factors. In this case, Yip discusses this balance through the following framework (see Fig. 2).

As one can see from the framework in Fig. 2, certain industries have a high potential for globalization, while others do not. Consider Business A versus Business D. While they are both operating in the

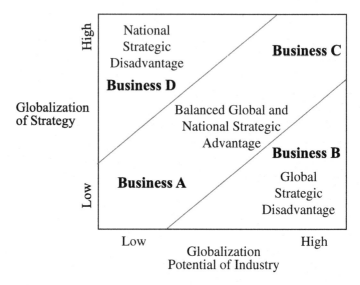

Fig. 2.   Globalization potential of industry vs. globalization of strategy.
Source: Yip (1989).

same industry, the less globalized Business A is outperforming the over-globalized Business D. On the contrary, in an industry of high globalization potential, the more globalized Business C is performing better than less globalized Business B.

Industry Globalization Drivers

If the globalization potential differs from industry to industry, what drives these differences? Yip identifies four broad categories of drivers: market, cost, governmental, and competitive:

- *Market Drivers* — Homogenous customer needs, global customers, global channels, and transferable marketing go under this category. A homogenous customer base leads to a global customer who is willing to buy the same product in multiple locations. This homogenization allows for uniform marketing since customers now react similarly to the standardized product.

Global channels of distribution link these market drivers to the producers.

- *Cost Drivers* — Obvious cost drivers are economies of scale and scope since global outreach allows firms to increase both of these elements. Another cost driver is enhanced sourcing efficiency from global outreach. Logistics also become more convenient and cheaper because the sales value relative to transportation cost increases.

- *Governmental Drivers* — These include government actions such as favorable trade policies, compatible technical standards, and common marketing regulations. Government globalization drivers depend on the rules set by the state and affect the use of all global strategy levers.

- *Competitive Drivers* — When activities are shared among countries, a competitor's market share in one country affects its competitive position in another country. This is similar to Porter's discussion of the nature of global competition. Yip describes further possibilities for firms to actually enhance the globalization potential of an industry through interactions of national differences and competitors' moves.

Considering these complex variables that decide whether or not a firm should globalize, Yip concludes that successful international strategies have varying shades and degrees. First, a firm must have a clear understanding of the industry in which it operates. As shown in Fig. 2, over-globalization can actually lead to a strategic disadvantage depending on the drivers present in an industry. Next, global strategies require a significant level of initial fixed cost. Although a firm may reap tremendous benefits after these costs are installed, a firm must have the muscle to incur the initial short-term disadvantage. Lastly, an organization's culture, structure, and people may not be suited for a global strategy. Firms from highly ethnocentric backgrounds may have difficulty in implementing global strategies due to insufficient human resources.

Analysis

Yip's analysis presents a fresh new look at the age-old debate between globalization and multi-domestic strategies. In the previous chapter, we saw scholars such as Levitt, Douglas and Wind, and Ghemawat argue for or against the globalization of a firm's strategy. Yip succinctly summarizes the pros and cons of both strategies and concludes that it is not a question of selecting one or the other, but of attaining the appropriate balance between the two, depending on the various exogenous and endogenous variables present. Yip's article essentially provides us with many answers to the questions that we may have had from the previous chapter. However, as is always true in the world of academia, Yip has also left us with more questions that need to be addressed.

One point that must be considered is Yip's framework of Total Global Strategy (see Fig. 1). The idea here is that a firm develops its core business strategy in its domestic market, internationalizes the strategy, and then moves on to globalize it through integrating the strategy in various countries. As logical as this may sound, this framework is quite inadequate to explain global strategy from the perspective of latecomers from less developed countries. Firms from the US and Europe may have taken this route as they developed a significant advantage from their domestic markets and then elevated their strategies to the global arena. As such, this method was plausible for advanced Western firms because they did not face any significant challenges from outside forces during their initial internationalization phases. Moreover, the global economic system evolved heavily in their favor and they may not need to modify their core business strategies too much in order to internationalize and then globalize.

Yet, when one looks at the evolution of latecomers, a different picture emerges. Given that these firms cannot enjoy the various advantages that most advanced Western firms have, these latecomers must simultaneously modify their core business strategies as they internationalize. Therefore, in order to explain the global strategy of latecomers, Fig. 1 must be slightly modified as depicted in Fig. 3.

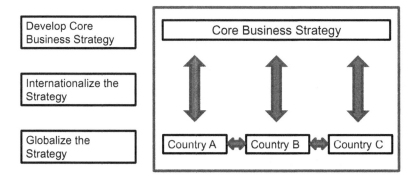

Fig. 3. Total global strategy for emerging multinational companies.

While the visual difference is merely one-directional arrows replaced with two-directional arrows, the implications are profound. Advanced Western firms simply duplicate their success in their domestic markets to the global stage, while latecomer firms dynamically formulate their global strategy during their process of globalization. This novel feature among latecomers has caught the attention of many scholars (Bartlett and Ghoshal, 2000; Mathews, 2002; Bonaglia *et al.*, 2007; Ghemawat and Hout, 2008; Khanna and Palepu, 2006).

This distinction is crucial because it becomes very important in explaining how emerging multinational corporations (EMNCs) from developing countries have been aggressively adopting international strategies in recent years. Since EMNCs start off in a more integrated global economy, they must simultaneously formulate their core strategy while they face global competition. This may seem disadvantageous at first glance, but latecomers do have certain advantages which they can exploit. As Bartlett and Ghoshal (2000) noted, EMNCs can quickly emulate the more established global players and then sidestep to produce a plus-alpha to their added value. For example, in mature industries such as the white goods industry, many corporations from emerging markets have acquired global competitiveness in a very short period of time and added their plus-alpha to create a "cheap and chic" line of white goods for global consumers (Bonaglia *et al.*, 2007). Hence, latecomers can take advantage of utilizing the emerging new technologies and also skip the trials and errors experienced by the first movers (Cho *et al.*, 1998). Mathews (2006) argued that such a learning process among latecomers is fundamentally derived from that of advanced-country firms.

Some scholars even proposed the "Born Global" model, which describes small and medium-sized start-ups that go global in the very early stage (first or second year) of their inception. The definition of a Born Global firm was first coined by McKinsey & Co. in a report that analyzed a sample of Australian exporting firms (McKinsey & Co., 1993). Born Global is defined as those that, from inception, pursue a vision of becoming global and often globalize their business rapidly without a previous long-term domestic or internationalization period (Luostarinen and Gabrielsson, 2004; Oviatt and McDougall, 1994). A more quantitative definition from Knight *et al.* (2004) describes Born Global as "firms less than 20 years old that internationalized on average within three years of founding and generate at least 25% of total sales from abroad." Moen (2002) defines Born Global as "firms having export sales higher than 25%."

Kudina *et al.* (2008) suggested that despite the differences in the definition, what is most intriguing is how firms became global so quickly. They argued that prior studies have found three key factors that drive the emergence of Born Global firms — new market conditions (the presence of global networks and alliances, global nature of business), technology advancement (communication technology, e-business), and management change (tapping into technological innovation from overseas operations). They further argued that, nevertheless, a remaining question is regarding why some new ventures go abroad from their inception whereas others do not. By examining the firms in the Greater Cambridge Area Cluster, they identified factors such as the importance of trust, personal relationships, social capital, and lack of fear of internationalization, which facilitate the international expansion of firms from an early stage. Therefore, the dynamic strategies of EMNCs and Born Global in the new integrated global economy leave us with another very interesting topic for further discussion.

10.2 Global Strategy: The Firm

If Yip presented us with an overarching view of the globalization phenomena, it is now time to look at how the firm itself should be managed under this context. Bartlett and Ghoshal (1989), in this seminal work, present a detailed look at the organizational model that firms should follow in this increasingly globalized world.

Still, before we look at the firm itself, it is important to clarify the differences in terminology. While Yip's analysis was based on "multi-domestic vs. global," Bartlett and Ghoshal use the term "transnational" to describe the new organizational model. This typological difference is important and Table 1 summarizes the categorization.

The key difference between the terms international and transnational is that assets and capabilities are dispersed yet interdependent for a transnational strategy. In other words, a transnational strategy has all the strengths of the multinational (e.g., local responsiveness) combined with those of a global company (standardization, scale economies, etc.). It does not simply centralize or decentralize, but makes selective and complex decisions which allow the organization to exploit the maximum benefit from both ends of the spectrum.

What emerges is a very different type of organization which can truly maximize the full benefit of global operations. It takes the best of everything and creates a formidable advantage against other firms. The interaction between the subsidiary and headquarters is not just one-sided but efficiently dynamic as a perfectly integrated yet diversified organization interacts extensively to take advantage of the various differences that exist among locations.

Building and Managing the Transnational

As attractive as the above proposition sounds, not many can actually achieve such a complex feat. Building and managing a transnational is not an easy task as it requires dealing with several delicate challenges. The three main sources of difficulties come from balancing diverse perspectives and capabilities within an organization, developing

Table 1. Organizational characteristics of the transnational.

Organizational characteristics	Multinational	Global	International	Transnational
Configuration of assets and capabilities	Decentralized and nationally self-sufficient	Centralized and globally scaled	Sources of core competence centralized, others decentralized	Dispersed, interdependent, and specialized
Role of overseas operations	Sensing and exploiting local opportunities	Implementing parent company strategies	Adapting and leveraging parent company competencies	Differentiated contributions by national units to integrate worldwide operations
Development and diffusion of knowledge	Knowledge developed and retained within each unit	Knowledge developed and retained at the center	Knowledge developed at the center and transferred to overseas unit	Knowledge developed jointly and shared worldwide

Source: Bartlett and Ghoshal (1989).

Table 2. Building and managing the transnational.

Strategic capability	Organizational characteristics	Management tasks
Global competitiveness	Dispersed and interdependent assets and resources	Legitimizing diverse perspectives and capabilities
Multinational flexibility	Differential and specialized subsidiary roles	Developing multiple and flexible coordination processes
Worldwide learning	Joint development and worldwide sharing of knowledge	Building shared vision and individual commitment

Source: Bartlett and Ghoshal (1989).

flexible coordination processes, and unifying diverse elements within the organization under a shared vision (see Table 2 for an overview).

- *Balancing Perspective and Capabilities* — As we can see from Table 2, a transnational firm's competitiveness is derived from dispersed and interdependent assets and resources. Therefore, managers must be able to aggregate diverse perspectives and capabilities without having one segment of the organization dominate the other.

- *Developing Flexible Coordination Processes* — Since a transnational firm requires increased integration between departments and nations, the organization takes on a much more multidimensional and complex landscape. In order to manage this properly the transnational firm must consider three issues: (a) flow of parts, components, and finished goods, (b) flow of funds, skills, and other scarce resources among units, and (c) flow of intelligence, ideas, and knowledge.

- *Unifying the Organization through Vision and Co-option* — All firms need to instill their employees with a common vision to direct the diverse resources toward one strategic direction. This becomes especially important when managing a complex organizational structure embedded in a transnational firm.

Analysis

The key contribution of Bartlett and Ghoshal is the conceptualization of an ideal firm that can exploit the maximum benefit of globalization. The transnational organization, like a chameleon, is a new kind of animal that can be highly standardized yet responsive at the same time. By introducing the organizational characteristics of different firms, the two authors have provided a typological categorization that can be used to distinguish firms according to their degree of internationalization.

In order to truly understand this implication, it is necessary to analyze these typologies from an all-encompassing framework (see Fig. 4). When we see the Bartlett and Ghoshal's typologies according

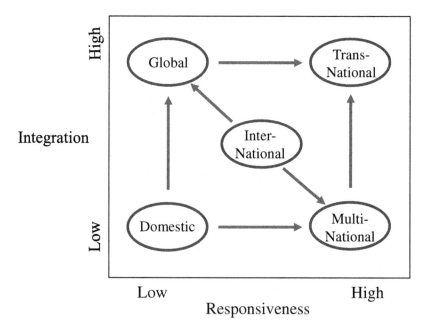

Fig. 4. Domestic, multinational, global, international, and transnational: The I-R framework.

to this framework, several questions begin to emerge. The first one is the authors' basic idea that a firm evolves from domestic → multinational → global → international → transnational. As we can see from Fig. 4, the authors' idea becomes problematic because it would mean that a firm evolves to the lower right-hand corner (multinational), moves to the upper left (global), comes to the center (international), and then mysteriously jumps to the final upper right corner (transnational). This point is crucial because the authors assume that a firm that used to have a federation of decentralized and nationally self-sufficient units will centralize its operation and then decentralize again. This seems highly complicated and inefficient even intuitively.

A better way to look at the evolution of firms is to think of multinational and global as different paths to reach the final stage (transnational) rather than viewing global as a more evolved form of multinational. Furthermore, rather than using the term multinational, it is typologically more precise to use the term multi-domestic since we are discussing individual markets. In correcting this flaw, we can see that a more organized and sensible framework emerges (see Fig. 5).

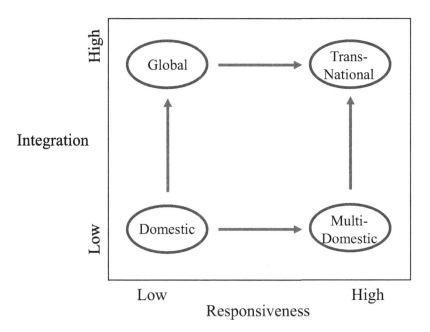

Fig. 5. Modified framework.

What we can see is that the ultimate goal is transnational, which is characterized by a high level of integration and responsiveness. Yet, the path to reach that goal can be achieved either through standardizing aggressively (global) or developing a high responsiveness to individual markets (multi-domestic). Afterward, in order to reach a transnational stage, companies in the global stage can gradually increase their responsiveness, while multi-domestic companies can integrate their previously decentralized units to reach the purely global stage. However, as it is difficult for firms to fully adopt both global and multi-domestic strategies simultaneously for all value chain activities at the entire organizational level, the transnational stage seems to be ideal yet difficult to achieve in reality.

10.3 Global Strategy: The Manager

If we liken this chapter to a plane journey, we can say that Yip has presented us with a detailed flight map, while Bartlett and Ghoshal analyzed the optimal aircraft that we will need to successfully navigate through this volatile world. Now, Kedia and Mukherji (1999) provide a detailed account on the type of the pilot we will need to fly the jet through the world of globalization.

It is apparent from our previous discussion that a firm that can exploit the full benefits of globalization is different from the organizations of the past. As such, the people who manage this multidimensional and intricately integrated organization must have a different mindset as well. Although global managers appear in greater number than ever, much less is known in either research or practice about how to globalize people for their international roles (Javidan and Bowen, 2013). Preceding studies often interchangeably use the terms of global manager and global leader (Suutari, 2002), and there is no collectively accepted definition for either global leaders or global managers (Osland *et al.*, 2006). The following shows Kedia and Mukherji's (1999) systematic and comprehensive description of the capability and competences of global managers.

Changing Orientation of Managers

In the past, managerial training was mainly focused on hard issues such as cost reduction, manufacturing, and budget allocation. However, these hard issues can no longer remain the most important sources of competitiveness as most valid competitors are increasingly competent in these basic factors. Therefore, the orientation is now changing to soft issues such as values, culture, vision, leadership style, innovation, and risks. The issues that global managers must deal with are far more eclectic and complex in scope, which require a different mindset from that of the past and are illustrated in Fig. 6. The important point to note in Fig. 6 is that this framework suggests a holistic orientation. Rather than focusing on hard or soft issues, a global manager must do both and balance the two aspects to the firm's best advantage.

Framework to Develop a Global Perspective

Now that we have an understanding of the shifting orientation, we must look at the necessary tools for achieving this change. Kedia and

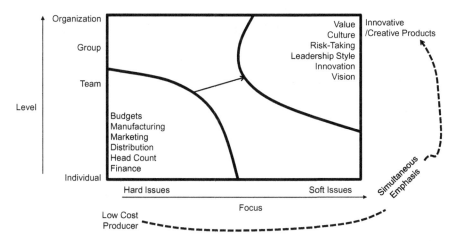

Fig. 6. Changed orientation of global managers.
Source: Kedia and Mukherji (1999).

Fig. 7.   Developing a global perspective.
Source: Kedia and Mukherji (1999).

Mukherji suggest that a global mindset is required to achieve this holistic orientation. In addition, two distinct aspects, knowledge and skills, need to be cultivated for this kind of mindset. The overall relationship is defined in Fig. 7.

Knowledge for a Global Mindset

In order to have a firm grasp of how various global issues affect the firm's operations, a global manager must be equipped with socio-political, economic, and cultural perspectives. Mastery of technology is also important because this has revolutionized various aspects of a firm's operation including manufacturing, processes, and services. The impact that technological development has is clearly exponential, especially when compared with the past.

Skills for a Global Mindset

If knowledge is the building block for a global mindset, skills allow the manager to execute his or her knowledge in the field. Acculturation, which means becoming privy to other cultures through constant interaction, is crucial because of the multicultural nature of global operations. It enables managers to map out this seemingly difficult task because it familiarizes managers on how to deal with this complex issue on a daily basis.

Developing a Global Mindset

As the above discussion set us with the end goal, we must now look at how to reach it. The authors suggest four concrete actions that can help: (a) foreign travel, (b) teams made up of people from diverse backgrounds, (c) training; and (d) transfers to foreign locations. The point of these measures is that exposure to diverse working conditions and constant training are all-crucial toward achieving a global mindset.

The Changing Mindset of Managers

In this section, the authors trace how managerial mindsets have evolved throughout history and present a typological framework to understand this evolution. Table 3 outlines the changes in managerial perspectives according to the evolution of a firm's strategy from ethnocentrism to geocentricism reflecting the transition from international to transnational.

Managerial Mindsets

Next, we must take a look at the typological distinctions of different mindsets and how they are evolving. Four categories are constructed in Table 4: (a) defender, (b) explorer; (c) controller, and (d) integrator; and, each has a different mindset on global perspective and identity.

Table 3. Changing managerial perspectives.

Mindset	Outlook	Strategy
Ethnocentrism: Home Country Perspective	Centralized/Controlled	International
Polycentrism/Regiocentrism: Host Country Perspective	Decentralized/Autonomous	Multinational
Geocentrism: Global Perspective	Networked/Interdependent	Transnational

Source: Kedia and Mukherji (1999).

- *Defender* — This is the traditional managerial mindset that was predominant before the wave of globalization. A defender maintains a world in which all outsiders are potential competitors and threats to its position. Therefore, a defender frequently asks for protection from foreign competition.

- *Explorer* — Explorers are more open to foreign opportunities, but are still cautious of allowing them into their own organization. Managers with this kind of mindset typically occupy a dominant position in the domestic market but have a weak presence outside.

- *Controller* — Managers in this category are more open and globalized than the former two categories and are willing to take more daring approaches in going abroad. However, the mentality is still dominated by control and is not fond of bestowing foreign subsidiaries with significant autonomy or decision-making power. Firms with these kinds of managers may have significant international presence, but will still prefer to retain much of the central decision-making authority in headquarters.

- *Integrator* — This describes the ideal mentality of global management as it integrates and leverages diversity. An integrator has the ability to organize and manage a complex web of multidimensional and multicultural operations and enjoys the full benefit of globalization. Overall, managers in this category possess a much more flexible, dynamic, and coordinated mindset.

Table 4. The four mindsets and global perspectives.

Mindset	Defender	Explorer	Controller	Integrator
Level of Global Perspective	None	Surface level	Intermediate level	Deep level
Global Identity Self	Maintain self-sufficiency	Define differences	Redefine self	Integrate
Others	Acknowledge	Explore	Control	Leverage diversity

Source: Kedia and Mukherji (1999).

Strategizing and Integrating Globally

A global manager requires specific skills that are necessary for integrating, coordinating, and leveraging (see Fig. 8). While each of the three actors in Fig. 8 has its specific field (specialization), all must keep a global perspective in mind at all times (integration), as represented by the rectangular box in the middle. More specifically, a global business manager is responsible for the coordination of the whole operation, while a country manager is responsible for local responsiveness. In terms of the integration and responsiveness framework, a global business manager integrates, while the country manager responds. The worldwide functional manager oversees the interaction between the two in order to ensure that the organization as a whole is moving toward a singular vision. The dynamics among these three actors demonstrate that no matter which function an individual performs in a transnational organization, he or she must be constantly aware that his or her action affects others and the organization as a whole.

Fig. 8. Integrating and strategizing globally.
Source: Kedia and Mukherji (1999).

Analysis

Perlmutter (1969) systematically categorized different types of worker attitudes and explained the various obstacles that prevented workers from acquiring a multicultural and globalized outlook. He identified three distinct types of worker orientations (which can be loosely interpreted as attitude, perspective, or outlook): (a) ethnocentric, (b) polycentric, and (c) geocentric. As the names aptly convey, the degree of global orientation increases moving from ethnocentric to geocentric. What Kedia and Mukhreji (1999) describe as the ideal worker is a further refinement and extension of Perlmutter's geocentric concept.

Human resources have always been the key to a firm's success and it will continue to be so. For this reason, all types of firms take great care in choosing the right person for the organization. In this sense, Perlmutter provides a very interesting and useful insight into what kind of person is suited to lead a transnational organization: a coordinator with an open mind and the ability to integrate complex tasks and elements into a shared direction. It is without a doubt that the profiles of desirable employees are rapidly shifting and will shift even further in the future. Attitudes expressed by traditional workers such as diligence and subservience, which are particularly favored among Asian companies, are becoming less desirable, while creativity and multicultural sensitivity are becoming more valuable.

East Asian companies, especially those with a strong collectivist and a vertical hierarchy structure, have difficulty accepting the need for a geocentric attitude. Unlike European nations or the US, which are mostly multicultural societies, East Asian countries such as Japan, Korea, and China are relatively homogenous in terms of their composition. Such homogeneity can sometimes lead to ethnic nationalism that also influences corporate culture to be more ethnocentric. While recent efforts by Japanese and Korean multinationals have been geared toward adopting geocentric company goals and hiring more geocentric employees, there is still a long way to go in terms of achieving a truly geocentric corporate culture because of the deeply ingrained ethnocentric practices and culture.

Another point that needs to be made regarding human resources is the need for strategic training. In the past, many assumed that formulating, implementing, and understanding strategy could only be done by a gifted, elite few. Therefore, the managerial structure was highly vertical, almost military format, in which top executives would unilaterally issue orders down to the bottom and require them to execute. It is unsurprising then that many corporate titles, such as Chief Executive Officer, have their roots in a military ranking system. However, this kind of vertical organizational measure is no longer desirable and could impede the adoption of a geocentric corporate culture. In an era of rapid globalization and an increased need for an agile yet multidimensional organizational structure, a vertical organizational dynamic will only lead to rigidity and failure. What is needed then is for all employees, from bottom to top, to have a firm grasp of the strategic direction that the company is heading toward. In order to achieve this feat, it is crucial to abandon the traditional, elitist attitude on strategy.

This may sound straightforward, but how do we actually achieve this? Terrell and Rosenbusch (2013) explored the experiences of global leaders, which were important for their development and training. They suggested that global leaders can develop through firsthand, personal participation in intensive cross-cultural and global leadership experiences. For this, the organization can provide developmental assignments to potential managers with regard to this type of experience. In addition, they stressed that global leaders should learn the importance and value of cultural sensitivity, relationships, and networks as well as adopt a desire to learn. These approaches and tactics are shown in Table 5.

The most important step would be to provide concrete training in utilizing and understanding analytical frameworks. Unlike theories, frameworks are highly applicable and can easily be understood. While some business managers lament the fact that business frameworks are abstract and unrealistic, such views are rather dismissive of their actual power. Frameworks are shortcuts toward understanding phenomena in the real world, and by having employees with a solid understanding

Table 5. Global leader learning approaches.

Attitude or stance toward learning	Learning approaches during experiences	Learning approaches after experiences
Openness to experience	Observation of people and organizational dynamics	Reflection-on-action
Motivation, willingness, and desire to learn	Learning from mistakes and failures	Transfer and generalization to other situations
Curiosity about working and living in other parts of the world	Learning "in the moment," accidental, incidental, and serendipitous	—
Discovery and exploration	Sett-reflection, reflection-in-action	—
Desire, intention, and willingness to gain something positive from experience	Listening and attending to others	—

Source: Terrell and Rosenbusch (2013), p. 1065.

of various frameworks, firms can mobilize their employees toward a desirable strategic direction with relative ease.

Case Study 1: Chinese Lenovo Goes Global[1]

In the early 2000s, Chinese firms began to vigorously pursue a global strategy (Peng, 2012). As such, their share of the Fortune Global 500

[1] Parts of this case study was extracted from the Lenovo Official Website (www. lenovo.com), Business Week (Beyond Outsourcing to Worldsourcing, May 29, 2008), International Herald Tribune (Interconnected we Prosper, June 25, 2008), Lenovo 2019/2020 Environmental, Social and Governance Report, 2020; https://www.csis.org/blogs/trustee-china-hand/biggest-not-strongest-chinas-place-fortune-global-500, https://business-review.eu/news-ro/lenovo-holds-24-pct-market-share-of-the-global-pc-market-206209, https://news.lenovo.com/smarter-technology-global-coordination-fuel-worlds-top-supply-chains/, and https://www.ft.com/content/a5f5f290-04c9-4776-ae8d-ee881b13bb3a.

list increased from 0 in 1990 to 124 in 2020, indicating that they have slightly outpaced both the US (121) and Japan (53). We have heard of scores of buyouts, takeovers, and mergers orchestrated by Chinese firms such as Huawei and Alibaba that have made names for themselves abroad. Although we have yet to see a truly global Chinese firm emerging from the formerly centralized economy, one firm that stands out from the rest of the crowd is Lenovo.

The firm was founded in 1984 by a group of eleven Chinese engineers and was originally known as the Legend Group Ltd. It set out as a fairly small domestic PC manufacturing firm and has maintained these roots as the firm has grown to become the largest PC manufacturer in the world followed by Hewlett Packard and Dell. In such a short span of time, the company has undergone a tremendous evolution and it is interesting to look at that evolution from the perspectives afforded by Yip, Bartlett and Ghoshal, and Kedia and Mukherji.

Yip stated that a firm's goal is to move from being multi-domestic to global. There are five areas in which a firm should desire to become global, which are market participation, product offering, location of value-added activities, marketing approach, and competitive moves.

In terms of market participation, Lenovo has seemingly moved away from a multi-domestic strategy. The company intentionally targeted markets not just for their potential but also for its own wider reaching strategic impact. Lenovo, as a Chinese firm, understands that in order to become a global firm it cannot be identified solely as a Chinese brand. Thus, Lenovo has continued to balance its revenues across four regions — Americas, Asia-Pacific, China, and the combined area of Europe, the Middle East, and Africa (EMEA) — with each reporting more than 20% of revenue. It also manages a highly complex global supply chain of manufacturing and delivering to more than 108 markets. Lenovo's overseas sales have become more important than ever, bringing in 79% of revenue in 2019. We can therefore identify Lenovo as being more global in this aspect.

As part of its global expansion, Lenovo has broadened its product range from PCs to workstations, servers, digital entertainment devices, and even mobile phones. Lenovo's core business remains personal computers, accounting for more than 70% of its revenue. The laptop models include ThinkPad, Ideapad, Yoga, and Legion. However, designs, colors, and options are fairly limited, which is why its product offerings are more standardized than tailored to local tastes. The company has further improved its product mix by selling more premium and high-end items. Therefore, we can also assume that Lenovo has a more global approach from this viewpoint.

The locations of value-added activities are multi-domestic when independent of each other and global when fully integrated and dispersed. Lenovo has developed a business model, which it dubs as "world-sourcing." Essentially, the firm's ideas, operations, and resources are literally borderless. It does not have a global headquarters, but rather has instituted a distributed management structure that places operational hubs around the world. The company has its key operational hubs in Beijing and Morrisville, North Carolina, while its research and development centers are located in China (Beijing, Shanghai, Shenzhen, and Xiamen), Japan (Yokohama), Taiwan, and the US (Chicago and Morrisville). These hubs interact fully with each other in a multi-way communication format. So, rather than seeing the typical hub-and-spoke setup that most firms have, Lenovo has a spider-web network through which resources can flow easily. In this way, Yip believes that Lenovo has a global strategy in its location of value-added activities. Because of such an approach to globalization, Lenovo has had little tension in the US, while many other Chinese firms such as ByteDance, Tencent, and Huawei have suffered from escalating restrictions amid the US–China trade war.

With regard to the marketing approach, a multi-domestic strategy would provide a more customized marketing approach for each country, whereas a global strategy would provide a uniform marketing approach. Lenovo pursues the latter, which is evident from its official website. It does not change this for each country, except for the language in which the product is sold. Therefore, the firm's marketing approach is also based on a global strategy.

Lastly, we must look at Lenovo's competitive moves. It is a highly integrated firm, which relies on "world-sourcing" as its business model. This means that every aspect of Lenovo's operation is integrated to a high degree and operations affect each other directly. Lenovo benefits from this high level of integration, making the company's strategy fairly global.

Therefore, according to Yip's framework, Lenovo can be identified as one of the first Chinese firms to truly go global in all aspects of its strategic endeavors. Still, his framework does not inform us of how Lenovo has achieved this level of globalization. Using the I-R framework, we can note that Lenovo is placed in the upper left-hand corner with a high level of integration and a low level of responsiveness. Now, we must ask whether the ultimate point is whether it should really be in that upper left-hand corner.

According to Bartlett and Ghoshal, the firm's ultimate move is to become a transnational firm. More specifically, they imply that the firm's total assets and capabilities must be dispersed yet interdependent. The firm should possess the strengths of a multinational as well as a global firm. For example, having a high level of local responsiveness while simultaneously possessing the strengths of a global firm shows a high level of integration. This requires a much more complex configuration of activities for the firm.

Again, utilizing the I-R framework, we can follow Bartlett and Ghoshal's logic when explaining the development of a firm. In the upper right-hand corner lies transnational. This is a high level of integration coupled with a high level of responsiveness. Having already applied the I-R framework to Yip's interpretation of a firm, we know that Lenovo lies in the upper left-hand side of the framework. Thus, we can determine that it can be classified as a global firm (see Fig. 9). However, a point of contention may be how Lenovo actually reached the global position. Was the firm able to bypass the multinational stage through its 2005 acquisition of IBM's ThinkPad division? In any case, Lenovo has yet to become a truly transnational firm.

Kedia and Mukherji (1999) offer a viewpoint from a management perspective on how to reach the final stage of transnationalism. They argue that management of days gone by was overly focused on hard issues such as cost reduction, manufacturing, and budget allocation. Today, soft issues such as firm values, culture, vision, and leadership are often more important than hard issues. Here, changing from one

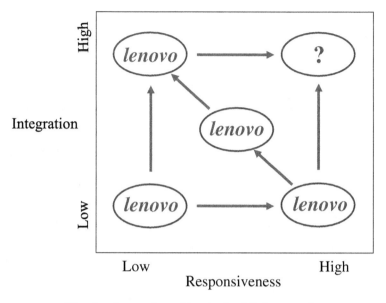

Fig. 9. Lenovo's position in the I-R framework.

focus to another is not the issue. Rather, finding the balance is the most important aspect for efficient management.

The authors identify four different types of managers: the defender, the explorer, the controller, and the integrator. Sticking with our I-R framework, we can place these four types into the framework in order to analyze current positions and future management strategy (see Fig. 10). The defender can be placed in the lower left (domestic) corner due to its emphasis on the domestic market and fear of the international market. The explorer can be placed in the lower right-hand (multi-domestic) corner due to its acknowledgement of the importance of foreign opportunities and its initial parlay into foreign markets. The controller can be placed in the upper left-hand corner (global), as it is willing to take a far more coordinated approach to going abroad. Finally, the integrator can be classified as a transnational manager (upper right-hand corner), as the integrator is able to integrate and leverage diversity, which is very different from the other management styles.

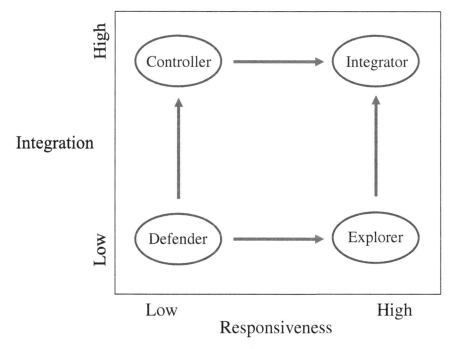

Fig. 10. Management styles from an I-R framework perspective.

According to Fig. 10, Lenovo is located in the upper left corner or controller. Its strategy has been successful, partly because in 2005, the company acquired the personal computer division of IBM, which was a well-established and internationally experienced company. If Lenovo had not purchased this division from IBM, the company might have gone through all the necessary international business and cultural experiences. The acquisition of Motorola in 2014 has also helped Lenovo achieve a breakthrough in the mobile phone market around the world. Furthermore, Lenovo acquired Fujitsu's PC business in 2017, by setting up a joint venture in which Lenovo took a majority stake of 51%. The acquisition is expected to help Lenovo enhance its product portfolio and enter high-end product lines. The purchase of renowned global companies, or alliances with them, may be a fast route toward becoming a global company for a latecomer, such as Lenovo.

Discussion Questions

1. Yip talks of five global strategy levers. Are any of the five elements now obsolete or can you think of an additional lever to add to the list? Explain.

2. Do you agree with Yip's benefits and drawbacks of having a global strategy? Why or why not?

3. What other factors do you think influence born globals to go abroad from their inception?

4. Bartlett and Ghoshal offer a framework of classifying multinational, global, international, and transnational firms. Do you agree with the definitions provided?

5. Previously, we have used the term multi-domestic. Where does "multi-domestic" fit into Bartlett and Ghoshal's framework?

6. According to Bartlett and Ghoshal, the final destination is not global but transnational. Do you agree with this perspective? Discuss.

7. In your opinion, is Lenovo a multinational, international, global, or transnational firm? Explain your choice.

CHAPTER 11

Dynamic Perspectives on Globalization

Chapter Guideline

In this final chapter, we will look at the critical relationship between the external environment and the firm itself. Are firms prisoners of the given environment or can they proactively change it? This is a critical question that must be examined because much of the existing literature is focused on explaining how firms can succeed in a given environment. The following articles will present different views on this critical issue so that we can get a firm grasp of the link between the exogenous and endogenous variables that determine the world of global business strategy.

Summary of Previous Chapters

Our long journey into the world of global business strategy is now approaching the end as we come to the final chapter. By now, we hope that you have been able to grasp a firm understanding of the cutting-edge issues related to global business strategy. While we have seen many viewpoints from various scholars on numerous subjects, the link between controllable and uncontrollable variables has yet to be analyzed. This chapter will raise the issue of how firms can influence the exogenous variables and change the very environment in which they operate. The answer to this may leave us with profound implications as to how we should perceive and execute global business strategy.

11.1 Controlling the Uncontrollable

Are we prisoners or masters of our destinies? This is a question which many scholars have pondered upon. Before the advent of scientific thinking and enlightenment, human beings were generally overwhelmed by the seemingly insurmountable power of nature and held a deterministic view on human destiny. This all changed following the enlightenment and renaissance period when scholars began to develop a more proactive mindset under the premise that humans are masters of their own destinies. Indeed, the human conception of the link between the endogenous and exogenous variables of life has significantly evolved throughout history. Such a perspective is reflected in the words of the great renaissance thinker Machiavelli who wrote, "God is not willing to do everything, and thus take away our free will and that share of glory which belongs to us" (Machiavelli, 2003, p. 82).

The discipline of international business is no exception to this general trend, and many scholars have pondered on whether strategic decisions can actually shape the business environment we operate in. Surprisingly, a majority of scholars and managers have assumed a more deterministic view and regard the business environment as fixed. This is quite surprising considering the modern and forward-looking nature of international business as a discipline. The root of this trend lies in its inherent volatile nature. Because myriads of variables interact on a daily basis to constantly create new and unfamiliar situations, scholars and managers have come to believe that the business environment is essentially uncontrollable.

This seems particularly true in the contemporary business environment, which is characterized by its dynamic nature and frequent changes and is referred to as VUCA or Volatility, Uncertainty, Complexity, and Ambiguity (Saleh and Watson, 2017). In such an environment, firms should not only provide quality products and services, but modify their strategies as well to better adapt to the changing conditions in a fast and responsive manner (Horney *et al.*, 2010).

Still, business is largely a human phenomenon, and we are all components of this apparently uncontrollable force. If the fundamental constituent unit of business is humans, it is then reasonable to argue that human will has the power to change the fundamentals of the phenomena we observe in international business. Of course, this is not to deny the immovable fact that business is significantly affected by uncontrollable variables such as pandemics, climate change, and politics. However, unlike natural science, the rationale for the social science is to derive general implications and prescriptions to provide shortcuts toward understanding the real world. Social science should not only concern itself with learning a theory but also provide a concrete guideline that can translate theory into practice.

As DeRond and Thietart (2007) noted, strategic management would seem pointless in a deterministic universe. Managers make strategic choices because they believe these will influence the course of events. Additionally, they must believe their choices to be freely made in principle even if they often remain subject to various constraints. In a similar vein, the strategic choice theory argues that external constraints are not sufficient to explain capabilities among decision-makers when exercising choices, and the characteristics of decision-makers such as mindsets should be considered as well (Jewer and Mckay, 2012). Still, the causation between strategic choice and outcome seems unclear at best. Some even argued that in the case of small and medium-sized enterprises, because of their small size, they are unable to induce much change through strategic choices and are largely bound to exogenous and endogenous constraints (Harvie and Lee, 2002; Kirby and Watson, 2003; Fogel *et al.*, 2006).

Professor P. Rajan Varadarajan has been instrumental in contributing to the theoretical development of marketing strategy. One of his research strengths is to develop theoretical issues into tangible issues linked to the real-world businesses (Bharadwaj, 2010). The influential research of Varadarajan *et al.* (1992) takes a deeper look into the power of strategic choice versus environmental determinism. The authors conclude that the most successful marketers can proactively create a favorable environment.

Environmental Determinism vs. Strategic Choice

According to Varadarajan *et al.*, the following are some representative analytical tools and frameworks derived from a deterministic view of business:

- *Product Life Cycle (PLC)* — Ever since Vernon introduced this concept in 1966, it has become one of the most important tools in marketing analysis.[1] The key to this concept is a stage model that maps the introduction, growth, maturity, and decline of an industry, product, or brand. This essentially leaves marketers with a passive role of managing the brand, product, or industry based on the cycle which they go through.

- *Matrix Approach to Product Portfolio Analysis and Planning* — The matrix approach is a very useful analytical tool, which organizes strategic objectives and direction in a readily comprehensible framework. For example, the Boston Consulting Group's growth share matrix designates the optimal strategic movement based on given market conditions. Similar to the PLC concept, the matrix approach assumes that market conditions are essentially uncontrollable as its purpose is to map out the consequences of certain strategic choices within the confines of given constraints.

- *Profit Impact of Market Strategy (PIMS)* — This approach aggregates and analyzes historical data from thousands of small business units to answer the following question: "Which strategy pursued under what conditions produces what results?" This is a useful tool as analysts and strategic planners can look back at past performances in order to devise the most effective strategies for the future. However, similar to the previous tools, it derives its assumptions from previous market conditions, which renders the analysis to be static.

---

[1] See Vernon (1966) for further explanations.

- *The Industrial Organization Economics Approach* — Porter's (1980) "Competitive Strategy" is a prime example of this school of thought. This approach focuses on structural determinants of an industry that induce the firm's actions to enhance their performance. Firm performance, therefore, is a function of structural elements such as the threat posed by competitors and barriers to market entry. Although Porter emphasized the power of firms to change the industrial structure in their given environment, many subsequent adherents of Porter's thoughts omitted this critical point and focused more on the deterministic aspects of his work.

The above discussion demonstrates how many adhere to the deterministic view of business strategy. Yet, there are some scholars and managers who have challenged this conventional view with innovative strategic tools that are outlined below.

Strategies to Influence Demand

- *Primary Demand Stimulation* — Demand can be divided into primary and secondary demands. The former refers to the absolute size of the demand, while the latter refers to the share. Therefore, primary demand stimulation focuses on enlarging the market itself. Rather than passively waiting for the market growth to fluctuate, this method attempts to proactively control the market growth

- *The Product Evolutionary Cycle (PEC)* — Clearly named as an antithesis for the product life cycle (PLC) concept, the PEC does not define a sequence of cycles. Rather, the PEC only defines a beginning and an end and believes that everything within these two extremes is controllable.

- *Strategic Self-Renewal* — This is designed as an antithesis to the Matrix Approach and is based on the premise that managerial action can actually influence the environment. Rather than looking at the past as fixed, this approach regards past market conditions as flexible and focuses on how managerial decisions could have altered the given environment.

- *Stimulational Marketing* — This is a very unique approach which attempts to create demand where there is none. For example, an Italian restaurant provided rolls of toilet paper branded with the restaurant's logo for customers who ordered takeout meals during the COVID-19 pandemic lockdown in 2020. As toilet paper was in great demand during the pandemic, such a marketing strategy has a positive impact in stimulating customers to order more meals from the restaurant (Edinger, 2020).

- *Mandatory Consumption Stimulation* — Firms can promote consumption through inducing regulatory and legislative changes. For example, smoke detector manufacturers have created mandatory consumption for their products after making lawmakers understand the importance of fire safety.

Strategies for Macro-environmental Change

- *Issues Management* — Issues management refers to identifying and managing issues that might affect the firm's operations. For example, firms with an environmentally unfriendly image can change this public perception through advertising and corporate social responsibility (CSR) activities.

- *Corporate Political Activity* — Commonly known as lobbying, firms can actively induce politicians to alter regulations and public policies to be more favorable to the firm's operations. For example, the Big Tech companies — Facebook, Amazon, Apple, and Google — combined to spend more than US$20 million on lobbying in the first half of 2020 with the focus on legislation, such as pursuing the enforcement of the state's new online privacy rules (CNBC, 2020; *The New York Times*, 2020).

- *Mega-marketing Strategies* — Firms can strategically coordinate their economic, political, and public relations activities in order to create a favorable operating environment. Mega-marketing strategies incorporate various tools to comprehensively manage and eliminate the barriers that inhibit the firm's activities.

- *New Game Strategies* — Similar to the Blue Ocean concept, this strategy creates new demands among populations that were previously untapped by satisfying a whole new set of customer needs. For example, the introduction of the iPhone by Apple in 2007 has shifted consumer demand toward smartphones from traditional feature phones.

While many of the above tools have been the source of political controversy, they are available for firms to shape their own destinies rather than to react passively in a given environment.

Analysis

Management scholars stress the adaptation among firms to the changing environment and the capability of exploiting their existing competencies and building new ones required for such a change (Helfat and Peteraf, 2003; Raisch and Birkinshaw, 2008). By contrast, strategy theorists pursue a more proactive approach and emphasize firms' ability to disrupt inertia by modifying or replacing their core competences to sustain the firm's performance for the long run (Agarwal and Helfat, 2009; Lechner and Floyd, 2012).

Bourgeois (1984) noted that if we followed the deterministic view on strategic management, we might as well resign ourselves to surrendering to the matrix of deterministic forces presented by environmental, technical, and human forces that impinge on the freedom of choice. At best, management becomes a computational exercise and at worst, it becomes a reactive waiting game, exploiting contingencies only as they arise through political forces. This is especially problematic because the very purpose of strategy is to distinguish one's firm from its competitors.

Therefore, the strategic decisions pursued by firms cannot be assumed to be the product of deterministic forces in their environment. In essence, strategic management itself, according to Bourgeois, cannot exist when confined within the boundaries of environmental determinism. Of course, this must not be misconstrued as neglecting the importance of environmental constraint. As a matter of fact, being overly confident in the power of humans could be equally misleading. As Hrebiniak and Joyce (1985) explain, strategic choice and environmental determinism are not mutually exclusive concepts, but are rather two separate independent variables that can be positioned on two separate continua to develop a typology of organizational adaptation.

Due to the growing global competition, shorter product life cycles, and accelerated technological breakthroughs, firms face new challenges with environmental scarcity (Schmitt *et al.*, 2016). This is defined as follows: "The decline in an ecological niche's size or shape, which leads to resource scarcity, has increased managerial complexity and organizational stress, which in turn have been found to affect a firm's ability to renew strategically" (Schmitt *et al.*, 2016). Facing these types of challenges and uncertainties, firms require initiatives for strategic alignment that are both proactive and reactive. The former initiative refers to firms that are proactive in anticipating future environmental changes or exploring emerging business opportunities in the future, whereas the latter initiative is marked by being responsive to the past or ongoing environmental changes (Eggers and Kaplan, 2009).

In this respect, excessive faith in one idea or the other will never lead to the optimal outcome. The "golden mean," or in Mandarin Chinese *zhong yong*, is always an important perspective that we should keep in mind. For example, if a strategist adopts an overly deterministic view, he or she may be limiting themselves to mediocre achievements at best. On the contrary, if a strategist becomes overly ambitious and believes he or she can override any constraints through strategy, then he or she will jeopardize his or her organization through reckless decisions. Somewhere in the middle, we may find the golden mean to strategic management.

This lesson can be applied to academic endeavors. For example, many young scholars are eager to incorporate bold and creative ideas in their academic pursuits. However, in many cases, they fail to obtain substantial progress because they forget that new ideas must be grounded on a thorough understanding of past studies. New ideas without a solid foundation are more than likely to end up being incoherent and incomprehensible. On the contrary, some students suffer from the polar opposite problem as they become overly prudent and limit themselves to previous studies. Any meaningful scholarly work must advance the state-of-the-art knowledge. The key, therefore, is to do both and keep a healthy balance without overly swaying toward one side. For this purpose, keeping the following formula in mind will help students achieve the difficult task of contributing to academia:

$$\Delta + \alpha = \square + ?$$

This seemingly cryptic formula summarizes the secret to inducing proactive change based on a solid understanding of the past. Δ represents the past, accumulated knowledge which scholars must acquire through thorough research. This provides a solid foundation for extending the frontiers of academia. For its part, α is the additional scholarly contribution to the existing body of knowledge. This represents the portion of the proactive change that we can induce through our ability. The combination of the two leaves us with $\square$ which represents the more advanced body of knowledge that is derived from integrating the existing knowledge with our contribution.

In any case, one cannot stand without the other and all young scholars must note that both elements, the past and the future, must be present to truly make meaningful contributions. Nothing though is perfect as there are always potential extensions that can be made by ourselves or by someone else, as represented by the symbol ? at the end. This will also enable students and scholars to take constructive criticism and further improve on their findings. Keeping this simple formula in mind will help us organize and understand our position as scholars in terms of how to make meaningful contributions to the academic discipline.

11.2 Standardization: Key to Success?

The rise of emerging markets is one of the most exciting topics in international business today. From the strategic management perspective, the big debate is centered on the appropriate strategy to adopt when entering these markets. In recent years, developing countries have become increasingly important destinations for developed-country MNCs, due to market liberalization, rapid growth of gross domestic product (GDP), increased consumption, improvement in labor skills, and institutional and political reforms (Hansen and Gwozds, 2015). In 2019, about 45% of global foreign direct investment (FDI) flowed into developing countries (UNCTAD, 2020).

Should multinationals simply elevate their existing strategies into these new arenas or should they customize their strategies to fit the specific market conditions in emerging markets? Khanna and Palepu (2006) noted that successful companies develop strategies for doing business in emerging markets that are different from those they use at home and often find novel ways of implementing them. However, scholars such as Springer and Czinkota (1999) urged that Western firms might find it beneficial to pursue a strategy of actually altering the emerging marketing environment step by step in order to move it closer to a functioning market economy. Rather than tailoring corporate strategy according to each market (as Khanna and Palepu prescribed), successful firms are those that change the market itself in order to create a favorable operating environment. So, what is the most effective way to achieve success in emerging markets?

A case in point for this section is the Central and Eastern European (CEE) region, which has emerged as an exciting new market with soaring consumer demands and rapid deregulation. The Czech Republic, Hungary, Poland, Slovakia, and Slovenia have all rapidly moved from a centrally planned economy to a liberal market democracy since the fall of the Iron Curtain in 1989. Their incorporation into the European Union (EU) also added to their market attractiveness significantly. Unsurprisingly, many international firms rushed in to gain a foothold in this arena because of the potentially lucrative payoffs. Yet, the fundamental dilemma for many of these firms has been whether to differentiate or standardize their marketing strategy into the CEE region. Intuitively, because this region is a distinct market sphere with different consumer tastes, income levels, and other elements, a strong case can be made for customization. At the same time though, a surprising number of firms in various industries have adopted the opposite strategy, i.e., a standardized approach in the CEE region. As Arnold, Chadraba, and Springer (2001) concluded, although the CEE region is in a transition period (albeit a rapid one), the region will ultimately converge to the standards of the industrialized Western countries. Springer and Czinkota (1999) went further to state that a successful transformation of the formerly planned economies to a vibrant market economy requires the development of a market orientation. This means that international firms can have further opportunities by helping restructure society and business processes in order to improve the standard of living in the CEE region.

Schuh (2000) presents the reasons behind why large multinationals have adopted a standardized approach in entering the CEE region. The main analytical framework utilized by the author is illustrated schematically in Fig. 1.

As can be seen in the above framework, both external and internal factors affect the decision of whether to standardize a marketing program or not. Furthermore, the variety of tools at the hands of a marketing manager that can help decide on the degree of standardization is illustrated inside the square box at the center of Fig. 1. Based on this framework, the author analyzed eight prominent companies, which entered the CEE region: 3M, Philips Electronics, McDonald's, Ogilvy & Mather, BBAG, Argana AG, Felix Austria, and Henkel CEE.

The key findings show that out of the eight companies, six have pursued a highly standardized marketing program, while the other two implemented a dual strategy of offering both localized and globally standardized products. This is a very interesting finding, considering the fact that all these companies operate in different industries.

How was this possible? The common reasoning behind this is that within the price-sensitive and mostly low-income CEE countries,

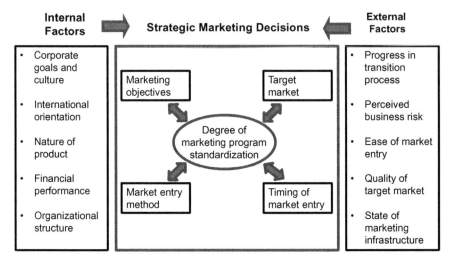

Fig. 1.   Framework for determining standardization of international marketing program.
Source: Schuh (2000).

there exists a relatively affluent middle- to high-income segment, which yearns for a global lifestyle, similar to the standards of advanced Western nations. In this sense, these companies were able to exploit that market segment through their global brand image as a way to satisfy the global product standard and lifestyle that this segment wishes to consume. Furthermore, by integrating the marketing operation into a globally standardized one, these companies opted to reduce coordination costs which could arise with an overly customized approach.

Of course, certain differentiating aspects such as labeling content, instructions, and certain product mixes, as McDonald's offers a different version of the local cuisine, are present. However, even this slight degree of customization is confined to marginal aspects. The overwhelming trend exhibited by multinationals operating in the CEE market is to standardize the basic platform and modify the periphery.

These case studies are very interesting as intuitive thinking would favor localization when marketing in this region. When analyzed with a comprehensive framework as in Fig. 2, the reasons for

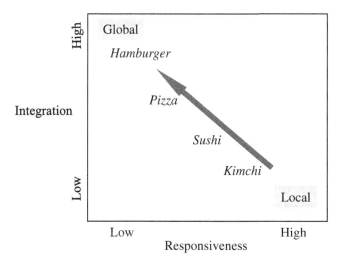

Fig. 2. Different strategic positioning.

Source: Moon (2005).

standardization can be easily understood. Another important point is the expectations among these corporations that customer preferences will evolve over time and will converge to the global standard. Increasing income in the CEE region will promote further integration with the rest of Europe, which will then lead to increased homogenization of customer needs. Most importantly, the corporations not only anticipate but accelerate this process through their strategic choice.

Analysis

Schuh's analysis presents a very vivid picture of international companies operating in the CEE region. The implications are quite profound as most of these firms are pursuing a global standardized operation rather than a regionalized or localized one. A more general lesson can be derived from this article. The classic debate between customization and standardization has sparked numerous offshoots in academia and many scholars have had heated discussions on this subject. As we have seen from Chapter 9, the debate is polarized between Levitt's position (standardization) and Douglas and Wind's position (customization), while Ghoshal and Bartlett have proposed a transnational solution as a synthesis. Schuh's study has added an interesting perspective to this debate, by observing a fairly standardized strategy in much differentiated markets. This is a compelling observation, which will be further looked at in the next section.

Another interesting aspect of the CEE region is the infiltration of firms from emerging economies — Emerging Multinational Companies (EMNCs) such as those from Brazil, China, India, Mexico, and South Africa (Kim and Park, 2015). These firms not only have the capabilities for providing products of global standard but they also have the ability to promote cost-competitive goods to cater to the lower-income segments which established corporations are reluctant to do. Despite their disadvantages, many firms from emerging countries have been successful in aggressively developing their own brands in the international arena (Erdğmus *et al.*, 2010; Luo, 2007; Moon, 2016a, 2016b). Case Study 2 that analyzes Arçelik's thrust into the CEE region will present a more detailed look into this phenomenon.

11.3 The World is Not Flat... But You Can Flatten It!

Over the years, scholars and researchers have examined standardization versus customization with regard to international marketing strategy. Despite this extensive discussion, the debate rages on and we are then left with often confusing and overlapping prescriptions. Other studies on topics such as glocal (Robertson, 1995), regionalization (Rugman, 2000), Metanational (Doz *et al.*, 2001), and Multiunit Enterprise (Garvin and Levesque, 2008) add to the already complex landscape of this age-old debate. Hence, the findings presented in the literature are still very fragmented and have yet to provide any clear insights (Tan and Sousa, 2013).

All of the above analyses in fact share a common limitation which reduces their explanatory powers: they adopt a static view of internationalization. While previous attempts have done remarkably well in terms of depicting a certain moment in time, not many have been able to accurately convey the dynamic and constantly evolving nature of internationalization. However, as we have seen in previous sections, the various forces that determine our settings are not set in stone. Rather, these forces can change, especially depending on our strategic choices.

Moon (2005) presents a different picture to this debate by adopting a dynamic perspective. In other words, the real issue is not to choose one of two extremes, nor to reach a compromise between the two, but how to increase the degree of standardization by enhancing the product values. We also need to clearly distinguish product standardization from that of other marketing mix elements. Coca-Cola, for example, may have different promotion and distribution strategies across borders, but the product itself is highly standardized. As a matter of fact, Coca-Cola has discontinued many of the products that it used to promote for local responsiveness. Cola Blak, which was promoted largely in the CEE region, was discontinued as well as Coca Cola C2 that was designed for Japanese consumers.

Consider the difference between a hamburger and kimchi. A hamburger is a highly global item which is consumed by billions of consumers all around the world. Kimchi, on the contrary, is a highly local product, which caters to a uniquely Korean preference for fermented vegetables fused with high-doses of garlic, red pepper, and fish extracts. This logic is mapped in Fig. 2.

Why is this so? Is the hamburger an inherently superior food to kimchi? Far from it; the health benefits of kimchi have been very well documented, while the various negative effects of hamburgers have been shockingly presented by numerous documentaries such as *Super Size Me*. The answer is quite simple; the hamburger provides a more convenient and comprehensive option at a much lower price than kimchi. While the hamburger was originally an American staple, it has rapidly gained prominence as a global food item due to its superior value in terms of low cost and good quality.

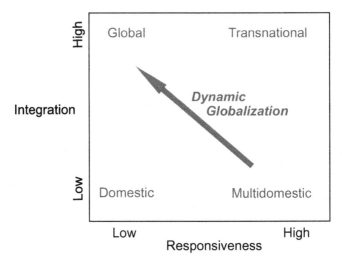

Fig. 3. Types of international strategies.
Source: Moon (2005).

Therefore, the real issue is not to choose between standardization and customization or to compromise between the two. Rather the primary concern should be on how to increase the degree of standardization. A truly successful firm does not choose one or the other, but boldly elevates the country-specific strategy to a global level through standardization. Thus, the firm can raise the timeless values of "low cost and high quality" to a degree which can override the national preferences and dissimilarities. One need not look any further but at the millions of Koreans, who are well known for their unyielding love for kimchi while also consuming Big Macs and Whoppers. If we ask any of these Korean consumers if they like hamburgers more than kimchi, the overwhelming majority will answer "No." But, why then do they flock to McDonald's or Burger King for a quick lunch? Simply because the utility generated from the good quality and low cost of hamburgers, as well as convenience in terms of time and location, overrides the national preference for kimchi.

As we can see in Fig. 3, the appropriate approach is to elevate a multi-domestic or even domestic strategy to the global level. This brings us to the last and most important point as the fundamental premise of all debates so far has been static and assumed the market conditions to be fixed. However, the reality is dynamic, and rather than simply treating the world as flat, individuals and corporations have the power to actually flatten it. Therefore, instead of dwelling on old certainties, it is important for firms to create new possibilities to induce changes that are more conducive to their operations.

The world's successful global products such as Coca-Cola, McDonald's hamburger, and Levi Strauss Jeans have all followed this formula of elevating a national- or local-level product to the global level. McDonald's has achieved worldwide success providing high economic value through its products based on a highly integrated and standardized formula. While the difference in national preferences for food is an important prevailing force, McDonald's was able to override the desire for non-economic factors by offering high economic factors, namely, good-quality and low-cost goods, convenience of time, and convenient location. Therefore, the real focus is not to choose between standardization and customization, but to elevate the country-specific strategy to a global level through enhancing economic values to a degree which can override the local preferences and dissimilarities.

Analysis

The final section of this book leaves us with an important topic for thought. How are we to view this ever-changing world? Most academic disciplines have had their fair share of debate on this common topic. Some emphasize the increasing differences among various cultural, societal, and economic groupings, while others perceive a converging and integrating world. In international relations, the end of the Cold War brought about the dichotomy between Huntington's *Clash of Civilization* (1996) forecast and Fukuyama's *End of History* (1992) thesis. Huntington argues that the world is heading toward the next great conflict in which the battle lines will be marked by cultural differences. On the contrary, Fukuyama insists that with the end of the Cold War we are witnessing a general convergence into

Western-style free market democracy, a process he calls the "end of history." In linguistics, Noam Chomsky (1976) suggests that a common pattern among all languages can be found which he dubbed "Universal Grammar," while others[2] believe that this is a limited phenomenon and only shows part of the story. In the world of international business, Douglas and Wind (1987) and Levitt (1983) form two opposing pillars, as has been explained extensively in the preceding sections.

On a more general level, globalization generates two apparently paradoxical trends, which have confounded many observers. On the one hand, globalization integrates the world into singularity while, on the hand, simultaneously accentuating the prevailing differences among national, cultural, and societal groups. The debate between standardization and customization and all the related discussions are derived from these two opposing phenomena. However, at least in the realm of international business, the fundamental question that we should never forget is as follows: "How to maximize profit?" Or put differently, "how to sell what to whom?" The best answer for both questions is to "find more important similarities and come up with ways to flatten other differences to your advantage."

Case Study 1: Globalizing China[3]

The key point of this chapter offers a number of methods and ways by which a firm can proactively stimulate business and alter the macro-environment in which it functions. Thus, firms are not necessarily passive entities subject to the uncontrollable forces of their

---

[2]For example, see Francis Lin (2017). https://www.sciencedirect.com/science/article/pii/S002438411730147X.

[3]Parts of this case study are extracted from the Air China Official Website (www.airchina.com; www.airchina.us), Euro-monitor (Coffee Brews a Future in China, September 2004), SINOPEC Official Website (www.sinopec.com), and https://www.theguardian.com/environment/2020/sep/10/pollutionwatch-air-pollution-in-china-falling-study-shows.

environment, but can be proactive and influence the very environment in which they operate to their advantage.

In previous case studies, we have presented particular firms and their experiences through a variety of frameworks and theories. But, for this case study we are going to focus on the experiences of a number of firms from or operating in a particular country, namely, China. Why China? Simply, it is a country where firms have been forced to shape the environment in which they function. This example offers us a unique opportunity to study the firms that have developed and expanded in new and exciting ways to incorporate the Chinese market into a global business, thereby expanding their scope of business.

Let us first look at Air China in the context of primary demand stimulation, which can increase one's market share using tools such as product promotion. When Air China first started out in 1988, it was a little known, mostly domestic airline company. But, over the years, it has managed to grow into a major international airline. As of the end of 2019, the company owned a total of 699 aircrafts of various types, mainly those manufactured by Boeing and Airbus. Air China flies to 43 countries and regions, and serves 187 airports, which include 65 international and 119 domestic cities. Air China is the largest airline by brand value in China (Valued at RMB167,876,000,000 by World Brand Lab in June 2019).

The main reason for Air China's remarkable growth had been the stimulation of consumer demand, both domestically and internationally through product/service promotion, although, like all other airlines, it has suffered since the COVID-19 pandemic. Initially, Air China negotiated with the Chinese government to become the only air carrier authorized to fly national leaders to its numerous destinations and transport foreign dignitaries and government leaders to China. Furthermore, Air China was one of the first airlines to develop regional hubs in Chengdu, Shanghai, and Guangzhou, rather than simply focusing on Beijing, thus extending its reach throughout China. The firm also attached great importance to cooperating with foreign airlines and has signed code-sharing agreements with domestic and foreign airlines, thus allowing the firm to offer domestic and foreign customers more convenient flight options. In 2008, Air China became the sole airline partner for the Beijing Olympic Games. In this respect, Air China knew it had to actively expand its own market through various promotional activities in order to avoid being perceived as a low-level domestic only service.

For another example, think back to Chapter 1 and recall the case study regarding Starbucks in China from a stimulation marketing perspective. China is renowned for its tea-drinking culture, yet the coffee culture that is so popular in the US has also spread to China. In recent years, Starbucks has opened more than 90 outlets around the country, and is set to open even more in the future. But, just how did Starbucks create and expand its demand? First, it appealed to adventurous, open-minded, young, and affluent urban consumers. This demographic already looked favorably toward Western lifestyles and was eager to try goods and services that gave them the utility of a sophisticated and modern outlook. Starbucks was able to reinforce this idea by further appealing to returnees or the huge number of Chinese students who have come back from Western countries in recent years. Many of these students lived abroad for an extended period of time and have returned with a Westernized consumer preference that is reinforced with high salaries and fashionable lifestyles. Lastly, Starbucks has tapped into the foreign expatriate communities and Western tourists, people who are generally big coffee drinkers.

Case Study 2: Back to Turkey's Arçelik[4]

If you recall, we have already looked at the case study involving Arçelik, and have highlighted its uniqueness and growth pattern. We are going back to look once more at the same Turkish white goods firm, but from a different perspective.

---

[4]Parts of this case study are extracted from the Arçelik Official Website (www.arcelik.com/tr), Appliancedesign.com (Arçelik Acquires Arctic of Romania, September 2002), and https://www.romania-insider.com/arctic-eur-1-bln-revenues (23 January 2019).

In the second section of this chapter, eight firms in the CEE region were analyzed in order to discover whether the firms used a standardized or differentiated marketing program for this particular region. Counterintuitively, it was discovered that six of the eight used a highly standardized marketing program, while the remaining two implemented a dual-strategy marketing program. Arçelik is another firm that once endeavored to enter the CEE region, and it is noteworthy to analyze how Arçelik has operated in this environment.

As mentioned in the previous case study, Arçelik has experienced rapid international growth. Through a variety of investments, acquisitions, and strategic alliances, in 2019 alone, Arçelik achieved a 19% revenue growth and international sales have increased by 17%. While Arçelik has been looking to expand into more advanced economies with the strategic focus on Europe, it has not ignored the underdeveloped potential market that exists in the nearby CEE region.

With a GDP of around US$249.6 billion and a GDP per capita of US$12,902 estimated for 2020 by the World Bank, Romania is an upper-middle-income economy and has been part of the European Union since January 1, 2007. This newly prospering nation offers a unique challenge for firms such as Arçelik. After the communist regime collapsed in late 1989 following the Romanian Revolution, the country experienced a decade of economic instability and decline, led in part by an obsolete industrial base and a lack of structural reform. It is, therefore, only since early 2000 that the nation has experienced any lasting form of stability. This is quite representative of the CEE region and provides a unique environment, as there is an emerging upper-middle-income band, but there still exists a significant lower-income band within the population.

After analyzing the unique environment of the CEE countries, and in particular Romania, Arçelik decided to opt for a dual marketing strategy in order to satisfy both kinds of consumers:

- Those who want a high-quality product, with a recognizable name brand, and do not mind paying extra for such product in order to emulate a more Westernized lifestyle (Type 1).

- Those who want a reliable quality product, with a reliable name brand at a reasonable price (Type 2).

Thus, when Arçelik first entered Romania, it sought to target the Type 1 consumer. Using its internationally recognized brand Beko, Arcelik signaled a standardized, global message to the upper-middle-income Romanian customers. In this way, Beko was able to garner success and has become an established, trusted, and desirable brand in the country.

Despite this achievement, Arçelik still needed to cater to consumer Type 2. Building a low-cost trusted brand in Romania would take the firm a considerable amount of time, funds, and effort, all of which Arçelik's management wished to avoid, especially since local low-cost white goods providers already possessed a remarkable ability to capture distinct local preferences. Without the image of a Western multinational or the advantage of a local firm, Arçelik would have been led astray. Its strategy in response was to set its sights on the local brand Arctic. This company was the most powerful name in Romania with 96% brand awareness and was the market leader with a market share exceeding 30%. In 2002, Arçelik acquired Arctic, and continued the tradition of catering to the lower-income population of Romania. Today, Arctic is the largest local home appliance producer. The company exports about 80% of its total production to 70 countries, which makes it one of Romania's largest exporters. In 2019, it completed the construction of a factory that focuses on the production of washing machines. The new production factory is expected to help the company double its production of household appliances.

Looking once more at Fig. 1 of Section 11.2, we can see that Arçelik carefully considered its marketing objectives, target market, market entry mode, and timing when deciding on the degree of marketing program standardization. In particular, the range of consumers that exists in this type of emerging economy and the possibilities for gaining a larger market share had a great influence on Arçelik's decision to expand into the market using both a standardized and customized approach.

Case Study 3: Green Tea and Hamburgers Go Global?[5]

Green tea has been around for centuries and its origins can be traced back to China. According to some legends, it dates back to approximately 2,700 BC, but a number of theories suggest an even more historic origin. Some claim that a man called Shien Non Shei discovered the plant, tasted a leaf from it, and found it to be perfect. He then decided to mix it with water and make a drink out of it, as he believed that the drink had medicinal qualities. However, another story goes that Emperor Shen Nung came upon the tea when a leaf from the plant fell into a cup of hot water he was drinking at the time. Whatever your belief of its origin, green tea has been used in China as a healthy and medicinal drink for thousands of years.

Based upon this, we can assume that green tea began its product life as a highly localized and customized product. Making a cup of green tea was regarded as a distinct Chinese art form. Appropriate utensils had to be used, the water temperature had to be monitored, and the leaves themselves were not processed, but had to be mixed with the water and then strained. The green tea then spread throughout the Northeast Asian region and became a highly popular pastime in both Korea and Japan. Yet, as these nations are somewhat similar in culture and values, the product itself maintained a high degree of regionalization and customization.

Over the years, the methodology behind brewing a cup of green tea has become a much simpler process, largely in part due to a desire to sell the product to other markets outside of the East Asian region. Thus, the simplification of the product has allowed it to essentially go global. In order to simplify it, the level of local responsiveness has

---

[5] Parts of this case study are extracted from the Tata Tea Official Website (www. tatatea.com), Zhejiang Tea Import and Export Company's Official Website (www. chinagreentea.com), Dr. Lee's Tea for Health Official Website (www.teaforhealth. com), https://worldteanews.com/market-trends-data-and-insights/green-tea-market-expected-to-grow, and History of the Hamburger (www.whatscooking america.net).

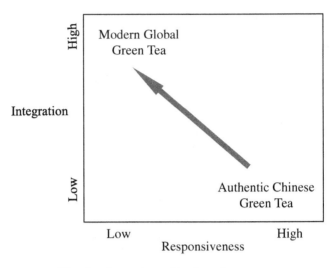

Fig. 4. Strategic positioning of green tea.

been decreased dramatically, thus making it more appealing to Western customers. Figure 4 represents this, in that the tea industry has moved from a multi-domestic strategy, which includes a high level of local responsiveness and a low level of global integration, to a global strategy. This is representative of a high level of global integration and a low level of local responsiveness.

Tata Tea, an Indian tea company, realized the potential of green tea in the global market. As part of this interest, it began a joint venture with Zhejiang Tea Import and Export Company in China. Their goal was to bring high-quality green tea at a low price and in a recognizable manner to the global consumer. Thus, the two firms have shifted their strategic positioning from multi-domestic to global by introducing a more standardized product, namely, the green tea bag, which is easier and more convenient for global consumers. This strategic shift is represented by the upper left-hand corner in Fig. 5.

According to the recent report from Global Industry Analysts (GIA) projects, Green tea bags have the potential to grow at more than 6.3% by 2025 and will also experience 4.9% growth in the US. What is interesting is that the US did not import tea from China between the 1950s and the 1970s. The imports were flat in the

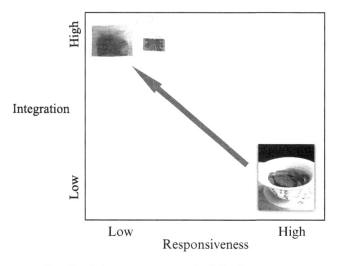

Fig. 5. Joint venture strategic shift of green tea.

1990s, but quickly increased since the mid-2000s. Nowadays, it has become one of the top three tea importers in the world. In addition to the instant tea bags, the recent versatility of the style of tea such as green tea lattes, iced green teas, and sparkling green teas has propelled its popularity among consumers around the world. Therefore, Asian firms have taken a traditionally purely local product and altered it slightly to appeal to the international consumers. They essentially flattened their world through dynamic global strategies.

While the case of green tea does prove our point, there exists an even better and far more recognizable example than this. The product in question is the hamburger. The hamburger's origins began in the late eighteenth century where sailors who visited the port of Hamburg in Germany were often tempted to eat the Hamburg-style steak, which was a hard piece of beef, often slightly smoked and was usually mixed with onions and breadcrumbs. The sailors enjoyed not only the taste but also the ease with which one could quickly consume the steak. Recognizing this potential market, Jewish immigrants quickly transferred the product to New York City Harbor, in order to attract hungry German sailors, who would line up next to eating stands to grab a quick bite (Moon, 2005).

While there continues to be much dispute in the US as to exactly who decided to place the meat between two pieces of bread or buns, the new style of hamburger became an instant success on the east coast of America and its popularity quickly spread throughout the country. It was then that restaurants such as the famous "White Castle," one of the earliest known hamburger chains, laid the path for the likes of the massively popular McDonald's and Burger King, to name but a few.

In this regard, we can see that while being sold in the port of Hamburg, Germany, the hamburger had a high level of local responsiveness. At this time, global integration was low as the product was only sold in Germany. It was only when it spread to America and then onto the world via the global fast food chains that the hamburger became a roaring success. In this way, its level of global integration moved from low to high as the product was little altered to specifically suit individual needs.

One might argue otherwise by pointing out the numerous localized versions of the hamburger. In Korea, the Bulgogi Burger (with the

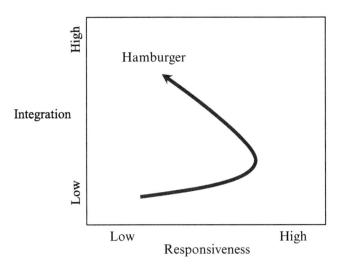

Fig. 6.   Dynamic globalization of hamburger.

patty marinated in a traditional Korean sauce) caters to local consumers, while in Japan, the Teriyaki Burger satisfies many customers in that country. However, the hamburger is a more homogenous than heterogenous product despite such variations. This is evident from the numerous McDonald's chains which provide the standardized flagships such as Big Mac, Double Cheese Burger, Filet-O-Fish, and McChicken. From a dynamic perspective, the hamburger has been more globally integrative than locally responsive, as illustrated in Fig. 6.

Discussion Questions

1. How effective are the various marketing tools discussed in this chapter in altering business environments? Discuss.

2. Which marketing tools, besides those mentioned in the above question, can effectively change the business environment? And, do they always change it for the better? Why or why not?

3. Are there any particular characteristics of the CEE region that make it receptive to standardized products? Could this strategy be simulated in other regions, such as Latin America?

4. Based on our discussions, which direction is better for a firm when going abroad, global integration or local responsiveness? Explain the reasons for your chosen approach.

5. How could kimchi change from a multi-domestic product to a global product? Detail the factors involved.

6. Is the hamburger a global or transnational product?

7. What are the most important lessons you have learned from the debate between standardization and differentiation?

References

Adner, R. (2017). "Ecosystem as structure: An actionable construct for strategy." *Journal of Management*, 43(1): 39–58.

Agarwal, R. and Helfat, C.E. (2009). "Strategic renewal of organizations." *Organization Science*, 20(2): 281–293.

Ahn, H. (2001). "Applying the balanced scorecard concept: An experience report." *Long Range Planning*, 34(4): 441–461.

Ansoff, H.I. (1965). *Corporate Strategy: An Analytic Approach to Business Policy for Growth and Expansion*. McGraw-Hill.

A.T. Kearney and Foreign Policy (2006). "The Global Top 20." *Foreign Policy*, November–December: 74–81.

A.T. Kearney and Foreign Policy. (2007). "The Globalization Index 2007." *Foreign Policy*, November–December: 68–76.

Argyres, N., McGahan, A.M., Barney, J.B., Brandenburger, A. and Bachmann, J.W. (2002). "Retrospective 2002, An interview with Michael Porter and related articles." *Academy of Management Executive*, 16(2): 41–65.

Arnold, S., Chadraba, P. and Springer, R. (eds.) (2001). "Marketing strategies for central and eastern Europe". Aldershot: Ashgate.

Backer, R. and Rinaudo, E.K. (2019). "Improving the management of complex business partnerships." *McKinsey & Company*, March 21. https://www.mckinsey.com/business-functions/strategy-and-corporate-finance/our-insights/improving-the-management-of-complex-business-partnerships.

Baig, A., Hall, B., Jenkins, P., Lamarre, E. and McCarthy, B. (2020). "The COVID-19 recovery will be digital: A plan for the first 90 days," May 14. https://www.mckinsey.com/business-functions/mckinsey-digital/our-insights/the-covid-19-recovery-will-be-digital-a-plan-for-the-first-90-days.

Balmer, J.M.T., Fukukawa, K. and Gray, E.R. (2007). "The nature and management of ethical corporate identity: A commentary on corporate identity, corporate social responsibility and ethics." *Journal of Business Ethics*, 76: 7–15.

Balmer, J.M.T., Powell, S.M. and Greyser, S.A. (2011). "Explicating ethical corporate marketing. Insights from the BP Deepwater Horizon Catastrophe: The Ethical Brand that Exploded and then Imploded." *Journal of Business Ethics*, 102(1): 1–14.

Banalieva, E.R. and Dhanaraj, C. (2013). "Home-region orientation in international expansion strategies." *Journal of International Business Studies*, 44(2): 89–116.

Barney, J.B. (1991). "Firm resources and sustained competitive advantage." *Journal of Management*, 17(1): 99–120.

Barney, J.B. (2002). "Strategic management: From informed conversation to academic discipline." *Academy of Management Executive*, 16(2): 53–57.

Bartlett, C.A. and Ghoshal, S. (1989). "Managing Across Borders the Transnational Solution: Chapter 4 The Emerging Organization Model." Boston: Harvard University Press.

Bartlett, C.A. and Ghoshal, S. (1989). "The emerging organization model." In: *Managing Across Borders: The Transnational Solution*. Boston: Harvard University Press, pp. 65–82.

Bartlett, C.A. and Ghoshal, S. (2000). "Going global: Lessons from late movers." *Harvard Business Review*, March–April: 132–142.

Bean, R. (2018). "How big data and AI are driving business innovation in 2018." February 5, 2018. https://sloanreview.mit.edu/article/how-big-data-and-ai-are-driving-business-innovation-in-2018/.

Becker, G. (1976). "The economic approach to human behavior." Chicago: University of Chicago Press.

Benedict, R. (1946). "The chrysanthemum and the sword." Boston: Houghton Miffin.

Bharadwaj, S. (2010). "On pluralistic scholarship: A comment on the research of P. Rajan Varadarajan." *Journal of Strategic Marketing*, 18(2): 103–111.

Bonaglia, F., Goldstein, A. and Mathews, J.A. (2007). "Accelerated internationalization by emerging markets' multinationals: The case of the white goods sector." *Journal of World Business*, 42: 369–383.

Boudreau, K.J. and Hagiu, A. (2009). Platform rules: Multi-sided platforms as regulators. In: Gawer, A. (Ed.), *Platforms, Markets and Innovation*. Cheltenham: Edward Elgar, pp. 163–191.

Bourgeois, L.J. (1984). "Strategic management and determinism." *Academy of Management Review*, 9(4): 586–596.

Brewer, P. (2002). "Putting strategy into the balanced scorecard." *Strategic Finance*, 83(7): 44–52.

Buckley, P.J. and Casson, M. (1976). *The Future of the Multinational Enterprise*. London: MacMillan Press.

Butler, A., Letza, S.R. and Neale, B. (1997). "Linking the balanced scorecard to strategy." *Long Range Planning*, 30(2): 242–253.

Cacciolatti, L. and Lee, S.H. (2016). "Revisiting the relationship between marketing capabilities and firm performance: The moderating role of market orientation, marketing strategy and organisational power." *Journal of Business Research*, 69(12): 5597–5610.

Carr, J.C., Haggard, K.S., Hmieleski, K.M. and Zahra, S.A. (2010). "A study of the moderating effects of firm age at internationalization on firm survival and short-term growth." *Strategic Entrepreneurship Journal*, 4(2): 183–192.

Cheng, B., Ioannou, I. and Serafeim, G. (2014). "Corporate social responsibility and access to finance." *Strategic Management Journal*, 35(1): 1–23.

Chesbrough, H. (2003). *Open Innovation: The New Imperative for Creating and Profiting from Technology*. Cambridge, MA: Harvard Business School Press.

Chesbrough, H.W., Vanhaverbeke, W. and West, J. (2006). *Open Innovation: Researching A New Paradigm*. Oxford: Oxford University Press.

Chesbrough, H.W. and Appleyard, M. (2007). "Open innovation and strategy." *California Management Review*, 50(1): 57–76.

Cho, D.S. (1994). "A dynamic approach to international competitiveness: The case of Korea." *Journal of Far Eastern Business*, 1(1): 17–36.

Cho, D.S. and Moon, H.C. (2000). *From Adam Smith to Michael Porter: Evolution of Competitiveness Theory*. Singapore: World Scientific Publishing.

Cho, D.S. and Moon, H.C. (2013a). *From Adam Smith to Michael Porter: Evolution of Competitive Theory*. Extended ed. Singapore: World Scientific Publishing.

Cho, D.S. and Moon, H.C. (2013b). *International Review of National Competitiveness: A Detailed Analysis of Sources and Rankings*. Cheltenham, UK: Edward Elgar.

Cho, D.S., Moon, H.C. and Kim, M.Y. (2008). "Characterizing international competitiveness in international business research: A MASI approach to national competitiveness." *Research in International Business and Finance*, 22(2): 175–192.

Cho, D.S., Moon, H.C. and Kim, M.Y. (2009). "Does one size fit all? A dual double diamond approach to country-specific advantages." *Asian Business & Management*, 8(1): 83–102.

Cho, D.S., Moon, H.C. and Yin, W. (2016). "Enhancing national competitiveness through national cooperation: The case of South Korea and Dubai." *Competitiveness Review*, 26(5): 482–499.

Cho, D., Kim, D. and Rhee, D. (1998). "Latecomer strategies: Evidence from the semiconductor industry in Japan and Korea." *Organization Science*, 9(4): 489–505.

Chomsky, N. (1976). "On the nature of language." In Harnad, S.R and Steklis, H.D. and Lancaster, J. Lancaster, (eds.), "Origins and evolution of language and speech." *Annals of the New York Academy of Sciences*, 280: 46–57.

Choo, C.W. and Bontis, N. (2002). *The Strategic Management of Intellectual Capital and Organizational Knowledge*. New York, NY: Oxford University Press.

Clausewitz, C.V. (1982). "On War." Oxford: Penguin Group (reprint from 1832).

CNBC (2020). "Big Tech spends over $20 million on lobbying in first half of 2020, including on coronavirus legislation." July 31, https://www.cnbc.com/2020/07/31/big-tech-spends-20-million-on-lobbying-including-on-coronavirus-bills.html.

Cochran, P.L. and Wood, R.A. (1984). "Corporate Social Responsibility and Financial Performance." *Academy of Management Journal*, 27(1): 42–56.

Cumming, D., Hou, W. and Lee, E. (2016). "Business ethics and finance in greater China: Synthesis and future directions in sustainability, CSR, and fraud." *Journal of Business Ethics*, 138(4): 601–626.

Dahlander, L. and Gann, D.M. (2010). "How open is innovation?" *Research Policy*, 39(6): 699–709.

Daniels, J.D. and Bracker, J. (1989). "Profit Performance: Do Foreign Operations Make a Difference?" *Management International Review*, 29(1): 46–56.

Delventhal, S. (2019). "How Xiaomi makes money." Investopedia, July 30. https://www.investopedia.com/news/how-xiaomi-makes-money/.

DeRond, M. and Thietart, R.A. (2007). "Choice, chance and inevitability in strategy." *Strategic Management Journal*, 28: 535–551.

Doshi, M. (2017). "Strategy Guru Michael Porter on the Companies he Admires, Donald Trump and Narendra Modi." *Bloomberg,* May 30. https://www.bloombergquint.com/business/strategy-guru-michael-porter-on-the-companies-he-admires-donald-trump-and-narendra-modi.

Douglas, S.P. and Wind, Y. (1987). "The myth of globalization." *Columbia Journal of World Business,* Winter: 19–29.

Doz, Y., Santos, J. and Williamson, P. (2001). "From Global to Metanational." Boston: Harvard Business School Press.

Dreher, A. (2006). "Does globalization affect growth? Evidence from a new index of globalization." *Applied Economics,* 38(10): 1091–1110.

Drucker, P.F. (1969). "The Age of Discontinuity; Guidelines to Our Changing Society." New York: Harper and Row.

Drucker, P.F. (1981). "Behind Japan's success." *Harvard Business Review,* (January–February): 83–90.

Dunning, J.H. (1977). "Trade, location of economic activity and the MNE: A search for an eclectic approach." In: Ohlin, B., Hesselborn, P.O. and Wijkman, P.M. (eds.) *The International Allocation of Economic Activity.* London: Macmillan Press, pp. 395–418.

Dunning, J.H. (1995). "Reappraising the eclectic paradigm in an age of alliance capitalism." *Journal of International Business Studies,* 26(3): 461–491.

Economist (2019). "The steam has gone out of globalization" January 24. https://www.economist.com/leaders/2019/01/24/the-steam-has-gone-out-of-globalisation.

Edinger, S. (2020). "4 ways to reconfigure your sales strategy during the pandemic." *Harvard Business Review,* October 20, https://hbr.org/2020/10/4-ways-to-reconfigure-your-sales-strategy-during-the-pandemic.

Efrat, K. and Shoham, A. (2012). "Born global firms: The differences between their short-and long-term performance drivers." *Journal of World Business,* 47(4): 675–685.

Eggers, J.P. and Kaplan, S. (2009). "Cognition and renewal: Comparing CEO and organizational effects on incumbent adaptation to technical change." *Organization Science,* 20(2): 461–477.

Eisenmann, T.R., Parker, G.G., and Alstyne, M.W.V. (2006). "Strategies for two-sided markets." *Harvard Business Review,* 84: 92–101.

Ekelund, R.B. and Hebert, R.F. (1997). *A History of Economic Theory and Method.* Singapore: McGraw-Hill.

Eng, T.Y. (2007). "Relationship value of firms in alliance capitalism and the implications for FDI." *International Journal of Business Studies*, 15(1): 43–68.

Erdğmus, I.E., Bodur, M. and Yilmaz, C. (2010). "International strategies of emerging market firms: Standardization in brand management revisited." *European Journal of Marketing*, 44(9/10): 1410–1436.

Ernst & Young (2020). "Are you reframing your future or is the future reframing you?" June 19. https://www.ey.com/en_gl/megatrends/how-megatrends-can-reframe-your-future.

Fogel, K., Hawk A., Morck, R. and Yeung, B. (2006). "Institutional Obstacles to Entrepreneurship." in Casson, M., Yeung, B., Basu, A. and Wadeson, N. (eds.), *Oxford Handbook of Entrepreneurship*, Oxford: Oxford University Press, pp. 540–579.

Financial Times (2013). "Hyundai: Time to abandon caution and push overseas?" May 3.

Friedman, T.L. (2005). "The world is flat." New York: Farrar Straus and Giroux.

Friedman, T.L. (2020). "How we broke the world." *The New York Times*, May 30. https://www.nytimes.com/2020/05/30/opinion/sunday/coronavirus-globalization.html.

Fukuyama, F. (1992). "The End of History and the Last Man." New York: Free Press.

Garvin, D.A. and Levesque, L.C. (2008). "The multi-unit enterprise." *Harvard Business Review*, June: 106–117.

Geringer, J.M., Beamish, P.W. and daCosta, R.C. (1989). "Diversification strategy and internationalization: Implications for MNE performance." *Strategic Management Journal*, 10(2): 109–119.

Ghemawat, P. (2001). "Distance still matters: The hard reality of global expansion." *Harvard Business Review*, 79(8): 137–147.

Ghemawat, P. (2003). "Semiglobalization and international business strategy." *Journal of International Business Studies*, 34(2): 138–152.

Ghemawat, P. (2007a). *Redefining Global Strategy: Corssing Borders in a World Where Differences Still Matter*. Boston: Harvard Business School Publishing.

Ghemawat, P. (2007b). "Why the World Isn't Flat." *Foreign Policy*, (March–April): 54–60.

Ghemawat, P. (2018). "Book highlight: Globalization in the long run." *Global Business and Organizational Excellence*, 37: 69–83.

Ghemawat, P. and Hout, T. (2008). "Tomorrow's global giants: Not the usual suspects." *Harvard Business Review*, November: 80–88.

Ghoshal, S. (1987). "Global strategy: An organizing framework." *Strategic Management Journal*, 8: 425–440.

Giuli, A.D. and Kostovetsky, L. (2014). "Are red or blue companies more likely to go green?" Politics and corporate social responsibility. *Journal of Financial Economics*, 11(1): 158–180.

Glaum, M. and Oesterle, M.J. (2007). "40 years of research on internationalization and firm performance: More questions than answers?" *Management International Review*, 47(3): 307–317.

Gould, A.M. and Desjardins, G. (2015). "A spring-clean of Michael Porter's Attic." *Competitiveness Review*, 25(3): 310–323.

Grant, R.M. (1987). "Multinationality and Performance among British Manufacturing Companies." *Journal of International Business Studies*, 18(3): 79–89.

Greenwald, B. and Kahn, J. (2005). "All Strategy is Local." *Harvard Business Review*, September: 95–104.

Gumbus, A. and Lussier, R.N. (2006). "Entrepreneurs use a balanced score-card to translate strategy into performance measures." *Journal of Small Business Management*, 44(3): 407–425.

Gygli, S., Haelg, F., Potrafke, N. and Stum, J.E. (2019). "The KOF globalisation index — revisited." *The Review of International Organization*, 14: 543–574.

Håkansson, K. and Snehota, I. (2006). "No business is an island: The network concept of business strategy." *Scandinavian Journal of Management*, 22(3): 256–270.

Hamel, G. (1991). "Competition for competence and inter-partner learning within international strategic alliances." *Strategic Management Journal*, 12: 83–103.

Hamel, G. (2009). "Moon shots for management." *Harvard Business Review*, (February) 91–98.

Hamel, G. and Prahalad, C.K. (1985). "Do You Really Have a Global Strategy?" *Harvard Business Review*, (July–August): 139–148.

Hamel, G. and Prahalad, C.K. (1994). "Competing for the future." Boston: Harvard Business School Press.

Hansen, M.W. and Gwozdz, W. (2015). "What makes MNCs succeed in developing countries? an empirical analysis of subsidiary performance." *Multinational Business Review*, 23(3): 224–247.

Hansen, E.G. and Schaltegger, S. (2016). "The sustainability balanced scorecard: A systematic review of architectures." *Journal of Business Ethics*, 133: 193–221.

Harvie, C. and Lee, B.C. (2002). "The Study of Small and Medium Size Enterprises in East Asia", in Havie, C. and Lee, B.C., *Globalisation and SMEs in East Asia: Studies of Small and Medium Sized Enterprises in East Asia*, 1: 1–9. Cheltenham: Edward Elgar.

Helfat, C.E. and Peteraf, M.A. (2003). "The dynamic resource-based view: Capability lifecycles." *Strategic Management Journal*, 24(10): 997–1010.

Herbold, R.J. (2002). "Inside microsoft: Balancing creativity and discipline." *Harvard Business Review*, (January): 143–178.

Horney, N., Pasmore, B. and O'Shea, T. (2010). "Leadership agility: A business imperative for a VUCA world." *People & Strategy*, 33(4): 32–38.

Hrebiniak, L.G. and Joyce, W.F. (1985). "Organizational adaptation: Strategic choice and environmental determinism." *Administrative Science Quarterly*, 30: 336–349.

Huntington, S.P. (1996). "The Clash of Civilizations and the Remaking of the World Order." New York: Simon and Schuster.

Ichijo, K. and Kohlbacher, F. (2007). "Global knowledge creation — The Toyota Way." *International Journal of Automotive Technology and Management*, 7(2/3): 116–134.

Institute for Industrial Policy Studies (2007). "IPS World Competitiveness Report." Seoul: Institute for Industrial Policy Studies.

Institute for Policy and Strategy on National Competitiveness (IPSNC) (2020). *IPS National Competitiveness Research 2019–2020*. Seoul: IPSNC.

International Institute for Management Development (IMD) (2010). *The World Competitiveness Yearbook 2010*. Lausanne, Switzerland: IMD.

International Institute for Management Development (IMD) (2020). *The World Competitiveness Yearbook 2020*. Lausanne, Switzerland: IMD.

Isenberg, D.J. (2008). "The global entrepreneur." *Harvard Business Review*, December: 107–111.

Javidan, M. and Bowen, D. (2013). "The 'Global Mindset' of managers: What it is, why it matters, and how to develop it." *Organizational Dynamics*, 42: 145–155

Jeurissen, R. (2004). "Institutional conditions of corporate citizenship." *Journal of Business Ethics*, 53: 87–96.

Jewer, J. and McKay, K.N. (2012). "Antecedents and consequences of board IT governance: Institutional and strategic choice perspectives." *Journal of the Association for Information Systems*, 13(7): 581–617.

Johnson, B.R., Connolly, E. and Carter, T.S. (2011). "Corporate social responsibility: The role of Fortune 100 companies in domestic and international natural disasters." *Corporate Social Responsibility and Environmental Management*, 18(6): 352–369.

Kalender, Z.T. and Vayvay, Ö. (2016). "The fifth pillar of the balanced scorecard: Sustainability." *Procedia — Social and Behavioral Sciences*, 235: 76–83.

Kaplan, R.S. and Norton, D.P. (1992). "The balanced scorecard — measures that drive performance." *Harvard Business Review*, 70(1): 71–79.

Kaplan, R.S. and Norton, D.P. (1996). "Linking the balanced scorecard to strategy." *California Management Review*, 39(1): 53–79.

Kaplan, R.S. and Norton, D.P. (2006). "Alignment", Boston: Harvard Business School Press.

Kaplan, R.S and Norton, D.P. (2007a). "Using the balanced scorecard as a strategic management system." *Harvard Business Review*, (July-August): 150–161 (reprint of 1996).

Kaplan, R.S. and Norton, D.P. (2007b). "The Strategy-Focused Organization". Boston: Harvard Business School Press.

Kawamura, K.M. (2014). "Kristine Marin Kawamura, PhD interviews Ikujiro Nonaka, Ph.D." *Cross Cultural Management: An International Journal*, 21(3): 613–632.

Kedia, B.L. and Mukherji, A. (1999). "Global managers: Developing a mindset for global competitiveness." *Journal of World Business*, 34(3): 230–251.

Kirby, D. and Watson, A. (2003). "Small firms and economic development in developed and transition economies: A reader." Aldershot: Ashgate.

Khanna, T. and Palepu, K.G. (2006). "Emerging giants: Building world-class companies in developing countries." *Harvard Business Review*, October: 60–69.

Kim, M., Lampert, C.M. and Roy, R. (2020). "Regionalization of R&D activities: (dis)economies of interdependence of inventive performance." *Journal of International Business Studies*, 51(7): 1054–1075.

Kim, M.Y. and Moon, H.C. (2006). "The global expansion strategy of Hyundai motor: A dynamic diversification-doordination (DCC) approach." *Journal of Strategic Management*, 9(2): 31–55.

Kim, C. and Park, D. (2015). "Emerging Asian MNCs." *Asia Pacific Business Review*, 21(4): 457–463.

Kim, E., Nam, D. and Stimpert, J.L. (2004). "The applicability of Porter's generic strategies in the digital age: Assumptions, conjectures, and suggestions." *Journal of Management*, 30(5): 569–589.

Kim, W.C. and Mauborgne, R. (2005). "Blue ocean strategy: From theory to practice." *California Management Review*, 47(3, Spring): 105–121.

Kim, W.C. and Mauborgne, R. (2015). Identify blue oceans by mapping your product portfolio. *Harvard Business Review Digital Articles*, February 12: 2–6.

Kim, W.C. and Mauborgne, R. (2017). *Blue Ocean Shift – Beyond Competing: Proven Steps to Inspire Confidence and Seize New Growth*. New York: Hachette Books.

Kim, W.C. and Mauborgne, R. (2019). Nondisruptive creation: Rethinking innovation and growth. *MIT Sloan Management Review*, 60(3): 46–55.

Kogut, B. (1985). "Designing global strategies: Comparative and competitive value-added chains." *Sloan Management Review*, (Summer): 15–28.

Knowledge@Wharton (2006). "Michael Porter Asks, and Answers: Why Do Good Managers Set Bad Strategies?" November 1st.

Knight, G., Madsen, T.K. and Servais, P. (2004). "An inquiry into born-global firms in Europe and the USA." *International Marketing Review*, 21(6): 645–665.

Kotler, P. (1986). "The prosumer movement: A new challenge for marketers." *Advances in Consumer Research*, 13(1): 510–513.

Koo, C.M., Koh, C.E. and Nam, K. (2004). "An examination of Porter's competitive strategies in electronic virtual markets: A comparison of two on-line business models." *International Journal of Electronic Commerce*, 9(1): 163–180.

Kuhn, T.S. (1962). "The structure of scientific revolution." Chicago: Chicago University Press.

Kudina, A., Yip, G. and Barkema, H. (2008). "Born global." *Business Strategy Review*, Winter, 39–44.

Lam, T. and Leung, L. (2018). "Xiaomi: From a mobile and technology company to a lifestyle and retail company." June. https://www.readkong.com/page/xiaomi-from-a-mobile-and-technology-company-to-a-lifestyle-3689046.

Laugesen, J. and Yuan, Y. (2010). "What factors contributed to the success of Apple's iPhone?" *2010 Ninth International Conference on Mobile Business*, https://ieeexplore.ieee.org/abstract/document/5494782.

Lechner, C. and Floyd, S.W. (2012). "Group influence activities and the performance of strategic initiatives." *Strategic Management Journal*, 33(5): 478–495.

Lee, Y.W., Moon, H.C. and Yin, W. (2020). "Innovation process in the business ecosystem: The four cooperations practices in the media platform." *Business Process Management Journal*, 26(4): 943–971.

Levitt, T. (1983). "The Globalization of Markets." *Harvard Business Review*, May–June: 92–102.

Lin, W.T., Liu, Y. and Cheng, K.Y. (2011). "The internationalization and performance of a firm: Moderating effect of a firm's behaviour." *Journal of International Management*, 17(1): 83–95.

Liou, J.J.H., Tzeng, G.H., Tsai, C.Y. and Hsu, C.C. (2011). "A hybrid ANP model in fuzzy environments for strategic alliance partner selection in the airline industry." *Applied Soft Computing*, 11(4): 3515–3524.

Lu, J.W. and Beamish, P.W. (2001). "The internationalization and performance of SMEs." *Strategic Management Journal*, 22(6–7): 565–586.

Luo, Y. (2007). "From foreign investors to strategic insiders: Shifting parameters, prescriptions and paradigms for MNCs in China." *Journal of World Business*, 42: 14–34.

Luostarinen, R. and Gabrielsson, M. (2004). "Finnish perspectives of international entrepreneurship', *in Dana, L.P. (Ed), Handbook of Research on International Entrepreneurship*, Cheltenham: Edward Elgar, 383–403.

Machiavelli, N. (2003). "The Prince." New York: Penguin Books (first printed in 1532).

Machiavelli, N. (1532, reprinted 2003). *The Prince*. New York: Penguin Books.

Magretta, J. (2011). "Understanding Michael Porter: The essential guide to competition and strategy." Boston: Harvard Business Review Press.

Makambe, U. (2015). "Perspectives on knowledge management — a literature review." *Information and Knowledge Management*, 5(1): 88–97.

Malbasic, I. and Marimon, F. (2019). "A simplified balanced 'balanced scorecard'." *European Accounting and Management Review*, 5(2): 38–60.

Marshall, V.B., Brouthers, L.E. and Keig, D.L. (2020). "RIMS: A new approach to measuring firm internationalization." *Journal of International Business Studies*, 51(7): 1133–1141.

Mathews, J.A. (2002). "Dragon multinational: A new model for global growth." New York: Oxford University Press.

Mathews, J. (2006). "Dragon multinationals: New players in 21st century globalization." *Asia Pacific Journal of Management*, 23: 5–27.

McKinsey & Co. (1993). Emerging exporters: Australia's high value added manufacturing exporters. Melbourne: Australian Manufacturing Council.

Mekić, E. and Mekić, E. (2014). "Supports and critiques on Porter's competitive strategy and competitive advantage." *International Conference on Economic and Social Studies*, 24–25. April, Sarajevo, Bosnia and Herzegovina.

Moen, O. (2002). "The born globals: A new generation of small European exporters." *International Marketing Review*, 19(2/3): 156–175.

Moon, H.C. (1993). "The Dynamics of Porter's three generics in international business strategy," *in Rugman, A.M. (ed.) Research in Global Strategic Management: A Research Annual*, 4: 51–64.

Moon, H.C. (1994). "A revised framework of global strategy: Extending the coordination-configuration framework."*The International Executive*, 36(September–October): 557–574.

Moon, H.C. (2005). "The new organization of global firms: From transnational solution to dynamic globalization." *International Journal of Performability Engineering*, 1(2): 131–143.

Moon, H.C. (2007). "Outward Foreign Direct Investment by Enterprises from the Republic of Korea." *in Global Players from Emerging Markets: Strengthen Enterprise Competitiveness through Outward Investment*, New York and Geneva: UNCTAD.

Moon, H.C. (2012). *Good to Smart*. Seoul, Korea: Rainmaker (In Korean).

Moon, H.C. (2016a). *Foreign Direct Investment: A Global Perspective*. Singapore: World Scientific Publishing.

Moon, H.C. (2016b). *The Strategy for Korea's Economic Success*. New York, NY: Oxford University Press.

Moon, H.C. (2018). *The Art of Strategy: Sun Tzu, Michael Porter, and Beyond*. Cambridge: Cambridge University Press.

Moon, H.C., Hur, Y.K., Yin, W. and Helm, C. (2014). Extending Porter's generic strategies: From three to eight. *European Journal of International Management*, 8(2): 205–225.

Moon, H.C. and Kim, M.Y. (2008). "A new framework for global expansion: A dynamic diversification-coordination (DDC) model." *Management Decision*, 46(1): 131–151.

Moon, H.C. and Parc, J. (2019). Shifting corporate social responsibility to corporate social opportunity through creating shared value. *Strategic Change*, 28: 115–122.

Moon, H.C. and Peery, N. (1995). "Competitiveness of product, firm, industry and nation in a global business." *Competitiveness Review*, 5(1): 37–43.

Moon, H.C. and Roehl, T.W. (2001). Unconventional foreign direct investment and the imbalance theory." *International Business Review*, 10: 197–215.

Moon, H.C., Rugman, A.M. and Verbeke, A. (1995). "The generalized double diamond model approach to international competitiveness." In: Rugman, A.M., Van Den Broeck, J. and Verbeke, A. (eds.) *Research in Global Strategic Management: Beyond the Diamond* (vol. 5). Greenwich, CT: JAI Press.

Moon, H.C., Rugman, A.M. and Verbeke, A. (1998). "A generalized double diamond approach to the global competitiveness of Korea and Singapore." *International Business Review*, 7: 135–150.

Mooraj, S., Oyon, D. and Hostettler, D. (1999). "The Balanced Scorecard: A Necessary Good or an Unnecessary Evil?" *European Management Journal*, 17(5): 481–491.

Morrison, A.J. (1990). "Strategies in global industries: How U.S. businesses compete." Westpoint, CT: Quorum Books.

New York Times (2020). "How tech's lobbyists are using the pandemic to make gains." April 3. https://www.nytimes.com/2020/04/03/technology/virus-tech-lobbyists-gains.html.

Nielsen, B.B. and Nielsen, S. (2013). "Top management team nationality diversity and firm performance: A multilevel study." *Strategic Management Journal*, 34(3): 373–382.

Nonaka, I. (1994). "A dynamic theory of organizational knowledge creation." *Organizational Science*, 5: 14–37.

Nonaka, I. (2007). "The knowledge creating company." *Harvard Business Review*, (November-December): 162–171 (Reprint of 1991).

Nonaka, I. and Takeuchi, H. (1995). "The knowledge creating company." Oxford: Oxford University Press.

Nonaka, I. and Takeuchi, H. (2019). *The Wise Company: How Companies Create Continuous Innovation*. New York, NY: Oxford University Press.

Nonaka, I., Toyama, R. and Hirata T. (2008). "Managing flow: A process theory of the knowledge-based firm." New York: Palgrave Macmillan.

Nørreklit, S.O. (2000). "The balance on the balanced scorecard – a critical analysis of some of its assumptions." *Management Accounting Research*, 11(1): 65–88.

Nucciarelly, A., Li, F., Fernandes, K., Goumagias, N., Cabras, I., Devlin, S., Kudenko, D. and Cowling, P. (2017). "From value chains to technological platforms: The effects of crowdfunding in the digital game industry." *Journal of Business Research*, 78: 341–352.

Ohmae, K. (1989). "The global logic of strategic alliances." *Harvard Business Review*, March–April: 143–154.

Ormanidhi, O. and Stringa, O. (2008). "Porter's model of generic competitive strategies: An insightful and convenient approach to firms' analysis." *Business Economics*, 43(3): 55–64.

Osland, J. S., Bird, A., Mendenhall, M. and Osland, A. (2006). "Developing global leadership capabilities and global mindset: A review." In: Stahl, G. K. and I. Björkman (Eds.), *Handbook of Research in International Human Resource Management*, Cheltenham: Edward Elgar Publishing, pp. 197–222.

Oviatt, B.M. and P.P. McDougall (1994). "Toward a theory of international new ventures." *Journal of International Business Studies*, 25(1): 45–64.

Parker, G., Alstyne, M. V. and Jiang, X. (2017). "Platform ecosystems: How developers invert the firm." *MIS Quarterly*, 41(1): 255–266.

Parnell, J.A. (2006). "Generic strategies after two decades: A reconceptualization of competitive strategy." *Management Decision*, 44(8): 1139–1154.

Paranjape, B., Rossiter, M. and Pantano, V. (2006). "Insights from the balanced scorecard performance measurement systems: Successes, failures and future — a review." *Measuring Business Excellence*, 10(3): 4–14.

Peng, M.W. (2012). "The global strategy of emerging multinationals from China." *Global Strategy Journal*, 2: 97–107.

Perkins, M., Grey, A. and Remmers, H. (2014). "What do we really mean by Balanced Scorecard?" *International Journal of Productivity and Performance Management*, 63(2): 148–169.

Perlmutter, H. (1969). "The tortuous evolution of the multinational enterprise." *The Columbia Journal of World Business*, 4(1): 9–18.

Polanyi, M. (1967). *The Tacit Dimension*. New York: Anchor Books.

Porter, M.E. (1980). "Competitive Advantage: Creating and Sustaining Superior Performance." New York: Free Press.

Porter, M.E. (1985). "Competitive Advantage: Creating and sustaining superior performance." New York: Free Press.

Porter, M.E. (1986). "Competition in Global Industries." Boston: Harvard Business School Press.

Porter, M.E. (1990). "The Competitive Advantage of Nations." New York: Free Press.

Porter, M.E. (1996). "What is strategy?" *Harvard Business Review*, November–December: 61–78.

Porter, M.E. (2001). "Strategy and the internet." *Harvard Business Review*, March: 63–78.

Porter, M.E. (2008). "The five competitive forces that shape strategy." *Harvard Business Review*, January: 79–93.

Porter, M.E. and Heppelmann, J.E. (2014). "How smart, connected products are transforming compeititon." *Harvard Business Review*, 92(11): 64–88.

Porter, M.E. and Kramer, M.R. (1999). "Philanthropy's new agenda: Creating value." *Harvard Business Review*, November–December: 121–130.

Porter, M.E. and Kramer, M.R. (2002). "The competitive advantage of corporate philanthropy." *Harvard Business Review*, 80(12): 56–68.

Porter, M.E. and Kramer, M.R. (2006). "Strategy and society." *Harvard Business Review*, December: 78–92.

Porter, M.E. and Kramer, M.R. (2011). "Creating shared value." *Harvard Business Review*, 89(1/2): 62–77.

Prahalad, C.K. and Doz, Y.L. (1987). "The multinational mission: Balancing local demands and global vision." New York: Free Press.

Prahalad, C.K. and Hamel, G. (1990). "The core competence of the corporation." *Harvard Business Review*, July–August: 55–70.

Prahalad, C.K. and Krishnan, M.S. (2008). "The new age of innovation: Driving cocreated value through global networks." New York: McGraw-Hill.

Prahalad, C.K. and Ramaswamy, V. (2000). "Co-opting customer competence." *Harvard Business Review*, January–February: 79–87.

PwC (2018). What the top innovators get right. October 30, https://www.strategy-business.com/feature/What-the-Top-Innovators-Get-Right?gko=e7cf9.

Qian, G., Li, L., Li, J. and Qian, Z. (2008). "Regional diversification and firm performance." *Journal of International Business Studies*, 39(2): 197–214.

Raisch, S. and Birkinshaw, J. (2008). "Organizational ambidexterity: antecedents, outcomes, and moderators." *Journal of Management*, 34(3): 375–409.

Ramaswamy, V. (2008). "Co-creating value through customers' experiences: The Nike case" *Strategy & Leadership*, 36(5): 9–14.

Ramaswamy, V. (2009). "Co-creation of value – towards an expanded paradigm of value creation." *Marketing Review St. Gallen*, 6: 11–17.

Ramaswamy, V. and Gouillart, F. (2010). "Building the co-creative enterprise." *Harvard Business Review*, 88(10): 100–109.

Ramaswamy, V. and Ozcan, K. (2018a). "Offerings as digitalized interactive platforms: A conceptual framework and implications." *Journal of Marketing*, 82: 19–31.

Ramaswamy, V. and Ozcan, K. (2018b). "What is co-creation? An interactional creation framework and its implications for value creation." *Journal of Business Research*, 84: 196–205.

Rangan, S. and Adner, R. (2001). "Profit and the internet: Seven misconceptions." *MIT Sloan Management Review*, Summer: 44–53.

Reich, B.R. (1990). "Who is Us?" *Harvard Business Review*, January–February: 53–64.

Rehder, R.R. (1979). "Japanese management: An American challenge." *Human Resource Management*, Winter: 21–27.

Retailing Asia (2018). "South Korean cosmetics to seduce Europe." March 2. https://retailinasia.com/in-markets/japan-korea/korea/south-korean-cosmetics-to-seduce-europe/.

Ridderstrale, K. and Nordstrom, J. (1999). "Funky business." Stockholm: Book House Publishing.

Robertson, R. (1995). "Globalization: Time-space and homogeneity-heterogeneity." *In* Featherstone, M., Lash, S. and Rolan, R. (eds.), *Global Modernities,* London: Sage, pp. 23–44.

Rosa, B., Gugler, P. and Verbeke, A. (2020). "Regional and global strategies of MNEs: revisiting Rugman & Verbeke (2004)." *Journal of International Business Studies*, 51(7): 1045–1053.

Rugman, A.M. (1981). *Inside the Multinationals: The Economics of Internal Markets.* Columbia: Columbia University Press.

Rugman, A.M. (2000). "The end of globalization." London: Random House and New York: Amacom-McGraw-Hill.

Rugman, A.M. and D'Cruz, J.R. (1993). "The double diamond model of international competitiveness: The canadian experience." *Management International Review*, 2: 17–39.

Rugman, A.M. and Verbeke, A. (2004). "A perspective on regional and global strategies of multinational enterprises." *Journal of International Business Studies*, 35(1): 3–18.

Sa, E.Y. (2008). "Stanford MBA to learn from Hyundai Motor." *Maeil Business Newspaper*, October 15. https://www.mk.co.kr/news/english/view/2008/10/607533/ (accessed April 19, 2021).

Saffo, P. (2007). "Six rules for effective forecasting." *Harvard Business Review*, July–August: 122–131.

Saleh, A. and Watson, R. (2017). "Business excellence in a volatile, uncertain, complex and ambiguous environment (BEVUCA)." *The TQM Journal*, 29(5): 705–724.

Schaltegger, S. and Burritt, R. (2018). Business cases and corporate engagement with sustainability: Differentiating ethical motivations. *Journal of Business Ethics*, 147: 241–259.

Schuh, A. (2000). "Global standardization as a success formula for marketing in central eastern europe?" *Journal of World Business*, 35(2): 133–149.

Schmitt, A. Barker III, V.L., and Raisch, S. and Whetten, D. (2016). "Strategic renewal in times of environmental scarcity." *Long Range Planning*, 49: 361–376.

Schwab, K. (2016). *The Fourth industrial Revolution*. Switzerland: World Economic Forum.

Sharma, P. (2011). "Country of origin effects in developed and emerging markets: Exploring the contrasting roles of materialism and value consciousness." *Journal of International Business Studies*, 42(2): 285–306.

Siebel, M. (2017). Why digital transformation is now on the CEO's shoulders. December 14. https://www.mckinsey.com/business-functions/mckinsey-digital/our-insights/why-digital-transformation-is-now-on-the-ceos-shoulders.

Springer, R. and Czinkota, M.R. (1999). "Marketing's contribution to the transformation of Central and Eastern Europe." *Thunderbird International Business Review*, 41(1): 310–326.

Suutari, V. (2002). "Global leader development: An emerging research agenda." *Career Development International*, 7: 218–233.

Tan, Q. and Sousa, C.M.P. (2013). "International marketing standardization: A meta-analytic estimation of its antecedents and consequences." *Management International Review*, 53: 711–739.

Tedlow, R.S. and Rawi Abdelal, R. (2004). "Theodore Levitt's 'The Globalization of Markets': An Evaluation After Two Decades." In: John A. Quelch and Rohit Deshpandé (eds.) *The Global Market: Developing a Strategy to Manage Across Borders*. San Francisco, CA: Jossey-Bass, pp. 11–30.

Terrell, R.S. and Rosenbusch, K.R. (2013). "How global leaders develop." *Journal of Management Development*, 32(10): 1056–1079.

Toffler, A. (1980). "The Third Wave." New York: Bantam Books.

Thurow, L.C. (1992). "Head to head: The coming economic battle among Japan, Europe, and America." New York: Warner Books.

UNCTAD (1995). *World Investment Report 1995: Transnational Corporations and Competitiveness.* New York and Geneva: United Nations.

UNCTAD (2002). *World Investment Report 2002: Transnational Corporations and Export Competitiveness.* New York and Geneva: United Nations.

UNCTAD (2012). "World Investment Report 2012: Towards A New Generation of Investment Policies." New York and Geneva: United Nations.

Vallentin, S. and Murillo, D. (2012). Governmentality and the politics of CSR. *Organization*, 19(6): 825–843.

Van Alstyne, M.W., Parker, G.G. and Choudary, S.P. (2016). "Pipelines, platforms, and the new rules of strategy." *Harvard Business Review*, 94(3): 54–60.

Varadarajan, P.R., Clark, T. and Pride, W.M. (1992). "Controlling the uncontrollable: Managing your market environment." *Sloan Management Review*, 33(2): 39–47.

Vargo, S.L. and Lusch, R.F. (2008). "Service-dominant logic: Continuing the evolution." *Journal of the Academy of Marketing Science*, 36: 1–10.

Verbeke, A. (2013). *International Business Strategy.* Cambridge: Cambridge University Press.

Verbeke, A., Coeurderoy, R. and Matt, T. (2018). "The future of international business research on corporate globalization that never was…" *Journal of International Business Studies*, 49: 1101–1112.

Verbeke, A. and Asmussen, C.G. (2016). "Global, local, or regional? the locus of MNE strategies." *Journal of Management Studies*, 53(6): 1051–1075.

Vernon, R. (1966). "International trade and international investment in the product life cycle." *Quarterly Journal of Economics*, 81(2): 190–207.

Vernon, R. (1971). "Sovereignty at bay: The Multinational Spread of U.S. Enterprises." New York: Basic Books.

Wall Street Journal (2015). "Hyundai Motor's profit falls again." April 23.

Wall Street Journal (2017). "The iPhone decade in 12 charts." June 29. https://www.wsj.com/graphics/iphone-10-years/.

Wall Street Journal (2020). "Post-pandemic, is the world likely to become less flat?", June 26, https://www.wsj.com/articles/post-pandemic-is-the-world-likely-to-become-less-flat-01593207487.

Weber, M. (1930). *The Protestant Ethic and the Spirit of Capitalism* (translated by T. Parsons). New York: Scribner.

WheelsJoint (2020). "2019 financial report of 28 mainstream auto companies in the world: Total profit decreased by 11% year-on-year", April 16, https://www.wheelsjoint.com/2019-financial-report-of-28-mainstream-auto-companies-in-the-world-total-profit-decreased-by-11-year-on-year/.

Wilson, J. and Oyola-Yemaiel, A. (2001). The evolution of emergency management and advancement towards a profession in the United States and Florida. *Safety Science*, 39: 117–131.

World Economic Forum (WEF) (2010). *The Global Competitiveness Report 2010–2011*. Geneva, Switzerland: WEF.

World Economic Forum (WEF) (2019). *The Global Competitiveness Report 2019*. Geneva, Switzerland: WEF.

Yip, G. (1989). "Global strategy... In a world of nations?" *MIT Sloan Management Review*, 31(1): 29–45.

Yip, G. (2000). "Global strategy in the internet era." *Business Strategy Review*, 11(4): 1–14.

Online Resources

1421 Consulting Group (2019). https://www.1421.consulting/2019/06/walmart-in-china-lessons-to-learn/ (accessed July 18, 2020).

Amore Pacific Online (2009). Our Story, http://www.amorepacific.com/usa/brand/story.jsp (accessed February 25, 2009).

Apple Asia Online. (2009). Support, http://www.apple.com/asia/support/ (accessed February 25, 2009).

Arçelik Online (2009). Arçelik A.Ş, http://www.arcelikas.com.tr/Cultures/en-US/Kurumsal/?MENUID=1 (accessed February 27, 2009).

Arçelik Global (2020). https://www.arcelikglobal.com/en/ (accessed October 4, 2020).

Balanced Scorecard Institute Online (2009). Examples and Success Stories, http://www.balancedscorecard.org/BSCResources/ExamplesSuccessStories/tabid/57/Default.aspx (accessed February 27, 2009).

Bank of Tokyo-Mitsubishi UFJ Online (2009) About the Bank, http://www.bk.mufg.jp/english/about/index.html (accessed February 27, 2009).

BBC Online (2001). Warren Buffett: "I told you so", March 13, http://news.bbc.co.uk/2/hi/business/1217716.stm (Accessed February 13, 2009).

Blue Ocean Strategy Online (2009). Partner Material, http://www.blueoceanstrategy.com/tools/partners.html (accessed February 25, 2009).

Business Week Online (2008). Beyond Outsourcing to Worldsourcing, May, http://www.businessweek.com/technology/content/may2008/tc20080529_101827.htm (accessed February 27, 2009).

Center for Management Research (2006). Tesco's Globalization Strategies and its Success in South Korea http://www.icmrindia.org/casestudies/catalogue/BusinessStrategy/TescoGlobalizationStrategiesanditsSuccessinSouthKorea.htm (accessed March 2, 2009).

Chosun-Ilbo Online (2001). Moon Kook-hyun, CEO of Yuhan-Kimberly, January 19, http://english.chosun.com/w21data/html/news/200101/200101190405.html (accessed February 25, 2009).

Dr Lee's Tea for Health Online (2009). History of Green Tea, http://www.teaforhealth.com/history.htm (accessed February 27, 2009).

Economist Online (2007). A Wobble on the Road to the Top, November 8, http://www.economist.com/business/displaystory.cfm?story_id=10097827 (accessed February 25, 2009).

Economist Online (2007). Revving Up, October 11, http://www.economist.com/specialreports/displaystory.cfm?story_id=E1_JJNRNVJ (accessed February 25, 2009).

Economist Online (2007). The Forbidden Latte, June 17, http://www.economist.com/business/displaystory.cfm?story_id=E1_JQJRSSG (accessed February 25, 2009).

Economist Online (2008). Charge!, May 8, http://www.economist.com/finance/displaystory.cfm?story_id=13136627 (accessed February 25, 2009).

Economist Online (2008). Asian Invasion, June 26, http://www.economist.com/business/displaystory.cfm?story_id=11632829 (accessed February 25, 2009).

Etude Online (2009). Etude Story, http://www.etudehouse.com/eng/etudeStory/etudeHouse.jsp (accessed February 25, 2009).

Giordano Online (2009). Our Company, http://www.giordano.com.hk/web/HK/ourCompany.html (accessed February 25, 2009).

Hindu Business Line Online (2006). Blue Ocean Strategy Helps HCL Tech Bag DSG Deal, January 20, http://www.thehindubusinessline.com/2006/01/20/stories/2006012001880600.htm (accessed February 25, 2009).

Hong Kong Trader Online (2001). Clothing Retailer Presses Ahead with Global Expansion, May 1, http://www.hktrader.net/200105/200102/200102s4.htm (accessed February 25, 2009).

Hyundai Motors Online (2009). Hyundai Worldwide, http://worldwide.hyundai.com/worldwide_index.html (accessed February 27, 2009).

Hyundai Motor Group Newsroom (2020). https://www.hyundaimotorgroup.com/About-Us/Group-Performance.hub (accessed October 12, 2020).

Inside Retail (2020). Giordano to Focus on Global Expansion as Sales Fall in Greater China, https://insideretail.asia/2020/03/11/giordano-to-focus-on-global-expansion-as-sales-fall-in-greater-china/ (accessed August 22, 2020).

Interbrand's Best Global Brands (2019). https://www.interbrand.com/best-brands/best-global-brands/2019/ (accessed September 7, 2020).

International Herald Tribune Online (2008). Interconnected We Prosper, June 25, http://www.iht.com/articles/2008/06/25/opinion/edamelio.php (accessed February 27, 2009).

Isehan Online (2009). Company Product Profile, http://www.isehan.info/ (accessed February 25, 2009).

Jiangsu Longliqi Group Online (2009). Homepage, http://longliqi.fuzing.com/ (accessed February 25, 2009).

Kanebo Online (2009). About Sensai, http://www.sensai-cosmetics.com/ (accessed February 25, 2009).

Kose Online (2009). About Kose, http://www.kose.co.jp/global/en//index.html (accessed February 25, 2009).

Lenovo Online (2009). Lenovo Locations, http://www.lenovo.com/planetwide/select/selector.html (accessed February 27, 2009).

Mi Website (2019). Xiaomi Makes Future 50 List for the First Time, https://blog.mi.com/en/2019/10/25/xiaomi-makes-future-50-list-for-the-first-time/ (accessed August 2, 2020).

Money Control (2019). How HCL Tech balances its organic and inorganic strategy will determine its growth, https://www.moneycontrol.com/news/business/companies/how-hcl-tech-balances-its-organic-and-inorganic-strategy-will-determine-its-growth-3967621.html (accessed September 14, 2020).

New York Times Online (2005). Starbucks Aims to Alter China's Taste in Caffeine, May 21st, http://www.nytimes.com/2005/05/21/business/worldbusiness/21coffee.html?scp=1&sq=Starbucks%20Aims%20to%20Alter%20China%27s%20Taste%20in%20Caffeine&st=cse (accessed February 25, 2009).

New York Times (2007). Bits, December 17, http://bits.blogs.nytimes.com/?scp=1-spot&sq=Bits&st (accessed February 25, 2009).

New York Times (2008). Sony Sets a New Course to Bolster Electronics, June 27, http://www.nytimes.com/2008/06/27/technology/27sony.html?scp=2&sq=Sony%20Sets%20a%20New%20Course%20to%20Bolster%20Electronics&st=Search (accessed February 25, 2009).

New York Times Online (2008). My Son the Blogger – An M.D. Trades Medicine for Apple Rumors, July 1, http://www.nytimes.com/2008/07/21/technology/21blogger.html?scp=1&sq=My%20Son%20the%20Blogger&st=cse (accessed February 25, 2009).

Palladium Consulting Group Online (2009). Bank of Tokyo-Mitsubishi UFJ BSC Hall of Fame, http://www.thepalladiumgroup.com/about/hof/Pages/overview.aspx (accessed Febraury 27, 2009).

Renault Online (2009). Suppliers and Partners, http://www.renault.com/en/Pages/home.aspx (accessed February 25, 2009).

Seattle Post Intelligencer Online (2005). Starbucks Adjusts its Formula in China, June 16, http://seattlepi.nwsource.com/business/228728_sbuxchina16.html (accessed February 25, 2009).

Shiseido Online (2009). Corporate Information, http://www.shiseido.co.jp/e/index.htm (accessed February 25, 2009).

Smith, M.K. (2003). Michael Polanyi and tacit knowledge, *the encyclopedia of informal education,* www.infed.org/thinkers/polanyi.htm. (accessed February 21, 2009).

Tata Tea Online (2009). Company Profile, http://www.tatatea.com/comp_profile.htm (accessed February 27, 2009).

Temasek Holdings Online (2009). Investment Themes, http://www.temasek-holdings.com.sg/our_portfolio.htm (accessed February 25, 2009).

Temasek Trust Online (2020). https://www.temasektrust.org.sg/Home.aspx (accessed August 22, 2020).

Toyota Online (2009). Various Company Information, http://www.toyota.co.jp/en/index.html (accessed February 25, 2009).

Toyota Supplier Online (2009). Supplier Diversity, http://www.toyota supplier.com/sup_diversity/sup_diversity.asp (accessed on February 25, 2009).

Wired Online (2002). The Civil War Inside Sony, February 11, http://www.wired.com/wired/archive/11.02/sony_pr.html (accessed on February 25, 2009).

Wizard Robotics Online (2009). Wizard Robotics Products, http://www.wizardrobotics.com/ (accessed February 27, 2009).

Woman Consumer (2020). http://www.womancs.co.kr/news/articleView.html?idxno=60812 (accessed December 5, 2020).

World Economic Forum Online (2007). World Economic Forum 2007–2008 Global Competitiveness Report, http://www.weforum.org/en/initiatives/gcp/Global%20Competitiveness%20Report/PastReports/index.htm (accessed February 27, 2009).

Yuhan Kimberly Online (2009). Social Responsibility, http://www.yuhan-kimberly.co.kr/ (accessed February 25, 2009).

Zhejiang Tea Import and Export Company Online (2009). Our Culture, http://www.chinagreentea.com/prog/about_e.asp (accessed February 27, 2009).

Index

Buffett, W., 66, 73
Burger King, 324, 334
business ecosystem, v, 17, 51
business environment, v, 1, 7,
16–17, 65–66, 79, 95, 103, 129,
170, 208, 210, 214, 310, 335
ByteDance, 304

C
Californization of need, 205, 219,
223, 260
Canon, 40
Carrefour, 22
Central and Eastern European
(CEE), 318
ceteris paribus, 109
Chesbrough, H., 209
China, v, ix, 4, 24, 28–31, 53, 57,
59–60, 89, 91, 158–159, 173,
181
Chomsky, N., 326
Clausewitz, C.V., 98
cloud computing, 67
Coca-Cola, 215, 260, 323, 325
co-creation strategy, 47, 49, 51, 59
coffee, 29–31, 205, 326, 328
collectivism, 39, 55
competition, 4, 6–7, 10, 16–18,
31, 63, 68, 70–71, 73, 91, 99,
106, 109, 120, 130, 137,
139–140, 142, 152, 198–199,
203–204, 208, 210, 223, 226,
230–233, 259, 263, 282
competition-based economy, 18
competitive advantage, 8–13, 15,
17–18, 24, 34–35, 43, 65,
67–69, 71–73, 78, 88, 90–91,
95, 98–100, 102–104, 108, 111,

123, 127, 137, 139, 142, 146,
148–149, 166, 171, 200, 206,
211, 213, 215–216, 221,
226–228, 230, 259–260
competitive drivers, 285
competitive moves, 282, 303–304
competitiveness, v–vi, 1–5, 8, 31,
54, 70, 72, 81–84, 117, 119–
120, 127, 136, 142, 155, 171,
177, 180, 198, 201–203, 213,
291, 295
competitive strategies, 2, 144
comprehensive global strategy,
141–142, 208–209, 215
cone of uncertainty, 182,
193–195
configuration, 100, 122, 213,
226–228, 230, 232–234, 236,
239, 241, 245–247, 250, 290,
305
cooperation, 4, 17, 55, 140, 204,
208, 210, 270
coordination, 15, 121, 169
coordination–configuration model,
226, 241
core business strategy, 280, 286
corporate political activity, 314
corporate social opportunity
(CSO), 84–85, 87
corporate social responsibility
(CSR), 65, 77–82, 84–87, 93,
95–97, 314
cosmetics industry, 159, 270–272
cost drivers, 285
cost focus, 8, 138–139, 142,
156–157
cost leadership, 8, 10, 23–25,
103–106, 138–139, 142, 144,

Printed in the United States
by Baker & Taylor Publisher Services